D1474020

ATHANASIUS

ATHANASIUS

Alvyn Pettersen

MOREHOUSE PUBLISHING

© Alvyn Pettersen 1995

All rights reserved. No part of this publication may be reproduced or
transmitted in any form or by any means, electronic or mechanical
including photocopying, recording or any information storage or
retrieval system, without prior permission in writing from the publishers.

First published in the UK by Geoffrey Chapman, a Cassell imprint

First American edition published by
Morehouse Publishing

Editorial Office
871 Ethan Allen Hwy,
Ridgefield, CT 06877

Corporate Office
P.O. Box 1321
Harrisburg, PA 17105

**A catalog record for this book is available from the
Library of Congress.**

ISBN 0-8192-1655-0

Typeset by York House Typographic Ltd
Printed bound in Great Britain by
Biddles Ltd, Guildford and King's Lynn

BR
1720
.A7
P47
1995

Contents

Editorial foreword

St Anselm of Canterbury once described himself as someone with faith seeking understanding. In words addressed to God he says 'I long to understand in some degree thy truth, which my heart believes and loves. For I do not seek to understand that I may believe, but I believe in order to understand.'

And this is what Christians have always inevitably said, either explicitly or implicitly. Christianity rests on faith, but it also has content. It teaches and proclaims a distinctive and challenging view of reality. It naturally encourages reflection. It is something to think about; something about which one might even have second thoughts.

But what have the greatest Christian thinkers said? And is it worth saying? Does it engage with modern problems? Does it provide us with a vision to live by? Does it make sense? Can it be preached? Is it believable?

This series originates with questions like these in mind. Written by experts, it aims to provide clear, authoritative and critical accounts of outstanding Christian writers from New Testament times to the present. It will range across the full spectrum of Christian thought to include Catholic and Protestant thinkers, thinkers from East and West, thinkers ancient, mediaeval and modern.

The series draws on the best scholarship currently available, so it will interest all with a professional concern for the history of Christian ideas. But contributors will also be writing for general readers who have little or no previous knowledge of the subjects to be dealt with. Volumes to appear should therefore prove helpful at a popular as well as an academic level. For the most part they will be devoted to a single thinker, but occasionally the subject will be a movement or school of thought.

The subject of the present volume was present at the Council of

Nicaea (AD 325), which produced the famous creed asserting the divinity of Christ. He was also an enormous influence on the shape of Christian teaching from the time of Nicaea. He is best known for his thinking about the divinity of Christ, but, as Alvyn Pettersen shows, he ranges over more topics than this. Athanasius was a Christian theologian concerned to provide an overall perspective on the Christian faith. And Dr Pettersen's book shows this very well. It also shows that Athanasius was a Christian thinker who has a great deal to offer today with respect to the notion that God is essentially good and the source of all that we can recognize as good.

Dr Pettersen is very well qualified to write about Athanasius. He has taught at Oxford University on the history of early Christian thinking. He is also author of a much-acclaimed study entitled *Athanasius and the Human Body* (Bristol, 1990). His new book will help readers to get a sense of Athanasius as a whole. It will help them to see why he is one of the greatest of Christian thinkers.

Brian Davies OP

Preface

A risk which any theologian faces is that in his work 'The Word made flesh here is made word again' (E. Muir, *The Incarnate One*).

The risk is doubled for anyone writing about a theologian. Athanasius of Alexandria, the great fourth-century Christian thinker, astutely and sympathetically avoided this hazard. I hope that I too have. I hope that the God known in the man Jesus, and shared with us by the Bishop of Alexandria, may not have been betrayed through this my appreciation. You, the reader, shall have done me honour if you turn from this book to Athanasius' own writings; and you shall have shown respect to Athanasius if you so reflect upon his thinking as to deepen your own sense of him who for our sake chose our form and fashion.

The editions of Athanasius' works used are R. W. Thomson, *Athanasius, Contra Gentes and De Incarnatione* (Oxford, 1971); J. P. Migne (ed.), *Patrologia Graeca* 25–26 (Paris, 1857); and H.-G. Opitz (ed.), *Athanasius Werke* II. 1 (Berlin, 1935/40). Translations are those of R. W. Thomson (op. cit.); A. Robertson, *Select Writings and Letters of Athanasius, Bishop of Alexandria* in the Select Library of Nicene and Post-Nicene Fathers, Vol. 4 (Michigan, USA, 1971); and C. R. B. Shapland, *The Letters of Saint Athanasius Concerning the Holy Spirit* (London, 1951), with occasional modifications. Standard divisions and subdivisions are used. The Revised Standard Version of the Bible is used for scriptural quotations.

My gratitude is due to Rowan Williams, who encouraged me to write this piece on Athanasius, to Peter Widdicombe, who so generously shared his ideas and insights, to Brian Davies, whose editorial advice was at once clear, kind and helpful, and to the people of the parish of Frensham, who not only were not afraid to accept as their vicar one interested in matters academic but also encouraged me to think and read and write. My gratitude is especially due to Judith. She neither researched nor typed nor proof-read this book. For that she was far too busy pursuing other equally important matters. Yet, without her continuous support, it would never have been completed. To her this book is dedicated.

Alvyn Pettersen
9 December 1994

Bibliography

T. D. Barnes, *Athanasius and Constantius* (Harvard, 1993).

G. Bebawi, 'St Athanasius: the dynamics of salvation', *Sobornost* 8.2 (1986), pp. 24ff.

J. Breckenridge, 'Julian and Athanasius. Two approaches to creation and salvation', *Theology* 76 (1973), pp. 73ff.

T. C. Campbell, 'The doctrine of the Holy Spirit in the theology of Athanasius', *Scottish Journal of Theology* 27 (1974), pp. 408ff.

P. Christou, 'Increated and created, unbegotten and begotten in the theology of Athanasius of Alexandria', *Augustinianum* 13 (1973), pp. 399ff.

F. S. Clarke, 'Lost and found: Athanasius' doctrine of predestination', *Scottish Journal of Theology* 29 (1976), pp. 435ff.

G. V. Florovsky, 'The concept of creation in Saint Athanasius', *Texte und Untersuchungen* 81 (= *Studia Patristica* VI; 1962), pp. 36ff.

R. P. C. Hanson, *The Search for the Christian Doctrine of God* (Edinburgh, 1988).

C. Kannengiesser, 'Athanasius of Alexandria and the foundation of traditional Christology', *Theological Studies* 34 (1973).

Politique et théologie chez Athanase d'Alexandrie (Paris, 1974).

A. Louth, 'Reason and revelation in St Athanasius', *Scottish Journal of Theology* 23 (1970), pp. 385–6.

R. J. Lyman, *Christology and Cosmology: Models of Divine Authority in Origen, Eusebius and Athanasius* (Oxford, 1993).

E. P. Meijering, 'Athanasius on the Father as the origin of the Son' in *God being History: Studies in Patristic Philosophy* (Amsterdam and Oxford, 1975).

Orthodoxy and Platonism in Athanasius: Synthesis or Antithesis? (Leiden, 1968).

J. Roldanus, *Le Christ et l'homme dans la théologie d'Athanase d'Alexandrie: Etude de la conjonction de sa conception de l'homme avec sa Christologie* (Leiden, 1968).

G. C. Stead, *Divine Substance* (Oxford, 1977).

K. J. Torjesen, 'The teaching function of the Logos: Athanasius' *De Incarnatione* XX–XXXII' in R. C. Gregg (ed.), *Arianism: Historical and Theological Reassessments* (Philadelphia, 1985), pp. 213ff.

T. F. Torrance, '*Spiritus Creator*: A consideration of the teaching of St Athanasius and St Basil' in *Theology in Reconstruction* (London, 1965), pp. 209ff.

P. J. Widdicombe, *The Fatherhood of God from Origen to Athanasius* (Oxford, 1994).

R. D. Williams, *Arius: Heresy and Tradition* (London, 1987).

F. M. Young, 'A reconsideration of Alexandrian Christology', *Journal of Ecclesiastical History* 22 (1971), pp. 103–14.

Abbreviations

Ad Adelph.	*Ad Adelphium*
Ad Drac.	*Ad Dracontium*
Ad Epict.	*Ad Epictetum*
Ad Max.	*Ad Maximum*
Ad Serap.	*Ad Serapionem*
C.Ar.	*Contra Arianos*
C.G.	*Contra Gentes*
De Decret.	*De Decretis*
De Fuga	*De Fuga Sua*
D.I.	*De Incarnatione*
De Syn.	*De Synodis*
Hist. Ar.	*Historia Arianorum*
Tome	*Tomus ad Antiochenos*
Vita Ant.	*Vita Antonii*

Introduction:
Athanasius' life and times

Alexandria was 'the crossroads of the world, serving it as a market-place serves a single city'. To a degree these words of the early second-century Dio Chrysostom[1] were still true in the very early fourth century. Alexandria certainly was still a place rich in ideas, culture and commerce. Power and prestige might be found there. Hence it acted as a magnet, attracting both rich and poor. In this cosmopolitan city, brimming with stimuli and overflowing with opportunities, Athanasius (c. 296–373) mainly lived and worked.

The picture of Alexandria as a city whose streets were paved with gold and of Athanasius as one living in an ideal time is, however, only partially accurate. Alexandria, the major seat of administration in Egypt, certainly was a great commercial centre, the chief port of the land, and the principal emporium for trade between the Roman empire and the markets of Asia and Africa. Two sheltered harbours on the Mediterranean side of the city, linked by a canal system to a third harbour, busier than the other two and landward of the city on Lake Mareotis, gave access from the Mediterranean to the Nile, and so to Upper Egypt, and central northern Africa. Indeed, the city's commercial importance was yet further under-lined when merchants discovered both that the westerly summer winds and the easterly winter winds of the Arabian Sea gave them direct access to India, uninterrupted by Arab middlemen, and that the unreliable winds of the northern end of the Red Sea might be avoided by routing goods via the Nile, as far as Thebes, and then via the roads, built by the imperial administration, linking the Nile with

1

the ports on the Egyptian south-eastern seaboard. In consequence through Alexandria passed goods from Egypt itself, from Ethiopia and central Africa, India and Sri Lanka. When this is noted alongside the facts both that Egypt was mainly desert — the only fertile areas being essentially the marshy land of the Delta, the narrow strip of land either side of the Nile, and the borders of Lake Moeris — and that cheap and reliable transport was mainly by water, we further appreciate the commercial significance of Alexandria for the whole province.

Whilst Alexandria had the necessary infrastructure of roads and waterways to benefit from it, such trade was, nevertheless, subject to the vagaries of climate, politics and tax. A large part of the goods which passed through Alexandria from Egypt itself consisted of fruits, nuts, wheat, papyrus — the principal writing material in antiquity, whose production Alexandria then virtually monopolized — flax and linen. Provided there was the annual inundation of the land adjoining the Nile, crops would be forthcoming. Those goods which came from beyond Egypt arrived in Alexandrian markets provided the winds were regular, and were sold and bought provided the peace and prosperity of the Empire prevailed. For these reasons Alexandria's prosperity was precarious. Fiscal and fiscally related matters could and did often further destabilize this prosperity. Rome's, and subsequently Constantinople's, growth was parasitic, their income directly and indirectly being tributary. Both cities valued and even exploited Egypt for its corn. The middlemen of Alexandria no doubt benefited; but the Egyptian workers on the land were much harmed, being drained of resources and kept firmly at the bottom of a rigid class system. Indeed, the imperial dependency upon Egypt is witnessed in the seriousness of the charge against Athanasius in 335 of his having delayed the sailing of the shipments of corn to Constantinople. Further, since the third century, expenditure, especially on the defence of the empire's frontiers, had consistently outrun revenue. Attempts to conceal the growing deficit by debasing the coinage only accelerated the inflationary process that finally destroyed the government's credit, hamstrung the administration and paralysed the economy. After several decades of monetary collapse Diocletian (284–305) and Constantine (306–337) sought to tackle the problem. The coinage was reformed. Silver issues were revived; and in 312 Constantine introduced his golden *solidus*. Indeed, in Alexandria in the reign of both there was a mint. Yet the re-establishment of the currency was dependent upon a balanced budget. Diocletian therefore attempted both to enforce stable prices by legislation and to put the whole empire on a new and more exacting scale of taxation. The consequences of this were several. The administrative effort needed to collect the required income was huge; the empire thus became a rigid, bureaucrat-ridden society living under martial law. The cost of collecting the taxes, as well as the taxes, was borne by those taxed. For the tax collectors made their money by collecting a total in excess of the sum due and of the amount that they had bidden for the right to harvest the taxes. This system only added to the inflationary pressures. Moreover, the taxes were levied mainly on the city dwellers, resulting often in increasing economic decentralization. The attempt to convert towns which had run a chronic but mild deficit into sources of revenue thus greatly weakened them. References to withdrawal to the Egyptian desert in order to escape taxation are as common in literature of the period as those to withdrawal for religious reasons. However, not only taxation was driving people into hiding. So too was the price fixing which made many professions profitless. The empire foresaw problems. To ensure professions and therefore taxes were not wanting, professions were made obligatory and professional liability hereditary. The professionals and smallholders reacted: to protect themselves from the summary requisitions of the tax gatherer, they often bought the protection of any local magnate by the gift of their profession or freehold. The responsible individual, whose economic success was to feed into the empire's financial recovery, was thus often replaced by a society stratified in terms of patron and client. Other peasants, being squeezed ever harder, simply forsook the land, where their toil no longer rewarded them. A common result, alongside the undermining of the largely agrarian-based Egyptian economy, was the Coptic peasants' growing hatred of their imperial political overlords, who left them little to nothing for the bounty of their land.

Intellectually Alexandria had long been an important centre. Upon Athanasius the legacy of Philo, the Jew (c. 20 BC–c. AD 50), and Origen, the Christian (c. 185–c. 254), both most significant in relating the Bible to Greek philosophy, especially prevailed. The dominant philosophical tone then was Hellenistic, but not in an aggressive form. For by the second century, Platonism was characterized by its predominantly religious and theocentric world-view. Such philosophy was then that which Christian theologians might employ in explaining and elaborating their tradition. An Athanasius may then be deeply indebted to Platonism. Yet his debt towards philosophy will not be at all simple. Like his predecessor Origen, Athanasius studied *as a Christian*. Not being a convert to Christianity like Justin Martyr (*c*. 100–*c*. 165) or Clement of Alexandria (*c*. 150–*c*. 215), Athanasius' attitude towards the intellectual climate was not one of uncritical welcome, but of usefully employing it for the profounder exposition of what he believed to be the Church's thinking. For the Christian theologian Alexandria thus provided an opportunity to press wisdom, wherever it might be found, into the service of the one Lord, to both the establishing of truth and the excluding of error.

Important as intellectual ideas of the time were both as a catalyst for deepening Christian understanding and as an aid for explaining the faith, especially to the intellectually curious, whether Christian or not, they were yet a mixed blessing. Sometimes this was because of a mismatch between certain sets or categories of ideas, and sometimes because philosophy, even as Christianity, was then developing in its own self-definition. An example of the former comes from the philosopher's supposition that the divine One, the Monad, not a chaotic nothing, was the source of all rational order in the universe. This influenced some Christians to think that God was completely simple and strictly immutable, a doctrine which lay rather awkwardly with the biblical picture of God as the creative, loving Father. To eliminate this awkwardness Christians tended then to link their idea of the one, immutable God with the Johannine concept of the divine Word, but as developed in a manner already foreshadowed by the Stoics. God the Father was thus seen as wholly transcendent. He exercised his providential care, not directly, but through his divine Word. Depending upon the varying understandings of the Father's simplicity, varying understandings of the Word's divinity were forthcoming, as were the degrees to which the Word might pervade the physical world, and suffer in and for it. An example of philosophy being a mixed blessing, because it, as Christianity, was then developing its own self-definition, surfaces in the use of terms like *ousia* and *hypostasis*. At the beginning of the fourth century the former could mean either individual or generic substance and the latter either a thing's underlying reality, which it probably held in common with other things, or its emergent, perceptible reality, which was likely to be understood as individual. Not surprisingly, confusion was rife amongst the church leaders, many of whom were not trained philosophers, when in 325 at Nicaea those who maintained that the Son was 'of another *hypostasis* or *ousia*' to the Father were anathematized. In short, the

4

philosophical terms which were available to fourth-century Alexandrian Christians carried various senses, the full meanings of which were not then wholly appreciated, and the openness of meaning of which was at the same time both a boon and a hindrance to theological expression. Further, as though this intellectual fluidity was not enough, there was the matter of Julian, who, while sole emperor (361–362), not only tolerated religious pluriformity but also promoted pedantic paganism. Exciting as the intellectual culture of fourth-century Alexandria was, its contribution towards Christianity's growth was complex.

Alexandria was the undisputed religious capital of Egypt. From the earliest times the Bishop of Alexandria had appointed virtually all the other Egyptian bishops, and by tradition had exercised an absolute authority over them. This outranking of fellow provincial bishops by the bishop of the provincial capital was an expression of the facts that Christianity in the early fourth century was still predominantly an urban religion, that Alexandria was the predominant commercial and intellectual Egyptian city and that proximity to political power strengthened an ecclesiast's hand. It comes then as no surprise that the sixth canon of the Council of Nicaea notes that the Bishop of Alexandria had a status not confined to the current civil province: the metropolitan of Alexandria had oversight of Egypt, Libya and Pentapolis.

A common metropolitan did not, however, necessarily mean unity throughout all Egypt. Certainly by the beginning of the fourth century Alexandria was a much-mixed population of Christians, Jews and Greeks. Already, by c. 300, it is estimated that half of all Egyptians may have been Christians. The Jewish community, which had suffered great losses in AD 115, was recovering. The Greeks were mainly descendants of Copts from the Egyptian hinterland who had been drawn by the wealth of Alexandria and who had gradually assimilated Hellenistic culture. Inland from Alexandria it was not Hellenism but the ancient Egyptian religion which offered a religious threat to Egyptian Christianity. This Egyptian religion, especially in regard to its beliefs that the desert was the domain of Seth, the embodiment of evil and disorder,[2] was still strong. When it is remembered that these Egyptians were largely dependent upon the land for their survival, were convinced that dishonouring the deities could result in divine anger manifest in unseasonable weather, and were not always averse to polytheistic religious practices, the full extent of the challenge may be better appreciated. Meanwhile, amongst those Egyptians who were Christians there were varieties of belief and practice. The Diocletian persecutions of 303 onwards were stubbornly resisted. Yet some Christians did lapse. In time a dispute arose whether or not to readmit to communion such lapsed. The followers of Melitius, Bishop of Lycopolis in Egypt, pursuing a rigorist line, refused readmission. Peter of Alexandria, however, who himself died a martyr during the persecutions under Maximin (311), held lenient views. This disciplinary dispute rumbled on for a number of decades. There was the doctrinal dispute between Arius and Athanasius, both eager to be true to their understanding of the inherited faith. For all the closeness of relationship between the patriarch of Alexandria and the monks of Upper Egypt, the latter, in their withdrawal from the Church's corporate life, were an obvious criticism of the Church's liturgy and piety. There may also have been tension between the Coptic-speaking Christians of Upper Egypt and the Greek-speaking Christians of the coastal area, resulting in a Coptic unwillingness to associate with hellenized Christians who had adopted an oppressive foreign government's language, thought, culture and church. It certainly seems that Coptic Christians did differ from their Greek fellow Christians. The former were generally simple countryfolk, whose lifestyle was necessarily somewhat austere. Their attraction to a severe doctrine which condemned indulgence can, however, more naturally be explained by their lifestyle than by economic pique with Alexandrian Christians, for whom indulgence was at least an economic possibility. Those of Upper Egypt did generally speak Coptic, the indigenous language, but probably as an index of their rusticity rather than of their disapproval of any Egyptian 'compromise' with alien powers. Whatever tension there may have been, it did not amount to disguised movements of social, political or economic protest by Coptic Christians against the Christians of the Delta. This seems confirmed by the *whole* Egyptian Church's maintaining a remarkable, enduring solidarity, tenaciously supporting the doctrines of its chief, the patriarch of Alexandria, through thick and thin, provided that the patriarch had been canonically elected and upheld his predecessor's doctrines.[3] These Coptic Christians seem then not to have been a divisive factor for the Catholic Church in fourth-century Alexandria. They do, however, further witness to the fact that this Church was anything but uniform. They are evidence of the differences in the Egyptian Church, even as the Melitians and the Arians are of the divisions, disciplinary and doctrinal respectively.

6

The impact of particular emperors upon fourth-century Egypt was various. In terms of ecclesiastical peace and prosperity Diocletian, Maximin (308–313) and Julian brought none; Constantine's three sons, Constans (337–350), Constantius II (337–361) and Constantine II (337–340), brought at best a precarious peace and at worst an enforced peace, the leading 'not contents' being exiled. Only Constantine, it may be argued, in 313 brought harmony. Certainly a reader of Eusebius of Caesarea's *Oration in Honour of Constantine on the Thirteenth Anniversary of His Reign* would think so. The existence of Constantinople as a Christian Rome, housing the court of a Christian ruler, evidenced the Kingdom's immanence. The Caesarean eulogist speaks of the Christian empire as an 'image' of the heavenly kingdom, with the Emperor as the 'Image' of the divine Word, from whom the universe draws its ordered and rational structure. The good of the Church and of the City were viewed as one. Life in the city under the king, Constantine, was supposed to be the Lord's ordinance of making humanity fit for his eternal kingdom. With this the peasant, not a citizen but a subject of a remote despotism, disagreed. With this identification of imperial and divine rule the hermits and monks disagreed: their withdrawal to the desert was not only a critique of certain forms of church life but also a protest to a worldly Church at her myopic identification of Church and empire. With this those who resisted both Constantine's commendation of Arius in 335 and later imperial supporters of Arianism disagreed. In short, the State allowed the Church possibilities: often it sought to direct the Church's choice of a particular possibility; and sometimes it caused the Church, or a part of the Church, to seek to declare its own self-definition, even when the State disagreed.

In this complex Athanasius was born, served as deacon, priest and bishop and wrote his theology.

Athanasius was born *c.* 295. His formal education was somewhat restricted; yet his ability and piety did draw him to the Bishop of Alexandria's attention. As a deacon he became Bishop Alexander's secretary, accompanying him to Nicaea (325). There, according to Gregory of Nazianzus, Athanasius, even though not yet a bishop, took a stand against the Arian 'plague'. Such, however, is unlikely. The claim seems to have resulted from the criticisms which Gregory felt needed answering in his panegyric rather than from history. For it is highly unlikely either that a young deacon would have had occasion to contribute directly to the public discussion of such a venerable assembly, or that he was indirectly

7

influential through Alexander, whose own role at the council was not crucial. Only after Alexander died in 328 does legend give place to fact.

Although contested by both Melitians and Arians, possibly illegally and probably enforced, at a little over thirty Athanasius was elected Bishop of Alexandria. The situation which he inherited from Alexander was volatile. The dispute between Melitius of Lycopolis and Peter of Alexandria had grown. Not only had Melitius stressed that lapsed laity should be readmitted to the Church's communion only after lengthy penitence, but also that lapsed clergy should be replaced. In Egypt, where the massive popular movement away from devotion to the traditional deities had tended towards the enthusiastic acceptance of differing forms of asceticism, the Melitian position was popular. Indeed, in 327 there was a Melitian bishop in all six episcopal towns in the Delta, and one in every two or three in the more purely Coptic-speaking province of the Thebaid. The Melitian mission extended south to Coptos. The Council of Nicaea had treated them gently: the Melitian clergy were to retain their functions and to be integrated with the clergy of Alexandria. Yet the division persisted, prompted and sustained by the seriousness with which the Melitians were seen to treat the sin of apostasy, by their asceticism, which was taken as symbolic of their saintliness — for by their fruits they shall be known — and by Melitius' practice of ordaining on his own authority persons to replace the lapsed clergy, deemed no longer worthy to be ministers of the true Church. The episcopal authority of Athanasius was at stake.

Arius, meanwhile, a senior priest in Alexandria, had begun to preach that the Son was not co-eternal with the increate Father; as Son he was created, an inferior deity, with a beginning as he was not unbegotten. For maintaining that the Son was then an intermediary between God and the world, Arius was denounced. Refusing to recant, he was deposed at an Egyptian synod in 323. Several bishops, including Eusebius of Nicomedia and Eusebius of Caesarea, however, supported Arius. The theological problem thus quickly spread beyond the Egyptian borders. It even threatened the Eastern peace. The emperor, Constantine, eventually summoned a council, wishing to solve the issue. In the spring of 325 a council met at Nicaea: Arius was condemned, and an expression of faith expressly anathematizing his thinking was approved. The term *homoousios* was included to define the Son's relation to the Father, a term which was long to be a thorn in Athanasius' side.

This issue had corollaries for the Melitian problem. The various rigorist groups in Egypt, orthodox monks and Melitians, gnostics and Manichaeans, were rivals. Yet they had much in common: they emphasized Christ's divine nature, the wholeness of his manifestation of the Godhead, and the complete character of the salvation of the believer, illumined by faith in, or knowledge of, him. Any compromise which may have been seen as 'Arian', any leniency towards the reception back into the Church of Arius, who had been unfrocked, would have much damaged Athanasius' credibility with these groups. There were also corollaries for relationships with a number of the Eastern bishops, who, though admiring Arius, stood as intellectual heirs of Origen. For them a mild form of subordination in the Godhead was a lesser evil than a modalistic understanding of God. The Nicene term *homoousios*, which sought to affirm commonality of Son and Father, appeared in the Nicene anathemata as an alternative to *hypostasis*, and thereby was capable of being interpreted as 'of the same person', an interpretation which did not accord with the revealed truth that the Word was the agent of creation, through whom one might know God, and so was in some sense separate from the Father. Athanasius therefore was in a situation where, for both theological and political reasons, he could not afford to sanction Arius' thinking. Equally, the language which was then available to him to this end was ambiguous and capable of bearing modalistic overtones, possibly resulting in censure by Eastern bishops. When Athanasius become bishop, then, he faced trouble both within and without Egypt.

Within two years of becoming bishop Athanasius faced major problems. Already pro-Arian bishops were being restored to their sees, and outspoken defenders of Nicaea, such as Asclepas of Gaza, Eustathius of Antioch and Marcellus of Ancyra, were being deposed. In 332 at the imperial court Arius signed a declaration of faith, while yet avoiding the term *homoousios*; and Constantine, believing Arius no longer held the extreme views condemned at Nicaea, directed Athanasius to readmit him to communion. Athanasius, however, was convinced that in his confession Arius was not simply thinking the same thoughts as Nicaea, only a little time after Nicaea had thought them. Truth and error, salvation and perdition were, for Athanasius, at stake. He refused the emperor.

Melitian resistance to Athanasius was also growing. The canons of Nicaea required gentle reconciliation with the Melitians. Athanasius does not seem to have facilitated their reconciliation. Alongside charges brought in 334 against Athanasius of levying a tax in Egypt to provide linen garments, a right previously belonging to the pagan priesthood, and of sending a purse of gold to a former high official, now disgraced, were those concerning dealings with the Melitians: his presbyter Macarius was alleged to have desecrated the church of the Melitian priest Ischyras and to have broken a chalice. Further, Athanasius was indicted with organizing the kidnap and murder of Arsenius, the Melitian Bishop of Hypsele, and of using his severed hand for magical purposes. Athanasius coped with this last charge. Arsenius had fled Athanasius' maltreatment; Athanasius' supporters found him, brought him from hiding and produced him safe and well at the inquiry at Antioch. Yet he was not able to cope with the former charges. Melitian and Arian opposition in Egypt to Athanasius, and prominent Eastern Bishops' support of this opposition, was disturbing the Empire's religious peace, a peace for which Constantine felt himself particularly responsible. The emperor was therefore easily persuaded to summon a council. In 334 Athanasius refused to attend a council at Caesarea, Eusebius' see, on the grounds that an impartial hearing would be impossible there. The emperor, though beginning to lean more towards Eusebius of Caesarea and his friends as those most likely to restore to the Church the blessing of peace — for they were in favour of using scriptural language, imprecise as it was, which was acceptable to the majority and resisted by the minority, at least in the East — was generous. Constantine, however, wanted a settlement by July 335, the thirtieth anniversary of his becoming emperor. In 335 another council was summoned. Although the council at Tyre was stacked against him, a hesitant Athanasius decided to attend. He set sail, accompanied by a large number of Egyptian episcopal supporters, who, not having been invited, were unable to attend the council itself. The old charges were raised; a hostile commission was deputed to investigate in Egypt; and Athanasius, convinced of the impossibility of receiving a fair trial, left Tyre for Constantinople. In his absence Athanasius was condemned, on disciplinary and not theological grounds: his consecration was deemed to have been uncanonical; and he was found guilty of sacrilege and of using violence against his opponents. He was sentenced to deposition and forbidden to return to Alexandria. Athanasius had been condemned on disciplinary grounds. Yet theological issues were not far below the surface. The bishops at the Council of Tyre were summoned to attend the dedication of the church of the Holy Sepulchre in Jerusalem in September 335. There they received Constantine's declaration of faith, which was the same as Arius earlier had made, and there they restored Arius and his followers to communion.

Athanasius, having absented himself from Tyre, had gone to Constantinople to petition the emperor on his return from the dedication in Jerusalem. Initially he received a kindly response from Constantine. Yet Athanasius' enemies were one step ahead. They dropped the earlier charges for the single and more damning one of delaying the sailing of the corn fleet from Alexandria to Constantinople. The emperor was convinced that Athanasius was becoming too powerful for the peace and stability of the empire in general and for Alexandria and Constantinople in particular. This irritant to imperial peace was to be removed; and in November 335 Athanasius was exiled to Trier. Unlike most exiled bishops, however, he was not replaced, and so remained more easily in contact by letter with his diocese.

On 22 May 337 Constantine died, leaving the empire split between Constantine II and Constans, both Nicenes, and Constantius II, who, under the influence of Eusebius of Caesarea and Eusebius of Nicomedia, was leaning towards a subordinationist theology. Initially this change of persons seemed to bode well for Athanasius. Almost immediately he and other exiled bishops were recalled by Constantine II. As is often the case, however, first impressions belied the truth. In November 337 Athanasius returned to the East, to Alexandria and to problems. Opposition to Athanasius had not died down. Indeed, Eusebius of Nicomedia, the long-time opponent of Athanasius, was now Bishop of Constantinople and had Emperor Constantius' ear. Athanasius' opponents pointed to the fact that Athanasius had been deposed, and by a council. The see of Alexandria was therefore legally vacant. Further, they accused him of embezzling corn set aside by the emperor for the poor in Egypt. Fruitless haggling between the opposing forces continued until a council in Antioch in 339 reiterated Athanasius' deposition, and the Eusebian party consecrated a cleric from Cappadocia, a certain Gregory, Bishop of Alexandria. Amidst scenes of violence, but protected by another Cappadocian, the Prefect of Egypt, Gregory was installed in Alexandria, and Athanasius, in March 339, once again withdrew, this time to the more sympathetic West, to Rome. There he gained the support of Pope Julius (337–352), as too did Marcellus of Ancyra, though not to the enhancement of Athanasius' cause. There too, in late 340 or 341, a council of bishops cleared him of the charges made against him at Tyre, and admitted him to communion as the lawful Bishop of

Alexandria. Again, however, Marcellus was a fly in the ointment. He too was readmitted to communion by the Roman council. The problem was that Marcellus had been accused of heresy, Sabellianism, while Athanasius had been charged with disciplinary matters, whatever theological motives there may have been. That both were cleared by the one council resulted for Athanasius in an unfortunate obscuring of the issues. Indeed, in time Athanasius had to refuse communion with Marcellus.

Matters were becoming yet more obscure for Athanasius. Varying power struggles, political and theological, and various matters of procedure were coming more to the surface. By 340 Constans, a Nicene supporter, had become ruler of two-thirds of the Roman world. While the rest of Christendom was then accepting a council of bishops, judicial or otherwise, as the voice of the Spirit, the papacy was more and more staking a claim to speak to colleagues on the authority of Peter alone. Hence rival theories of church authority were in play, and in play in the Eastern and Western halves of an empire whose Church was bitterly divided between Nicene, Eusebian and Arian parties, and varying intermediate theological positions.

It was against this background that the ecclesiastical battles, fought mainly through creeds and formulae, developed.

In the autumn of 341 the Eastern bishops met in Antioch to celebrate in the emperor's presence the dedication of the church of the Golden Dome. They availed themselves of this occasion to alert Pope Julius, who had invited the East to reopen the case against Athanasius, that both East and West had respected each other's verdicts, and that it was unheard of for Eastern bishops to be judged by Westerners. Further, they denied that they were followers of Arius and laid down exactly what they believed the Church's faith to be. This was to be the first of many creeds promulgated during Constantius' reign to rid the Church of the term *homoousios*. It came close to the Nicene position, asserted the Trinity, three individual persons, united by mutual harmony in a single will, and each with its own function within the Godhead. It further confined itself strictly to the terms used of Christ that could be found in Scripture. Having anathematized specific Arian teaching, it concluded, 'for all that has been delivered in the divine Scriptures, whether by the prophets or Apostles, we do truly and reverentially both believe and follow'.

The following autumn Constans, the senior emperor in the West and a supporter of both Athanasius and Pope Julius, forced his brother, Constantius, to assemble a conference at Serdica, just inside the Western frontier. Ninety-six Western and seventy Eastern bishops presented themselves, but to no immediate avail. For the Eastern bishops were unwilling to sit with the deposed bishops Athanasius and Marcellus of Ancyra, both supported by the West. Indeed, the Eastern bishops could have done so only if they also denied the validity of their ideas and decisions of the previous decade. Hence, as soon as possible, on the pretext of congratulating Constantius on his victory over the Persians, they withdrew from the West to Philippopolis in Thrace. There they quickly anathematized Athanasius and Marcellus, their Western supporters, including Pope Julius and also Hosios of Cordova, the leader of the Western bishops at Serdica and the one-time central figure at Nicaea. The Western bishops, meanwhile, continued at Serdica: Athanasius and Marcellus again were vindicated; and those who had taken over the sees of those rehabilitated by the West were deposed. They asserted, against Arian and pluralistic thinking, but in a form very open to Sabellian interpretation, belief in the 'oneness of the *hypostasis* and the unity of the Father and Son' and, rejecting the Eastern practice of passing appeals from smaller to larger synods for decision, they granted the Bishop of Rome important, if limited, appellate jurisdiction in the event of disputes between bishops.

Quickly matters were relaxing. In 344 the East met in Antioch. Their creed, the *Macrostichos*, acknowledged Christ to be 'like in all things', a phrase which, while not yet, would in time allow 'likeness' to extend to 'substance' and so involve 'being of the same substance'. They rejected both Marcellus, by name, as monarchian and Jewish, and every confession open to Sabellian interpretations. They did not, however, mention Athanasius. Meanwhile, under enduring pressure from his brother Constans, Constantius relaxed persecution against Athanasius' Eastern supporters and invited Athanasius to his court. In June 345 Gregory, Athanasius' supplanter in Alexandria, died. Only then, the see vacant, did Athanasius accept the invitation to Constantius' court. In April 346 Constantius and Athanasius were formally reconciled — although it ought to be noted that the act of reconciliation was one by the imperial government and not by the Church — and the latter passed via Jerusalem to Alexandria. In October 346 he arrived home to a hero's welcome.

No sooner had matters improved than they worsened. Constans, the emperor advocating Athanasius' cause, was murdered in the revolt of Magnetius in 350; and in September 351 a critical event in Mursa occurred. Valens, Bishop of Mursa, was devoted to Emperor Constantius' cause. This devotion did not, however, preclude his using information to improve his own standing in the imperial eyes. When, then, he discovered that a battle at Mursa was turning in Constantius' favour, he was the first to inform the emperor, adding the gloss that an angel had brought him the news in a vision. Constantius accepted this as a sign of divine favour, although, importantly for Athanasius, the deity here was of a semi-Arian hue. The result was that as long as Constantius lived, Athanasius' and Nicaea's opponents were to be in the ascendant. Matters were, however, to worsen still more. In August 359 the usurper Magnetius committed suicide in Lyons, leaving Athanasius' opponent Constantius the sole emperor in the Roman world, and, moreover, suspicious that Athanasius had been the recipient of an emissary from the late Magnetius. The result was that, and now for political reasons as well, the emperor sought Athanasius' condemnation. Although Arianism had not troubled Gaul, of the Gaulish bishops only Paul of Trier, where Athanasius had been exiled eighteen years before, refused the emperor's request to condemn Athanasius. At Arles (353) and Milan (355) the Western bishops were further pressured to stand against Athanasius. Even Pope Liberius, Julius' successor, was exhorted, though vainly, to confirm the condemnation passed at the council he had summoned to Milan. The case of Athanasius was difficult. On the theological level, Athanasius could be seen to be defending the Nicene *homoousios*. Yet it must be remembered that Hilary of Poitiers, one of Constantius' most influential opponents, admitted that before he went into exile in Phrygia he had never heard of the Nicene formula.[4] He then noted that while Scripture allowed both *homoiousios* and *homoousios* the Church Fathers preferred the latter. On the political level, Athanasius recognized that the emperor had powers to summon councils and to legislate to protect the Church against pagans and heretics. What he, and many Western bishops, opposed was the imperial attempt to integrate the Church within the State, with the resulting state intervention in ecclesiastical law and decisions. The two issues, theological and political, were clearly distinct but not separate. For even the imperial power to defend the Church depended upon a particular view of what constituted the Church; and while Athanasius viewed Constantius as a Christian, he felt him to be heterodox; and as long as Constantius continued his policy of establishing religious unity around a creed acceptable to as many as possible, Athanasius felt him to be gaining greater political stability at the cost of less theological truth.

After a while Constantius resorted to force against Athanasius. Neither rescinding his earlier permission for Athanasius to return to his see, nor dismissing him directly, he stood neither for Athanasius nor against local hostility. Although Athanasius had produced letters sent by Constantius to him at the beginning of the war with Magnetius, assuring him of imperial protection, and showed them to Syrianus, the new military commander in Alexandria, they had little effect. On the night of 7/8 February 356 Athanasius was president at a vigil in St Theonas' church in Alexandria. Syrianus surrounded the church, and his troops entered it. In the confusion Athanasius escaped to the monasteries of Upper Egypt, there to hide for the next five or six years.

By 358 events were again beginning to improve for Athanasius. The rise of Aetius, with his assertion that if the Son was a creature and did not share the Father's substance, he was 'unlike' the Father, was too much for even Constantius. In 357, at Sirmium, on the Danube frontier, a powerful council had assembled under Valens of Mursa, his companion Ursacius of Singidunum, and another Illyrian, Germanicus of Sirmium. The West was also represented. Its confession cut through the debate:

there is one God almighty, and Father, as is believed throughout the world, and his only Son, Jesus Christ, the Lord, our Saviour, begotten of the Father himself before all ages.

It precluded 'two Gods'. Prudent agnosticism was deemed to be the only proper attitude towards the relationship of the two divine beings. 'Who shall declare his generation?' the council said, quoting Isaiah 53:8. There was then no mention of either *homoiousios* or *homoousios*. They should not be mentioned even in preaching. All that the preacher should say was that 'there is no question but that the Father is greater than the Son in honour, dignity, splendour and majesty', as the Son witnessed and John 14:28 recorded. The agnosticism, the lack of formula, the reliance on Scripture and the suggestion that the Son was subordinate to the Father only in a secondary sense made the creed attractive. Yet, with time, people realized that even it could not meet the questions raised. By the spring of 358 the episcopal heirs of Eusebius of Caesarea found a leader in Basil of Ancyra. In April of that year, in Ancyra *ousia* was

15

restored to theological respectability and anathemata were aimed against both Aetius and Marcellus. The third Council of Sirmium clearly favoured *homoiousios* as the correct definition of the Son's relation to the Father and condemned *homoousios* when used, as they feared, in a Sabellian sense. Basil himself used *homoiousios* as the stick with which to beat those who asserted that the Son was 'unlike' the Father. In short, when faced with the prospect of tolerating Arianism, many in the East preferred to move towards Athanasius' position.

On the political front matters were again improving. George of Cappadocia, a man who made his name as a profiteering pork contractor to the army, had filled the vacated place of Athanasius in Alexandria in 357. There he had used violence against Athanasius' supporters and had handed churches to the Arians. Such actions, however, aroused such resistance that, in fear for his life, George withdrew from Alexandria in 358.

Despite these theological and political changes Athanasius could not yet return to Alexandria. The emperor Constantius still opposed him: for Athanasius was still unwilling to accept the emperor's rule in all matters and was still supported by the West, which was unwilling to accept the role of the emperor as the 'bishop of bishops', dictating their attitude to both Athanasius and the State's power to intervene in church matters. Further, Constantius was still unhappy to use the term *ousia*. He had again turned to those prepared simply to accept that the Son was 'like' the Father. Another creed was promulgated at Sirmium, *ousia* being avoided as an unscriptural term. A version of this creed was placed before Eastern and Western bishops, in Seleucia in Isauria and in Ariminum. The West eventually asserted that Christ was 'like the Father', without any definition of 'how'; even the original 'in all things' was omitted. In October 359 the East came to the same conclusion, and their and the West's conclusions were further ratified at Constantinople in January 360. Valens and Ursacius had effected a great triumph.

The longer-term outcome of this was that the theological alternatives now seemed to be Constantinople or Nicaea. Hence Constantius, finding Aetius unwilling to accept the Constantinopolitan creed of 360, stripped him of his rank as deacon and exiled him. Athanasius and Hilary of Poiters, both in exile, were increasingly convinced by Constantius' unwillingness to accept Nicaea that the emperor was anti-Christ. The change in attitude to Constantius in Athanasius' writings is marked, from being deferential to him in his *Defence Addressed to Constantius* (356/7), to reproving him in his *History of the Arians* (358), to condemning him in *On the Synods* as 'most irreligious'.

Matters changed greatly in the early 360s. Julian was proclaimed Augustus. George of Alexandria returned to Egypt, but only, on the news of Constantius' death, to be imprisoned and murdered by the mob. In time, in accordance with Julian's permission for bishops exiled by Constantius to return to their sees, Athanasius returned to Alexandria in February 362. Quickly he summoned a council. Faced with the possible reversal of their situations, supporters of both the *homoousios* and the *homoiousios* positions were prepared to look at their differences. Athanasius was more concerned for theological than verbal accuracy: 'like in all respects' was taken to imply *homoousios*, but with two provisos, that no Sabellianism was implied and that the distinction of the *hypostaseis* of the Trinity was acknowledged. The Spirit's consubstantiality with the Father and Son was also recognized: for how else might baptism in the three-fold name be understood? The council also considered the issue of how, if the Son was consubstantial with the Father, he could also be one with us. The former Homoiousians had become Homoousians. Those who through fear had signed the creeds of the recent councils of Seleucia and Ariminum were pardoned; and the terminology separating the two anti-Arian groups in Antioch was discussed, though the generosity of the discussion did not heal this particular ecclesiastical rift during Athanasius' time.

Julian died in June 363; and Jovian, the new emperor, recalled Athanasius from the desert, where he had been hiding from Julian since October 362. Athanasius' life, however, was not much easier. For Jovian died in early 364 and was succeeded by Valentinian, a supporter of Nicaea who yet appointed his brother Valens, an Arian sympathizer, as Augustus in the East. Valens (364–378) favoured the creeds of Seleucia and Ariminum; and with the support of successive Bishops of Constantinople — the Arian Eudoxius (d. 370), by whom he was baptized in 367, and Demophilus (370–380) — he attempted to enforce these creeds upon the Eastern bishops. Nicaea had no standing; and Valens ordered all those bishops exiled by Constantius and recalled by Julian to leave their sees. The result for Athanasius was a brief exile, from October 365 to February 366. Valens' commandment was then suddenly rescinded, to conciliate opinion at the time of Procopius' revolt. Thus, for the last seven years of his life, Athanasius stayed in Alexandria.

Seventeen years, out of forty-six as bishop, Athanasius had spent in exile. Politics and theology had ever intermingled. So Athanasius lived, defending his understanding of the Catholic faith, as declared at Nicaea.

Notes

1   Dio Chrysostom, *Discourses* 32.35–36.

2   J. G. Griffiths, 'A note on monasticism and nationalism in the Egypt of Athanasius', *Texte und Untersuchungen* 129 (= *Studia Patristica* XVI, part 2; 1985), pp. 24ff.

3   A. M. Jones, 'Were ancient heresies national or social movements in disguise?', *Journal of Theological Studies* N.S. 10 (1959), pp. 280–98.

4   Hilary of Poitiers, *De Synodis* 41.

1

Creation and providence

CREATION

As the local said to the visitor, if I were trying to get there, I would not start here. So we do not start with creation itself but God. For Athanasius does not understand the world as a thing in itself but as that which owes its existence, and even the quality of that existence, to God. So Athanasius understands it in the light of God. This God, being sovereignly free, is not forced to create. Eternally good, God will neither envy anything its existence nor create anything contrary to his bountiful nature. Simple and unchanging, God will be neither impaired not improved when he creates. Indeed, what benefits through the creative act is that which is brought into being, even as through the act of recreation, as we shall see, what gains is not the Saviour but that saved.

The world, then, is understood by Athanasius as originally good, and its proper end is to share in God's life and blessedness. Yet its goodness adds nothing to God's goodness; and its blessedness is no means by which to establish a claim upon God and so to assert a measure of independence over against its Creator. In every aspect it is properly dependent upon its divine Creator, not only for its having been called into being, but also for its being held in being, and in orderly being. The stars, for example, owed to God not only their very existence but also their harmonious order. People, once created, found their well-being in their service of God, a service which, while owed as an absolute right of the essentially sovereign deity, is neither forced nor unwelcome. For all are recognized even

19

by the sovereign deity as free; and in people freely recognizing their debt to God's gracious sovereignty, and in responsibly voicing their gratitude not only with their lips but also in their lives, these servants of God remain in the blessed state to which God first called them. Love of God, worshipful recognition of God for who God is and for what God has magnanimously done, and faithfully keeping the divine will, not for God's benefit but creation's well-being, are closely intertwined in Athanasius' thinking.

Further, being simple, unchanging and sovereignly free, the Creator's relationship to creation, whatever creation's to God, is constant. God never absents himself from this totally dependent creation, not even to the extent of creating it good and then leaving it to fend for itself. Being unchangeably good, God ever wishes all creation to be and never tires of wishing its continuing well-being. Hence, once God has called creation into being, he shows continuous providential care for it in its natural dependency. Creation thus has in its Creator an enduring basis for hope.

The issue of God's simple sovereignty had for long been an issue for early Christian theologians, and concerned the relationship of God to creation. Origen, the Alexandrian biblical thinker, exegete, theologian and spiritual writer, allowed that God's fatherhood was logically prior to all other attributes and that the 'Father–Son' relation was logically prior to all other relationships. Yet he maintained that the eternal 'Father–Son' relationship is the matrix for the eternal expression of God's goodness and power, evidenced in the eternal existence of rational creation. Had rational creation not existed eternally, God would either have been unwilling or unable to create; and if that were so, God would be either not eternally good, or mutable. Methodius, Bishop of Lycia (d. 311), a critic of Origen, would not tolerate belief in creation's eternity. Eternal non-divine creation, he maintained, infringed the Christian belief in God's self-sufficiency. Matter's eternity implied a rival, self-subsistent reality over against God. Rather, he asserted, God created through free, gratuitous love. Arius, the Alexandrian priest condemned for denying the Son's eternal and essential divinity with the Father (c. 250–c. 336), while referring to God as Creator, rejected any argument from correlativity, that 'Creator' and 'creation' are by definition simultaneous,[1] and so rejected creation's eternity. Arius wished primarily to preserve the idea of God as the ingenerate First Principle, indivisible, unique, above all limitations, absolutely free and unconstrained from without. Hence, creation was seen as the product of God's free will and not as arising from

God's divine being. That God was Creator was then not part of God's essential definition; and creation's description as essentially contingent and complex, generated from nothing, the result of divine, sovereign free will, is central to the Arian understanding of God, the only Ingenerate One, essentially independent of all contingencies.

Athanasius wished to preserve God's free sovereignty. Like Methodius, he rejected the idea of creation's co-eternity with God the Creator. His argument is not however the 'third man' theory, that the ascription of 'unoriginateness' to both Creator and creation necessitates the existence of a 'third', prior and higher than both, which accounts for their distinct existences. Rather he argues that otherwise God's power is limited. Like Arius, he asserts that God wills creation from nothing, though especially emphasizing God's goodness, founding, as Origen did, this good will in God's good nature as eternal Father and Son.

It comes as no surprise then to note that although Athanasius has much to say about God's creative and providential action, he is not particularly interested in the subject for its own sake. He views creation from God's perspective and treats it as the backcloth against which the Incarnation may be rightly seen; and he covers providence, creation's continuing sustaining, as that which furnishes an appreciation of the godly life. This does not mean that Athanasius is discreet in elaborating his thought. In the *De Incarnatione*, one of Athanasius' earliest works, the theories of the Epicureans, the Platonists and the Gnostics are considered and curtly dismissed as contrary to what 'the divinely inspired teaching of faith in Christ [reveals]' (*D.I.* 3). They all lack divine authority and propose bad theology. The Epicurean theory that the universe came into being of its own accord, by chance, is incompatible with creation's harmony, ordered by a purposeful God. The Platonic deity of the *Timaeus*, who fashions the world from pre-existent, disordered matter, is weak. He is but a craftsman, unable to make anything unless the raw material to be crafted already exists; and he is dependent upon the pre-existent material, even if that matter cannot shape itself and is itself dependent upon the divine Fashioner. For Athanasius, the God of Christian tradition is not so limited, both forming and shaping all. The Gnostic thesis, that the universe is the creation of one other than the Father of Jesus Christ and is therefore alien to the only source of goodness, is opposed to Scripture's witness to creation's goodness, whose beginning and end is God, the Father of Jesus Christ.

Having swiftly dismissed what he sees as private notions, individual likings standing in arrogant contrast with the corporately acknowledged ecclesiastical tradition, Athanasius notes that

the divinely inspired teaching of faith in Christ ... teaches that ... God, through the Logos, brought the universe which previously subsisted in no way whatsoever into being from non-being. (*D.I.* 3)

Initially Athanasius' assertion of 'creation from nothing' may appear to be a slogan, used polemically to differentiate him from others, but whose meaning is unclear. Yet Athanasius seems thereby not only to differentiate himself from the Epicureans, Platonists and Gnostics, but also to break new ground in giving meaning and substance to this phrase. For he extends that doctrine emerging slowly and uncertainly in early Christianity. When earlier Christians maintain such a doctrine, it is uncertain whether a strict sense of creation from nothing is implied.[2] In Athanasius' case there clearly is a strict doctrine of creation from nothing. He enumerates other options and rejects them; and the ideas held and not just those who held them are at stake. Hence Athanasius rejects, by implication, both the assertion of the early Christian apologist Justin Martyr that creation is from nothing, where 'nothing' is tantamount to pre-existent but unordered matter, and Origen's eternal creation of the eternal Creator. Creation is not God, nor God's contemporary, nor an emanation from God; it is not form imposed upon unformed matter. It is the result of God's calling into being what formerly was not. This 'was not' is the very antithesis of God, he who is. Whereas God is Life and the Giver of all life, the 'nothing' is void, a vacuum of emptiness, as it were, which not only is nothing, but ever pulls that created away from its God-given life and orderliness to its formless, chaotic void. It is in appreciation of the 'power' of this nothingness that Athanasius gives meaning to creation being truly miraculous, to the universe's order and harmony being the hallmark of God's gracious activity, and to death's power.

Athanasius further expands creation from nothing's meaning by employing the concept to maintain a complete and essential distinction, although not division, between God, the Self-existent, and that called and held in being solely by God's gracious will. He denies an intermediate sphere between God and his creation: the intermediary Logos is now consigned to the strictly divine; and the spiritual, the human soul included, is of the strictly creaturely. Creation is recognized as having no rights or value in itself, being dependent entirely upon its Creator and Sustainer. Revelation is dependent upon God's initiative; salvation is not concerned with some direct relationship between the soul and God, as in Origen, but with the restoration to conformity with the Logos *by the Logos himself condescending to creation in the Incarnation*; and contemplation is no longer that which 'divinizes' but is the response to the divine act of grace wherein the self-existent Creator stoops to wholly dependent creation. Indeed, the corollaries of Athanasius' extensive insistence upon the uniqueness of God and the dependence of the created order upon the Deity stress Athanasius' certain employment of a more developed doctrine of creation from nothing.

In keeping with this statement of creation from nothing, and its attendant theological ideas, Athanasius cites 1 Corinthians 8:6, 'there is one God, the Father, from whom are all things'. He is not content, however, merely to note that all is of God. He is concerned to explain why creation, which was not necessary to God being God, came into being. Reflecting the *Timaeus* of Plato, the Greek philosopher (427–347 BC) whose ideas in a modified form became so important for early Christian theologians, and echoing the reference to it by Irenaeus, the important Catholic theologian and Bishop of Lyons (*c.* 130–*c.* 200),[3] Athanasius maintains that

> God is good, or rather the source of goodness; and the good has no envy for anything. Thus, because he envies nothing its existence, through his own Logos, our Lord Jesus Christ, he made everything from nothing. (*D.I.* 3)

This thought's concern is, however, with more than a deity who will not deny others existence, or with a tolerant, well-meaning deity. It is concerned with God's very nature. The Father, perfect in nature, can only express his generous, joyous nature with a subject, equally perfect, who is able perfectly to return that joyous life. The Father, as P. Widdicombe notes,[4] thus delights in seeing himself in his own Image; and, conversely, the Son rejoices in seeing himself in the Father. The divine life consists then in a communion of goodness, and in a plurality and mutuality in which there is a wealth of intentional delight and gift, arising from the Father's eternal generative nature and the Son's dependency as the ever Only-Begotten. This understanding of the divine being prompts

Athanasius to see it as the source of all existence. The generous Father and the loving Son freely and joyously will to bring a creation into being which is reflective of that divine life's nature, but is yet distinct.

God's good nature and creative will are then closely related. For Athanasius, however, God does not choose either to be Creator, or even to will creation's existence. For God does not decide to be what he is. Equally, however, God is not constrained either by his nature or from without to be or do anything. Rather, what God is and does, God is and does consciously and intentionally and eternally.

Especially when working with such an understanding of God, Athanasius is compelled to consider whether the arguments that he marshals regarding the Son's eternal generation from the eternal Father transfer to those regarding creation's origination from the Father. So he reflects: 'God was always a Maker ... Does it then follow that because he is the Framer of all that his works are also eternal?' (*C.Ar.* 1.29; cf. Tertullian, *Adversus Hermogenem* 3.1). The issue is the more pointed if the general thesis of the Greek philosopher Aristotle (384–322 BC) is accepted, of the contemporality of relations. Athanasius' consideration begins by distinguishing the Son from the works of creation. 'What likeness', he asks, 'is there between the Son and works, that [the Arians] should parallel a Father's with a Maker's function?' (*C.Ar.* 1.29). He notes a crucial distinction between what is begotten and what is willed. The Son is the proper Offspring of the Father's essence and not the product of the Father's will. Indeed, Athanasius asserts, by analogy, that paternity is not a matter of will but essence, and a man can only be a father if and when his son exists. In contrast, creating is a matter of will, a work being external to its maker's being. It is, for Athanasius, external to a maker's definition. For a work need not exist for a person to be called a maker, it being sufficient that that person may fashion the work as and when he wills. In short, essential sonship is contrasted with willed creation. As the Father always is, so what is proper to his essence, the Son, must always be; but whereas God is always called Creator, God's works, not being proper to his eternal essence, but the result of his good will, need not be nor are always.

A subsidiary question then arises. If God always was good and ever had the power to create, why did he not always create? Athanasius' answer lies in his understanding of creation. Being originate, it wants the power to be eternally. It has a beginning.

Further, having a beginning, it is perishable; it may return to that nothing whence it emerged. That created from nothing cannot therefore be co-eternal with God, who knows and can know neither beginning nor end. Given his sense of God's goodness Athanasius does not, however, leave the matter there. He continues 'God, looking to what was good for [things], made them at that time when he saw that, when brought into existence, they were able to abide' (*C.Ar.* 1.29). Recognizing their natural bias towards the 'nothing' whence they arose, God brought all things into existence and providentially held them in being when it was most to their advantage. Goodness directs that things may be; and goodness informs when they should be. The interlocking of God's nature, creation and providence is evident.

A corollary of this is, of course, that the creative act was for the creatures' and not the Creator's benefit. The world, and not God, was therein fulfilled; and not even the latter's goodness suffered detraction or disparagement through creation's once not existing. For God is God, whole and sufficient in himself. The creative God is not dependent upon things external to himself existing eternally to realize his eternal goodness. That is eternally and fully expressed within the loving communion of Father and Son. Realized, logically first, in the relation of the Father and Son, this form of divine goodness is then expressed through the Logos in his willed act of creation.

For Athanasius then creation is both very fragile and most wonderful. Considered by itself, it is weak, unstable and mortal; apart from the Creator's sustaining power it dissolves, not, as Plato would maintain,[5] to that infinite space of dissimilarity, but to non-existence. Such a naturally unstable world[6] renders the world considered by itself of little value. Certainly trust in it is futile; and worship of it is vain. Considered under God's creative hand, it is, however, recognized as worthy. This sense of creation being as nothing and yet of sublime worth is reinforced in Athanasius' picture of the creative Logos. He is absolute Power, absolute Light and absolute Truth, epithets whose simplicity is highlighted by creation being described as powerful and wise, not absolutely nor in itself but through its participation in the self-same Logos. Its worth lies then in God, the source of its existence and of its goodness. Creation is from the world's side a continuous receiving of God, who gives all that it is and has. It therefore has responsibilities towards God, whom it is to serve, and towards itself, whose God-given and life-enhancing harmony no part should disturb.

25

This harmony is noteworthy. For it refers not solely to the world not being at variance with itself, but also to creation's God-given settled being. For it is in the Logos that the works of creation remain settled, not working their own downfall. Apart from God they slip inexorably back to chaotic nothingness. So creation's parts are to be united in relation to one another *in the Logos*. They are no longer to have exclusive regard to their individual nature, but are to recognize their sovereign Creator, whose good will is that their movement and relationship should not be haphazard and meaningless. Indeed, prospering in their harmony, they will know their true nature as creatures of the fatherly Creator. For creation, in all its variety, including the invisible powers which pagans often saw as divine in themselves, is seen as dependent, in a responsible contingency which is not deadly but life-enhancing. The world is recognized not as an end in itself but as living through, in and for the Logos and Father, the world's Beginning and End, who never envy the world its well-being. This harmony is therefore correlative with the universe's welfare; it is also a celebratory witness to the Divine Harmonizer.

Creation is then living and contingent; for God, the only source of life, offers life to all in giving himself to all. It is good; God, who cannot work evil, made it. It is reasonable, being formed by divine Reason, God's Logos. In all this, creation reflects its Maker. Here we have the basis upon which Athanasius resists the tendency both to drive a wedge between grace and nature, and to present Christ as the antithesis of nature rather than its completion and key to meaning. In teaching that the Logos was the agent of creation, Athanasius allows that to live after Christ is the natural life, that the Creator is the Saviour, and that nature and grace are related and not antithetical. Certainly he hardly ever turns in Wordsworthian fashion to nature's 'Old Felicities' for illustrations. Yet his thought of the Logos as agent in creation permits the conviction that there is not mere analogy but an inward affinity between the natural order and the spiritual. As we will periodically see, Athanasius does not need to invent artificial illustrations for the religious truths that he wished to teach. He finds them even in secular life. Hence he will use the image of a teacher stooping to his pupil's level, to enhance a sense of the Incarnation; of a king who is no more or less king for his subjects' loyalty or infidelity, to stress the impossibility of God's being changed by either true worship or idolatry; and of asbestos, the ultimate, secure protection against fire, to illustrate the security offered by the incarnate Saviour. He can also use non-biblical terms such as *homoousios*, 'of the same substance', and *hypostasis*, 'person', to guard the truth of Scripture. Athanasius' sense of God being the Creator of all is the premise behind these moves.

People are part of this wider creation and yet they are peculiar within creation. Hence, while what is true of the wider creation is true of people, that is not the whole truth. The point is made immediately in Athanasius' description of God's action towards them.

> Of all those on earth God had special pity for the human race; and seeing that, by definition of its own existence, it would not be able to persist for ever, [God] gave it extra grace, not simply creating men like all irrational animals on earth, but making them in his own image and giving them also a share in the power of his own Logos; so that, having as it were shadows of the Logos, and being made rational, they might be able to abide in felicity and live the true life in paradise, which is really that of the saints. (*D.I.* 3)

For all such extra grace, people's dependency is not lessened but is rather intensified. Certainly it is the case that they are 'superior' to the rest of creation in that they alone are rational. Yet they are so through being granted a share in the power of the divine Logos. Nor is that grounds for boasting or for self-confidence. For they participate in the divine Logos on the grounds not of their merit but of God's mercy. The motive again is God's goodness, which envies none existence. People are given this added grace that they may be able to live the true, paradisial life. Indeed, such phrases as 'a share in the power of [God's] own Logos' and 'shadows of the Logos' reinforce the sense of their increased dependency. People are powerful and rational by participation, while the Logos is the Father's Power and Wisdom 'not by participation, nor do these properties accrue to him from without' (*C.G.* 46). People have, as it were, 'shadows of the Logos', while the Logos is he whose shadow is cast. Indeed, the Creator's benevolent lordship is further manifest in God's provision of a ring fence against people's abusing their God-given free will. By placing them in paradise, and by warning them against misusing this faculty, stating the glorious results of obedience and the dire consequences of turning from God, God further sought to secure the additional grace given. Significantly, just as people's dependence does not deprive them of responsibility, so this example of God's lordship is not so dominant as to render them but puppets. In being so guarded by God, their freedom is not removed. Rather, its importance is the more stressed in that God graciously seeks to protect them from abusing their God-given liberty, calling upon them to use their freedom for establishing and maintaining their goodness. Equally significantly however, by rightly exercising their God-given freedom, people do not establish their independence from God, not even to the extent of having a basis for boasting. For in that, they use in obedience to God a God-given faculty, with the promised God-given result, the blunting of their natural corruption, and their living henceforth 'as God' (*D.I.* 4).

Given not only that the whole person is held in being but also that each of his aspects is maintained in its right relationship to all others, it is not surprising that Athanasius rejects the common Platonic antithesis of spirit and matter, of soul and body. The soul, it is true, is immortal, and thus akin to the Immortal. Yet this soul is also created; it is the product of the divine will, use of the word 'will' being one of Athanasius' means of indicating that which is onto-logically distinct from the divine Creator. Further, Athanasius' 'soul', unlike Plato's, is seen as not exterior to the creaturely body but bound to it by God's good will. There is no sense of the soul being punished or hampered by its being one with its body. Rather, the soul orders its body, and orders it for the harmonious well-being of each person, soul and body, and not for the soul's emancipation from its body. There is no Origenistic sense of the soul being purified by the short, sharp shock of being embodied. In short, there is no awkwardness relating a soul to its body.

With this human soul Athanasius often connects the idea of God creating an individual after his own Image; God granted each a 'likeness' to himself, an idea deriving from the Septuagint Greek version of Genesis 1:26, and referring to rationality.[7] This ration-ality is seen as God's continuous gift, held in trust, and not as a human 'possession'. It amounts to being enabled to understand oneself and one's world rationally, or as God's Reason, the Logos, does, and thereby to appreciate the world as created, good and valuable, although not to be worshipped as God himself is wor-shipped; and it consists in being empowered to recognize creation's harmony and the Harmonizer of all creation.

This rationality is not cold and calculating. For it is properly secured by a 'desire' for God, the very antithesis of any covetous longing for creation. God, for Athanasius, is 'limitless'. In essence God is outside the universe, not constrained by anything, though by his providential power containing everything. In consequence people relate to a limitless Being, ever approached but never fully reached. Their religious journey necessarily never comes to an end. Yet this journey is not towards an abstract, infinite absolute, but towards an infinite Goodness, a boundless Source of life and grace. Their never ending pilgrimage is, then, one always marked by desire and hope, and is never coloured by possession or control of that sought. This desire is, if one wishes, a corollary of God's sovereign freedom and human contingency, because of which human nature is seen as essentially restless. Not solely was it drawn from nothing, and but for God's continuing grace would return there, but also its orientation is towards a deity who creates and sustains it, meets it through the world and yet extends endlessly beyond it. People's movement towards the boundless Creator arises, then, from neither fear nor natural necessity. They are attracted to God by God's goodness and by the longing to share in the divine generosity, the basis of all true existence.

The true creature then respects the divine self-existence; the humble being manifests a trust or faithfulness directed away from himself and towards a Creator to whom none will ever be adequate and whom no one will ever fully comprehend. Humble people are those who recognize their own provisionality, their excellent yet pale reflection of the infinite Excellence. In short, a person's restless and precarious life and history is made both possible and meaningful by reference to the Creator and Sustainer, who meets each in history and yet extends beyond history. So human rationality is marked by desire, a righteous jealousy for God and God's creation.

It almost goes without saying that creation delights in God; what must be said is that it is that in which God rejoices. This latter point means neither that creation is, in any sense, an end in itself and so a rival to the Father, nor that God, in delighting in it, adds somehow to his well-being. Athanasius will not relinquish the belief that God is perfect and complete, wanting nothing. Athanasius will, however, assert that God's delight in the world is explained in relation to the Father's eternal delighting in the Son. For God's perfection is not abstract, but that known in the 'Father–Son' relationship. The Father delights in seeing himself in his own eternal Image, the Logos, a joy which is not 'added' to the Father. Delighting in the world is consistent with this eternal delight. For when the Father delights in creation, he delights 'in seeing the works made after his own Image; even this rejoicing of God is on account of his own

29

Image' (*C.Ar.* 2.82). The fact that creation is made after God's own Image is the cause of the Father's delighting in it. The Father's delight is then neither new nor dependent upon creation. Creation does not need to exist for this joyous delighting of Father in Son and Son in Father. The delighting is eternal and simple. With creation, only the arena where the joy is reflected is new.

PROVIDENCE

In his account of God as Creator Athanasius has stressed God's unrivalled sovereignty and the dependent and orderly creation. Focusing on the world as having been called into being, Athanasius is no less eager to stress these same two themes. He resists any belief that the world is like a clock, wound up and left to run a predetermined course. Such a belief would have the advantage of not being open to the charge that the world, once brought into existence, is the helpless butt of change. Yet it has the disadvantage of allowing the world a degree of independence which would challenge both the Creator's being the sole and continuous source of life and the world's contingency. Hence Athanasius cites Matthew 10:29 (*De Fuga* 9; 15) regarding not one sparrow falling into a snare without the Father's knowledge. The idea of providence is advanced. In keeping with the Matthean text, Athanasius is concerned with both the immediacy and particularity of this providence. Hence, for example, he will write of the Creator Logos, by his angel, commanding Joseph to take his infant son, the child whom the Logos had become in becoming incarnate, to Egypt to escape Herod's fury (*De Fuga* 12).

Athanasius senses that the Creator knows and is involved not only in what is and has happened, but also in what shall happen. For while it is important for him to assert that the Logos is the creator of 'time', it is equally important to maintain that the Logos created 'times'. Even as in creation the Logos fashioned according to the Father's will, so in his providential care the Logos, in accordance with the Father's wishes, allocates to each a time to live and a time to die. This is evidenced especially in the Johannine account of Christ's life, where, when Christ's hour was come, he obediently accepted exaltation upon the cross. Each person knows, according to Athanasius, that 'a certain time is measured to every man, but . . . no one knows the end of that time' (*De Fuga* 15). For particulars of each person's life span are unknown unless God reveals them.

More flesh may be put upon this providential skeleton. In *C.Ar.* 2 Athanasius is concerned to explain the providence lying behind salvation. A number of themes are interwoven here, amongst which are the ideas that redemption was appropriate, and the Creator fittingly the Recreator. For God our Creator,

> knowing our destinies better than we, and foreseeing that, though having been made good, we should in the event be transgressors of the commandments and be thrust from paradise for disobedience, being philanthropic and good, prepared beforehand in his own Logos man's salvation. (*C.Ar.* 2.75)

Indeed, Athanasius argues, it would have been improper not to allow that a person's salvation should be prepared 'even before the world's foundation' (*C.Ar.* 2.75, quoting Ephesians 1:4). Otherwise God would have appeared ignorant of people's fate, open to an increase in knowledge, and mutable, God taking counsel after their fateful demise. Indeed, God would have appeared less prepared than any wise architect, who,

> proposing to build a house, consults also about its repair, should it at any time after being built become dilapidated; and counselling about it, he makes preparation and gives the workmen material for repair. So, prior to us, is the repair of our salvation founded in Christ, that in him we may be created anew. The will and the purpose were made ready 'before the world' but have taken effect when the need required, even when the Saviour came amongst us. (*C.Ar.* 2.77)

In his understanding of providence, the emphasis is upon the divine purpose, which is eternal, and upon its realization in time; both the eternity and immutability of God and the temporality of the assumed finite humanity are thus preserved.

Even when God's eternal saving purpose is effected in and through the Incarnation in space and time, it is clear that providence is not exhausted. In his *De Fuga Sua* Athanasius further treats the matter of providence, this time considering primarily the providential God's continuing relationship with Christians. There it is widely recognized that each one's weal comes of living in accordance with the divinely willed times, and that ill befalls the non-compliant. Yet these 'times', measured to each, are not imposed mechanically. There is no determinism. Athanasius, it is true, does have a strong sense both that God eternally envies none fullness of existence and that 'the Logos himself, as Logos, knows all things even before they come to be' (*C.Ar.* 3.38[8]). Only so is God's immutability in will and wisdom preserved. Alongside these beliefs, however, Athanasius has an equally strong sense of people being free. Hence the immutable God who cannot change his mind allocates the proper 'hour' of Christ's death; and the Logos in his mutable flesh obediently accepts his sacrificial death. In this case the freedom of the assumed flesh and the possibility of disobedience may seem slight. Yet, Athanasius does know of John 10:18 and admits that 'though able to prevent [death, the Logos] did not do so' (*Ad Epict.* 6). As man, the Logos could have resisted death, and so have prevented his dying for all. Yet, though he could have been so disobedient, he was not disobedient. Freely he complied with the providential will. Before the hour, appointed by the divine, providential Logos, for his arrest and crucifixion came, the Logos as man, when sought, hid himself. When, however, it came,

> he announced it to the Father, saying, the hour is come; glorify thy Son. And then no longer he hid himself from those who sought him, but stood willing to be taken by them. (*De Fuga* 15)

In short, Christ's life and death is shot through with willing obedience, and the implied responsible use of freedom.[9] In the case of Christ's servants, the possibility of disobedience is more pronounced, partly because Christians, unlike Christ, have been and are less responsible in freedom's use. Christians should, Athanasius maintains, always be ready freely to live in accordance with the divine will, and the hours it allocates. Yet their will is not determined. All are capable of resisting their 'hour', by either postponing or anticipating the 'hour', both of which are equally wrong, as the time given by God is wisely and accurately given. Both amount to missing the right time. Athanasius' point is that the life led under God's providence should concentrate upon freely and responsibly conforming one's whole life to the times measured to each individual. The emphasis is upon obedience to God's sovereign purpose. Hence Christ, who lived obedient to the 'hour' given him, is the exemplar of proper human behaviour. He

> neither suffered himself to be taken before the time was come; nor did he hide himself when it came, but gave himself up to them that conspired against him. (*De Fuga* 15)

Standing for the Truth, whether or not it resulted in death, was all-important. Fear, the opposite of trust in God, was to be resisted.

Athanasius does speak of man being 'represented beforehand' in the Logos, being 'predestined unto adoption', being 'chosen before we came into being' and having 'an inheritance which is pre-destined', terms echoing the Pauline passages to which he refers (e.g. Ephesians 1:3–5; 2 Timothy 1:8–10). He also writes of saints hiding until they were delivered into the persecuting hands, according 'as it seemed to God to be good' (*De Fuga* 16). Yet he interprets all this in relation both to God's eternal purpose for good and life, and to man's possibility, though not necessity, to accept such. Athanasius does not preclude the unwise choice, the irresponsible use of freedom. Indeed, he does not hesitate to speak of people being

> transgressors of the commandments, of their being thrust out of paradise for disobedience and of their receiving in the final judgement the inheritance 'according to [each one's own] conduct'. (*C.Ar.* 2.76)

He readily recognizes people's freedom, and its possible use in a manner contrary to God's good, providential purpose for their well-being.

Clearly Athanasius believes therefore that there should be free, culpable, human co-operation with the providential God. Yet this co-operation is not that between two equals. Nor is it centred so much upon particular acts, important as they are. For the object of living under God's providence is to subdue one's own will, to trust God, and to allow the Logos who eternally purposes man's good to take over the self. The aim is to banish the selfish, self-concerned activity of the *ego* and to let God's will be done, on earth as in heaven.

By relating God's sustaining providential care not only to Christ but also to the apostleship of Paul and to 'our own calling' to serve God (*C.Ar.* 3.61), Athanasius domesticates the subject. Belief in providence is not only important on the wider theological canvas, safeguarding the unchanging goodness and sovereignty of God; it is also a belief significant for the mundane leading of Christian life. This latter point is made clear in Athanasius' *Festal Letters*, annual epistles announcing both the date of Easter and the manner of

Lenten preparation. It is also especially manifest in his *De Fuga Sua*. Initially the matter of subduing one's own will to God's providential will seems straightforward; but, when it is remembered that the providential times measured to each person are unknown to each unless God reveals them, the matter is seen to be not so straightforward. Athanasius meets this difficulty head-on. Being ignorant of the providentially appointed 'hour' of death, the saints of old were unwilling to deliver themselves immediately into the power of those conspiring against them. They therefore hid themselves from their persecutors, either until the appointed time of their death by natural means, or until God stayed their persecutors' hand, or until they were delivered into the persecuting hands (*De Fuga* 16). Rightly the saints of old so acted. For they did not want to tempt God, in whose hand they knew their portions lay, but what these portions were they knew not. Moreover, they did not wish to hand themselves over to their persecutors 'without reason'. For to hand themselves over even prematurely would be contrary to the will of God's Logos, or Reason, would be tantamount to suicide, and could be deemed to be cowardly or untrusting. Seeking a premature death, rather than accepting the providentially appointed 'hour' of death, even at the hands of persecutors, would amount to seeking escape from the greater hardships of flight, wherein a godly life might be learnt and shared. To the deluded eye, so ready a self-surrender might appear to be an act of courageous witness to the Lord. In reality it amounted to a betrayal of the patient, suffering Christ. Therein is known an untimely death, a counterfeit martyrdom, rather than the patient, costly enduring until the God-given hour of death. Thus, neither shrinking from death when it came nor forestalling it, both of which were marks of infidelity, the saint was to follow the general rule of fleeing when persecuted, hiding when sought, and waiting, ready and alert, for the time of death.

It is worth noting that providence, though closely associated with the good Creator, is unlike the creative act, in not being 'from nothing'. God's providential acts, and especially the saving Incarnation, are conditioned by space and time. The Providential One works with history, transfiguring and transforming it. This One works with ignorant man, and knows that virtue is worked on the anvil of experience. Hence God works even with and through particular people's irresponsibility. While Athanasius does not commend people misusing their God-given freedom, he acknowledges that God seeks to bring good out of the evil born of their folly. Thus, reflecting upon the manner of Christ's death, Athanasius maintains that Christ's captors freely chose crucifixion; and insofar as killing, and especially killing most cruelly, is evil, Christ's death is evil, the result of a misuse of human liberty. Yet that misuse of freedom is especially fitted to God's revelatory and saving purposes. For in the choice of the very worst, and in the triumph of the Logos over it, Christ's divine lordship is made all the more manifest to disbelieving mankind. Providence, for Athanasius, works through the world; it does not cancel out the world.

Given this sense of God's providence, Athanasius leads his followers to have faith both in the original goodness of creation, despite its terrible appearances, and in God's good purposes for the world; and he gives the basis to cultivate and recollect an awareness of the unchanging and untroubled eternal glory in which that faith is grounded and in which the world has some share even here and now. This faith in creation suggests the importance of seeing the world, and each and every person in it, as in some sense imaging God the Creator. Here is the *raison d'être* of the world being holy, of seeing God in it, because this is what it is in God. Indeed, without providence, the continuing of God's self-manifestation in the world, complex, ambiguous and mutable as it now is, would be highly problematic. Further, here is the basis for a right understanding of people's dominion in creation. Given that the divine Wisdom left his imprint on *all* creatures, 'that what was made might be manifestly wise works, and worthy of God' (*C.Ar.* 2.78), and that people were, of all creatures, further made capable of perceiving that divine imprint in all, and the witness of all to the divine Wisdom and to Wisdom's Father, a person's relation to the rest of creation cannot be one of superiority. Our distinction lies not in our being granted the divine imprint and the rest of creation not; in fact even our distinct capacity to perceive God is ours by grace, and not by either nature or right. Our relation to the rest of creation is then one of responsibility. We are not to denigrate nor to idolize it, but to venerate it as that which both bears God's imprint and witnesses to him who would have all creation not only existing but existing worthily of its Maker. In short, we are to view it as 'sacramental'.

Notes

1 Compare Aristotle, *Categories* 7B.15: 'relatives seem to be simultaneous by nature; and in most cases this is true. For there is at the same time a "double" and a "half", and when there is a "half" there is a "double"; and where there is a "slave" there is a "master". Similarly

with the others. Also, one carries the other to destruction.' Compare also Aristotle, *Metaphysics* 5.15, where Aristotle cites the relation between a 'father' and a 'son', but uses this example as an illustration of *agent* and *patient* as it arises as a result of a *temporal* act.

2 Compare R. M. Grant, *Miracle and Natural Law in Graeco-Roman and Early Christian Thought* (Amsterdam, 1952), pp. 133–52.

3 Irenaeus, *Adversus omnes haereses* 3.41; 4.63.1.

4 P. J. Widdicombe, *The Fatherhood of God from Origen to Athanasius* (Oxford, 1994), pp. 206–8.

5 Plato, *Politicus* 273E–F.

6 Athanasius' understanding is shared with Albinus (*Epitome* 2.1), Athenagoras (*Supplicatio* 22.2) and Numenius (*Fragments* 17).

7 Compare C. McL. Wilson, 'The early history of the exegesis of Genesis', *Studia Patristica* 1 (*Texte und Untersuchungen* 63; 1957), pp. 420–7.

8 C. Kannengiesser, *Athanase d'Alexandrie évêque et écrivain: une lecture des traités contres les Ariens (Théologie historique* 70; Paris, 1983), suggested that *C.Ar.* 3 was written not by Athanasius but by the young Apollinarius (*c.* 310–*c.* 390), another vigorous critic of Arianism, who wrote a number of works which yet were attributed to Athanasius. G. C. Stead, in a review of *Athanase d'Alexandrie* in *Journal of Theological Studies* N.S. 36 (1985), pp. 220–9, questions Kannengiesser's thesis.

9 Athanasius does refer to John 10:18:

> The Logos, being himself immortal, but having a mortal flesh, had power, as God, to become separate from the body and to take it again, when he would. (*C.Ar.* 3.57)

This passage is not primarily concerned with human obedience to divine Providence, but with countering the Arian belief that the Logos is a creature. Hence here Athanasius contrasts the Logos, who may put down or take up life, as he wills, with a creaturely man, who dies when his nature dictates, even if he then does not wish to die. The will of the Logos is effective against death; a man's is not. The Logos is the source of life; creatures are its recipients. The passage is about the divine status of the Logos, and not the synergistic sense of a person's life in God.

2

Revelation and resistance

GOD'S SELF-REVELATION

Athanasius' presentation of God's self-revelation stems from his understanding of both God and man. God is not solitary, but naturally gives of himself, firstly in the divine triune community, and secondarily in the acts of creating and sustaining. He is good and thus wishes all to live fully in the knowledge and loving obedience of their Maker. Revelation is then not a necessity for God, but an important consequence of God's good nature. Humans, meanwhile, were made that, never abandoning their conception of God, they might ever enjoy in the saints' company a joyful converse with 'divine' things, living an idyllic, truly blessed and immortal life; those however who freely but foolishly cut themselves off from the Truth lack even in this life a 'profitable existence' (*D.I.* 11), and in the hereafter deprive themselves of immortality. Hence, God's readiness always to reveal himself to each and for every person's benefit, our God-given capacity to appreciate God revealed, and the importance for all of knowing and the folly of ignoring God are themes central to Athanasius' writing on the subject of knowing God. This knowledge of God is, however, more than mere knowledge about God. It is knowing God, with the corollaries of a godly life in this earthly life, and of immortality in the life hereafter. It is then no wonder that Athanasius notes that when God, the source of all goodness who denies no one existence, creates people, God does not leave them destitute of knowledge of him 'lest even their own existence should be profitless to them' (*D.I.* 11).

To deny no one existence means to deny no one a full and rich existence. To exist *and* to know God grants people a quality of life even now, let alone in the hereafter. This quality of life is highlighted in the comparison of people with animals. The latter know nothing more than things terrestrial; they are unaware of the Father's Logos, by whom they are created and held in being. The former, however, cognizant of their Maker, know both the material world and its meaning; and knowing the Source of all meaning and value, they judge all through the Creator's perspective. The issue of knowing God is not then just one of theological debate; and human wisdom, the obverse of knowing God through his Reason, is not just the human reasoning capacity. These are matters of utmost seriousness and consequence. They are to do with human definition, with being and knowing oneself to be a creature of the Creator. Those who know God and live reasonably, obeying the divine Reason, live a happy and truly blessed life; and they know their wholesomeness in being true to their nature as a creature and child of the good and generous creative Father.

This creative God is unknown in himself and known only in his 'power'. This is not an early version of the later Byzantine theory that to know God is to know him in his 'acts', which flow from the three divine persons, God's divine substance remaining entirely transcendent and incommunicable. Rather, believing that God in himself is beyond man's comprehension, God being increate and people creaturely, Athanasius employs an idea something like that of Philo the eclectic Jewish thinker and exegete and of Origen, who find God in the harmony of the created order. This is an imprecise idea. Yet it is a useful tool in securing, especially later on, a proper doctrine of divine transcendence; and it is important for stressing Athanasius' understanding of a relational knowledge of God, the limitless One who is known but never comprehended, loved and desired but never possessed nor reached. Consequently, matter is rendered God's vehicle of self-manifestation. Drawing no substantial distinction between space and time, as God creates each, between things spiritual and material, as God fashions all, between acts and thoughts, as they too ultimately are 'from nothing', Athanasius leads his reader to believe that God reveals himself everywhere and at all times: all things, living, moving and having their being in him, bear witness to their Creator, Sustainer and Harmonizer. Hence all those then who with an upright understanding, according to the Wisdom given them, come to contemplate the creatures, are able to say for themselves, by thy appointment all things continue. (*C.Ar.* 2.81)

God's gracious revelation is thus continuous with matter's continuity, ever enabling all to know fullness of existence.

Athanasius does then reject the substantial Hellenistic division between soul and body, spirit and matter, thought and act and so on. Yet he is willing to recognize a hierarchy of means of revelation. For while he recognizes that soul, spirit and thought are all creaturely, and thus ontologically distinct from their common Creator, he also acknowledges that these are more akin to the Creator than the body, matter and act. In the former, God's self-manifestation is more patent, and in the latter more latent.

Certainly revelation's existence may be denied. Such denial is, however, the result of delusion, 'the same kind of delusion as if one were to depreciate the sun when it is hidden by clouds' (*C.G.* 1). People are graciously made capable of appreciating God's epiphany; yet they are not compelled to appreciate it. Irrationality, the consequence of not exercising the Wisdom given them, can have its field day, awful as the result may be. The result is, however, the ending not of God's revelation but of a person's fullest existence in knowing God.

God's self-revelation comes via four main instruments: a human soul, created in God's image and likeness, a harmonious creation, the Old Testament Scriptures, and Christ. God's goodness, already evidenced in his self-disclosure, is thus further reflected in there being more than one vehicle of revelation. 'The grace of being "in the image" was sufficient for one to know God the Logos, and through him the Father' (*D.I.* 12). Yet God was aware of human mutability; God foresaw people's possible negligence wherein they might dull this divine image in themselves, fail to recognize God therein and turn to that nearer them, creation, and venerate it. Yet creation, to which they might turn, God so ordered that it might turn people back to God; it was so made that it, as it were, exhorted them 'Worship not me but him who made us both'. Even then, however, the divine mercy and generosity found not its limit. Indeed, it could not. For, being infinitely good, its goodness knew no bounds. God therefore gave law and sent prophets,

39

so that if [people] were reluctant to raise their eyes to heaven and know the Creator, they would have schooling from those close by. For man can learn more directly from other men about more advanced things. (*D.I.* 12)

For those, however, who misread or forgot the law and prophets, and so exchanged the Truth for a lie, and worshipped the creation rather than the Creator, the Lord of the law and the prophets took creation upon himself that

those who supposed that God was in corporeal things might understand the truth from the works that the Lord did through the actions of his body, and through him might take cognizance of the Father. (*D.I.* 15)

God's merciful goodness thus was reflected; it took seriously both the natural weakness of people's nature and the freedom of their will; and it graciously sought to instruct them at that level of instruction best suited to their present state. Indeed, it is fair to say that God sought not to compel nor to impress but to woo people with the Truth, and always and only for their benefit. These vehicles of divine courtship we now shall consider more closely.

KNOWING GOD THROUGH ONE'S SOUL

Especially in *C.G.–D.I.* Athanasius stresses this theme. To know the way to the truly existent God, each needs nothing but their own self.

For the road to God is not as far from us or as extraneous to us as God himself is high above all, but is in us ... and this road ... is each person's soul and the mind within it. (*C.G.* 30)

Nor is this capacity to know God limited to an élite. All have a soul.

All have stepped on that road [to God] and know it, even if not all wish to follow it, but rather abandon it because of this life's pleasures which drag them aside. (*C.G.* 30)

This God-given way to God is then explained. Being rational, the soul is akin to God's Reason; being immortal it is akin to the Eternal One; and as long as the soul remains pure, its rationality and immortality remain as earnests of the immortal Logos and his

Father. So the soul, pure and unruffled by bodily desires, may know God.

This idea is enhanced by the introduction of the term 'mirror'. To understand the metaphor of the soul being a mirror which when pure reflects the Logos, and in the Logos the Father (*C.G.* 34), it is necessary to appreciate Hellenistic thinking about mirrors and images. According to Plato (*Timaeus* 46A–C), light from the eye meets light from an object seen, the two rays of light mingling on the mirror's surface to form the image seen. The mirror's image is then not an illusion caused by the rays of light reflected by the mirror's surface, but actually exists, truly formed thereupon. When therefore Athanasius speaks of the pure soul's mirroring God, he is using a metaphor to explain people's being in God's image, a person's soul being a real, although dependent, image of God. True self-knowledge, profound appreciation of the soul having been made in the image of God's image, thus is a way to God.

This metaphor, faintly hinted at in Theophilus, the late second-century Bishop of Antioch, a Christian apologist,[1] and in Plotinus (205–270), the Neoplatonist philosopher and mystic,[2] is introduced clearly and distinctively, and it is embellished. It is Reason itself in whose image the soul was created. Reason enters and binds and harmonizes creation in all its pluriformity. Not limited by creation, the unmoved Logos enlivens and moves and judges all. The soul mirrors this Logos. It is reasonable; it enters its creaturely body, but is not limited by its body's bounds. It moves and governs and judges its body. So it is that in knowing the pure soul's true relationship to its body the observer knows the mirrored reflection of him in whose image the soul was made. This symmetry, whereby one may know God through self-knowledge, is no mere coincidence. For creation is not by chance. Creation, even of the soul and its relationship to its body, is deliberately and divinely willed, for its own good and for its knowing its Maker and Sustainer.

In *C.Ar.* 2 Athanasius illustrates this selfsame knowledge of God through introspection. A king's son, wishing to build a city, 'might cause his own name to be printed upon each of the works ... to make them remember him and his father' (*C.Ar.* 2.79). So God has, as it were, written his own Wisdom in humans. Human wisdom is 'as if it were the Logos' own' (*C.Ar.* 2.78); the impress of the Logos in us is 'as if it were himself' (*C.Ar.* 2.80). Thus,

a man, entering, as it were, upon this way first ... then advancing upwards in his thought, and perceiving the Framing Wisdom

41

which is in creation, will perceive in it also its Father. (*C.Ar.* 2.80)

Within this context the importance of the soul's purity is stressed. Generally speaking, this purity is the soul's being unimpaired by passions, an idea common both to churchmen like Theophilus of Antioch[3] and Clement, the one-time head of the catechetical school at Alexandria,[4] and to philosophers like Philo[5] and Plotinus.[6] More precisely, this purity derives its meaning from the recognition that while thoughts of, for example, immortality 'never leave the soul but remain in it' (*C.G.* 33), external influences may disturb the soul's mind and prevent it seeing in its soul, as in a mirror, God Immortal (*C.G.* 34). Hence searchers after God are to

> cast off the stain of all desires ... and wash themselves until they have eliminated every addition foreign to the soul and show it unadulterated, as it was made, in order that thus [they] may be able to contemplate [in their souls] the Father's Logos, in whose image [they were] made in the beginning. (*C.G.* 34)

Rather than allowing God's impress in a person to be overshadowed by irreverent thinking, the Christian is to retain that openness to the divine Logos, that intellectual integrity which allows himself to be blessed and God to be him who blesses. Thus, by retaining, or returning to purity of soul, rational people may see God mirrored. In that simplicity, as divinely willed and created, the soul is established in its right longing for God. As like to like, it reflects its Creator and Lord. This 'like to like' is a common Hellenistic idea, used to note the real similarity between the pure soul and God, yet without introducing any natural relationship between the soul and God, between mirror and that mirrored.

This purity does not, however, effect the revelation. It only puts the human soul in the position of being open to God, of being able to know the Logos, mirrored there.

When writing of the 'unadulterated [soul], as it was made' Athanasius does refer to the pure mind having intercourse with divine things and not with the body; he comments upon a person being superior to sensual and bodily impressions and clinging by the mind's power to heaven's divine and intelligible realities; he notes that when the mind is whole, it transcends the senses and all human things, rising above the world to behold the Father through the Son. Athanasius' ideas do not, however, imply that the pure individual lives in awareness of the divine, intelligible world, which, *separated from the sensible world*, truly is. His pure individual is not the Platonic philosopher who 'ought to try to escape from here to there as quickly as possible. And the way to escape is to become as nearly as possible like God' (*Theatetus* 176A–B). Pure human life for Athanasius lies not in separation from sensible things, but in detachment from a wrong relationship of soul and body. The soul was created unadulterated by, but not separated from, its body. The one good God is the Creator and Sustainer of both, and the created body is then not to be fled. The human soul is not to be careless of its body: it is to recognize its God-given relationship to it. It is to remember that it is properly soul to its body, governing and directing its body's wishes and desires, but not being dominated by its body. Only in this right, God-given relationship to its body does the soul mirror the relationship of the Logos to the world; only so may the soul know God properly mirrored in itself.

Certainly Athanasius does mention that the soul is 'other' than its creaturely and transitory body. Yet it would seem that even here Athanasius does not abandon his clearly articulated doctrine of creation from nothing, with its complete ontological distinction between the increate God and creation. He does not here reject the soul's natural, proper relationship to the created body. When Athanasius refers to the soul as 'other' than its body, he refers not to a substantial but a functional distinction. For while the body is naturally and uncritically attached to the present, transitory world, its soul critically assesses the body's relation to the world. Indeed, that the soul is 'other' than its body may well point, not to the soul's divinity, but to God, naturally other than the soul, and to which it and its body witness. For Athanasius knows the principle that the harmonious relationship between opposites points to God, through whom alone is order, unity and symmetry (*C.G.* 37). The soul, other than but in harmony with its body, would then point beyond itself. The cause of a person's harmony, that is, the soul, would reflect God, the cause of the soul's harmony. Such is but a variant upon Athanasius' clear assertion that 'by [God's] providence ... the rational soul is moved and possesses reasoning and life' (*C.G.* 44), an assertion most inappropriate for anything that is naturally other than the creaturely body, but most appropriate for a created soul which is functionally distinct from the creaturely body, through the orderly governance of which it witnesses to its Creator and Harmonizer.

This complex of ideas ties in with the Hellenistic view that the mind is the governing principle in the body, which is not to be entrapped by inferior, sensible desires. It also fits the Hellenistic belief that the mind properly relates to the intelligible world, which points the mind beyond itself to God. Yet Athanasius' views do differ in that both the sensible and intelligible worlds, the soul and its body, are created, their right union being a basis upon which God grants knowledge of himself.

There is then a real similarity between the soul and the divine Logos, and between, on one hand, the soul and its body and, on the other, the divine Logos and the world. There is, however, no natural kinship between the two. Hence the soul may be a road to God, but is not God. Knowledge of the self is not knowledge of God as it is, for example, with Plotinus, where the self is a true emanation of the One, and self-understanding is knowledge of the Divine.[7] Athanasius here radically adapts a common Platonic theme, in consequence of his adopting a clear doctrine of the human soul's creation from nothing. Without God's grace there is no revelation, nor vehicle of revelation. The 'image' of God in humans, a point of contact between God and man, is not then a self-existent possession in them, given to be used as and when they wish. It only exists in and through God's eternally creative will. Thus it is that their soul does not have the right to know God; the knowledge of God, people's wisdom, is given through the impress of the divine Wisdom's seal; it is received; it is 'created'.[8]

When then Athanasius speaks of self-knowledge being itself a way to knowing God, 'the soul ... [being] its own path, taking the knowledge and understanding of God the Logos not from without but from itself' (*C.G.* 33), he is not contradicting himself, denying the necessity of grace and asserting the soul's self-sufficient power to apprehend God. Rather, he is suggesting that the soul can know God in itself in the sense of seeing God graciously mirrored in this particular part of creation. What is true of the whole world, whose harmony points to the divine Harmonizer, is also true of a part of this whole creation, the creaturely soul in its body.[9]

KNOWING GOD THROUGH CREATION

Athanasius shares the Philonic thought that while one may gain knowledge of God through the mind set free from all sensible things, one may know God indirectly through creation.[10] So Athanasius asserts.

it is possible to gain knowledge of God from visible phenomena, since creation through its order and harmony, as it were in writing, indicates and proclaims its Master and Maker. (*C.G.* 34)

Athanasius' exposition assumes that the human race, being made from nothing, by itself cannot attain to any knowledge of the Increate One. Such knowledge comes not of climbing up to God, but of God magnanimously descending in humble self-revelation. God ordered creation because he was good; and although invisible by nature, he may be known through his having so ordered it. This argument is, of course, not new. Stoics, to whom God is the immanent, all-pervasive energy by which the natural world is created and sustained; Apologists, like the second-century Christian philosopher Aristides of Athens[11] and Theophilus,[12] and Irenaeus[13] all use it. Yet Athanasius' argument is the more significant for its complete exclusion of any ontological kinship whatsoever between the world and God. The doctrines of a God who is naturally invisible and incomprehensible, being above all created being, and of creation from nothing only emphasize that knowledge of God is by unconditioned grace alone and not through any natural kinship.

Athanasius employs a four-part argument to maintain the thesis that the contingent world manifests its increate Maker and God. 'In [the Wisdom's] impress the works [of creation] remain settled and endure for ever' (*C.Ar.* 2.80). Given that matter has an innate tendency to slip back to the nothingness whence it was formed, the appreciation that creation remained 'settled' involved the recognition that it remained so not through its own nature, but solely through the power of One who so held it (*C.Ar.* 2.81). Not being an efficient cause (*C.Ar.* 2.21), the whole world witnesses to him who is its continuous Framer. Indeed, when the ever-threatening, destructive nothingness is remembered, the world's precarious but continuing nature and its fragile harmony and beauty are appreciated as all the more marvellous and revelatory of the graciously vivifying Creator and Sustainer. But for the grace of God, it would not ever be, let alone be orderly. Nature's elegant contingency thus witnesses to God's existence and warns against giving creation the worship properly due only to its Creator (*C.G.* 45).

This argument is then further honed. The world's continuing existence witnesses not only to a non-contingent Being upon whom it depends, but also to this Being's generous character. Echoing

Plato (*Timaeus* 29E), Athanasius notes 'A good being would be envious of no one. So he envies none existence but rather wishes all to exist' (*C.G.* 41). The stability of this naturally unstable, transient world points then to One who exercises kindness and delight in creating and sustaining all. The third aspect of the Alexandrian's argument recognizes that opposing things in creation — hot and cold, spring and autumn, male and female — are not at variance but in concord, and ordered for the common good (*C.G.* 40; *C.Ar.* 2.81). Athanasius then introduces the principle that where there is no leader there is chaos. Given the world's order, there must therefore be a god; and as the universe is created with reason and wisdom, arranged with complete order, it is manifest that this governing and ordering God can be none other than God's Logos, Reason and Wisdom (*C.G.* 40). The fourth aspect of his argument is that it is obvious from the world's harmonious existence that God is one. For whilst where there is no leader, there is chaos, where there is more than one leader, there is anarchy. The world's harmony denies such anarchy and asserts God's oneness. Athanasius corroborates this argument by asserting that 'the single and perfect entity is superior to the disparate' (*C.G.* 39.24–25). To suppose then that there were more than one deity and only one world would be to suppose that the one world was superior to the many creator gods. This, to Athanasius' mind, would be nonsense. For 'gods' are superior to 'matter' and 'creators' to 'creatures'. Hence he concludes that 'if creation is one and the world is one and its order is one, then we must consider that it has one Lord, its King and Creator' (*C.G.* 39).

This understanding of the divine Wisdom making his impress on all matter not only allows Athanasius to appreciate that God is ubiquitously present and to be seen through all. It also permits a sense of the world being 'sacramental'. God can be known in and through matter and history, through people and deed, and through baptism and the eucharist. It also undergirds Athanasius' sense of God revealing himself through the different levels of creation, the human soul, the wider world and the words and works of Christ, levels appropriate to the perspicacity of each believer.[14]

Here again purity of mind in the beholder of the world is necessary. Through people's retaining their rational likeness to God and so viewing the world from the divine perspective, they are able to appreciate the creation's harmony and thereby discern the divine Harmonizer. Or, putting it negatively, when people are not overwhelmed by material desires, they do not become possessive of creation and so neither covet nor idolize it. They do not exchange the truth of God for a lie, and worship the creation more than the Creator. Rather, they enjoy creation as a good gift and worship its Creator as the gracious Giver. For

> all those who with an upright understanding, according to the Wisdom given them, come to contemplate the creatures, are able to say for themselves, by thy appointment all things continue. (*C.Ar.* 2.81)

Purity is then related not only to not breaking creation's harmony but also to not misreading creation's harmony. This purity is not only moral but also intellectual simplicity. Here Athanasius' argument is both like and unlike the Neoplatonism of Plotinus. He is like Plotinus both in having little but contempt for those who vilify the cosmos, and in recognizing the worshipper's important ability to let go and pass beyond the fragmentary and transient to the Source of all. This is the intellectual generosity of which J. Trouillard[15] speaks, which leads Plotinus and Athanasius from this world to this world's Origin. Athanasius is, however, unlike Plotinus in that the latter can speak of 'beauty perceived in material things [as] borrowed' (*Ennead* 5.9.2). Beauty is lent to the material world but does not inhere in it. 'It announces in its own being the entire content of the Good ... of which this is the expression, already touched by multiplicity' (*Ennead* 5.9.2). For Athanasius, however, the harmony and beauty of this world is contingent; it is not substantially one with God the Beautiful, God the Harmonious, even though touched by multiplicity. A kinship between creaturely harmony and divine Harmony exists, but no ontological continuity.

KNOWING GOD THROUGH SCRIPTURE

The Scriptures, Athanasius believed, not only complement God's general revelation through creation but in fact give 'fuller teaching'. Quoting various Old Testamental texts Athanasius establishes to his satisfaction that God is one and alone to be worshipped. He discovers that, in his universal, all embracing providence, God, through his Logos, creates, forms and orders the universe. He also infers that the Logos therefore necessarily pre-exists all that he brings into being and so is other than creaturely. The New Testament, he concludes, confirms the Old.

A general but important point is being pursued: it is God's good will that people may delight in knowing God, and since they by themselves cannot know God, God reveals himself, variously – through introspection, harmonious creation and Scripture – and constantly. Wherever people turn, they find God expressing himself. The force of these arguments, found especially in the *C.G.–D.I.*, is to underline the fact that no one has a reason for ignoring God. Unstintingly God reveals himself, and in a form comprehensible even to the most myopic.

THE MESSIAH AND KNOWING GOD

Not surprisingly Athanasius believes that God reveals himself in the Christ, the Messiah. Yet, before he will elaborate upon this, he feels compelled to explain that the Messiah has now come. Some of his audience do not so much misunderstand the significance of the Old Testamental messianic texts as fail to realize that they have already been fulfilled, and in Christ. Athanasius therefore calls upon his readers no longer wrongly to await the Messiah's advent. Arguing in line with the thinking of Justin Martyr's *Dialogue with Trypho* and Irenaeus' *Epideixis*, Athanasius asserts that the messianic prophecies have been fulfilled. The signs and times of the advent of God, as prophesied in Isaiah 35:3–6, are no longer awaited: at and only at Christ's coming do 'the blind see, the lame walk, the deaf hear and the tongue of the stammerer is loosed' (*D.I.* 38). Daniel 9:24–25 also, he maintains, has found its end in Christ. The text, he maintains, contends that the Messiah is not merely a man but the Holy of Holies, that Jerusalem will stand only until this Holy One's coming, and that from the time of this One's coming onwards prophecies and signs will cease. Until Christ's coming, Athanasius suggests, many were anointed; they were called 'holy men', but not the 'Holy of Holies'. In time past Jerusalem stood firm, and prophets prophesied and saw visions. Since Christ's coming, however, prophets no longer arise; visions are no longer seen; and Jerusalem, which had stood for so long, has fallen (*D.I.* 40). And understandably have these things passed away.

For when he who was announced has come, what need is there of those who announce; when the Truth is at hand, what need is there of the shadow? For this reason they prophesied until Justice itself should come . . . for this reason Jerusalem stood for so long, in order that they might first meditate there on the types of the Truth. Therefore, since the Holy of Holies is at hand, rightly have visions and prophecies been sealed and the kingdom of Jerusalem has ceased. Kings were anointed amongst them only until the Holy of Holies should be anointed. (*D.I.* 40)

The Christ is indeed the long-awaited Messiah, in the light of whom the Old Testament is to be read. Again, the idea of right-mindedness, or intellectual purity, surfaces, here in an exegetical context.

What seems clear from this argument from the prophecies' fulfilment is that while even in Old Testament time God reveals himself, he even then points through shadows and types to a future more decisive self-manifestation in Christ. Christ's works cry out, revealing the divine Saviour 'clearly' (*D.I.* 32). Indeed, the manifestation of God's justice and goodness is so intimately connected with Christ's own words and works and person that, for Athanasius, God's justice and goodness *is* Christ. Yet, interestingly, Athanasius still understands the divine epiphany to be, in a sense, future. He contrasts the 'apparent degradation through the cross' (*D.I.* 1) with

> [Christ's] second glorious and truly divine manifestation . . . when he will come no more with simplicity but in his own glory, no more with humility but in his own greatness, no more to suffer but thenceforth to bestow the fruit of his own cross on all. (*D.I.* 56)[16]

We must be chary of explaining Athanasius' understanding of the manifestation in Jesus and the glorious manifestation still to come in terms of a contrast between partial and complete. It is rather a contrast between veiled and manifest. According to Athanasius, God is manifest in Old Testamental times. This manifestation became, however, more patent in Christ. For Christ is fully God and truly came to this earth. What is now awaited is not then something more complete than God incarnate, but rather God incarnate, manifest in glory and power. In Christ God's self-manifestation is complete; it is decisive; and in that sense all are without excuse if and when they deny that divine Truth. For through the Incarnation people then had at hand not just the imprint of Wisdom from which to perceive Wisdom, but that which makes that imprint, Wisdom itself; no longer had they but the shadow of Truth from which to surmise Truth, but Truth itself, which yet still casts its own shadow over the whole creation (cf. *C.Ar.* 2.81). Yet God veils the Truth in incarnation, even as a good teacher veils the truth for the poorer student, not in such a way as to make acknowledgement impossible, but in such a way as to leave room for even the most obtuse person to appreciate the Truth. Thereby the oracle of Isaiah 11:9 shall be fulfilled, that the universe may be filled with the knowledge of God, as the waters cover the sea.

Though Athanasius willingly speaks of the fullness of God's revelation in Christ, over against the shadowy revelation in the law and the prophets, he does not forsake his theology of the cross for a theology of glory. God in his mercy is unwilling to dazzle mankind by his self-manifestation in Christ; hence the assumption of a humble body. Athanasius wishes to stress that God has become man in Christ and that therefore all who hesitate to acknowledge the Messiah's advent are in error. He also wants still to concern himself with what is radically distinct from the Creator, the worldly; he recognizes what this truly is, the window into God, and yet that this is at the same time what God humbly accepts to hide his blinding glory. The completeness of God is met in what 'hides' him, a creaturely life, a mortal body, an inglorious death.

When explaining God's revelation Athanasius speaks of various arenas of revelation: the pure soul, creation's being and harmony, Old Testamental teachers and prophets, and the Christ. Just as it is important to note that it does not follow that God is only partially present in the 'earlier' instruments of revelation and fully present only in the 'latest', so it is important to stress that, while God 'moves' from one arena of self-revelation to another, he does not thereby absent himself from a former one when he moves to a subsequent one. Nor does it follow that God is absent from a particular creaturely instrument whereby revelation may be effected, and only comes upon it when he decides so to use it. For the Logos, being infinite, is limited neither by the whole creation nor a part of it. 'He contains all things and is at once with all and in each part, invisibly revealing himself' (*D.I.* 42). Nor is it inappropriate that he who is in all may be recognized through a part of this all.

> The mind, which is throughout a man, is known by a part of the body, I mean the tongue, and no one says that the essence of the mind is thereby diminished. Just so, if the Logos who is in all things, were to use a human instrument, this would not appear unseemly. (*D.I.* 42)

Just as when the Logos becomes incarnate he does not thereby
absent himself from sustaining the whole world of which the
assumed humanity is a part, so when God reveals himself through a
particular part of creation, he does not render himself invisible in
the rest of creation. The principle issue here is not God's self-
revelation, but man's appreciation of God's self-revelation.

The particular then is only preferable to the all, the material to
the spiritual, the near to the distant, in so far as man's capacity is
such that he finds God more knowable through that which is near to
him. Man may appreciate God more readily in the particular than in
the general, despite the fact that God is fully and equally present in
both the particular and the general. To cite A. R. Peacocke,

> God is not more present at one time or place than at another ...
> nevertheless man finds that in some sequences of events in
> created nature and history God *unveils his meaning* more than in
> others. God is equally and totally present to all times and places
> but man's awareness of that presence is uniform neither in
> intensity nor in content ... So, though in one sense, God as
> Creator acts in all events, yet not all events are received as 'acts of
> God'.[17]

The sense that the omnipotent Logos providentially reveals himself
in the varying levels of creation is especially significant for the sense
that revelation is still possible in and *through* a fallen world. In
Athanasius there is a certain antinomy: there are the beliefs both
that through the fall creation is affected and that in this fallen
creation God's eternal power is still visible. However warped by
humanity's sinful perspective and action, creation is still the divine
Wisdom's medium. Only so can sense be made of Athanasius' call
to those who have abandoned God to turn back to him (*C.G.* 34).

Athanasius' sense of God's self-revelation, of God's sharing
himself with people in order that they might know, and not simply
know about, God, is a useful counterbalance to certain modern
trends. Rightly, increased emphasis may be laid upon the reality of
evil and the otherness of God; wrongly, there may be an increasing
insistence upon a discontinuity between nature and grace. Hence,
for example, God's revelation in Christ is set over against the
knowledge of God that nature gives, although not as its focus but as
something other. Athanasius' stress upon Christ as the Wisdom of
God and upon creatures as witnessing to the Agent of their creation
encourages one to see a strong continuity and not discontinuity

51

between God's work as Creator and as Redeemer. It exhorts one to trace in this world, sinful as it is, the marks of God's Wisdom, and so to claim truth in all disciplines as God-given. It evokes in one the memory that salvation is to include this world: renewal in God's image is effected in this world; and the knowledge of God is reflected in a holy life, transforming this world.

HUMAN DISREGARD

As created, a person

> had his mind fixed on God in unembarrassed frankness and lived with the saints in the contemplation of intelligible reality ... and so God wished him to remain. (*C.G.* 2–3)

Athanasius therefore saw any turning from this good state as contrary to God's will, and to the person's detriment, and as an inversion of the proper hierarchy of God, the human mind, the human body and its world. Yet turning there was.

Athanasius' understanding of such is not based in the Hellenistic view that material existence itself already constituted an individual's fall, nor in an Origenistic pre-mundane fall. Rather, the fall is that of an already existing being, mind, soul and body, explained thus:

> The devising of idols was the beginning of fornication and the invention of them the corruption of life; for neither were they from the beginning, neither shall they be for ever. For by the vaingloriousness of man they entered into the world. (Wisdom 14:12–14, mentioned in *C.G.* 9)

Created good and for a godly purpose, people were yet no puppets. They were made free and responsible, with the option of choosing either good or evil. More precisely, they could 'just as well incline to the good as turn away from the good' (*C.G.* 4). For in the world, as created, evil itself did not exist, only the possibility of evil. Where all things are possible but not all are expedient, each individual's choice then was to serve or not to serve God, to use or to abuse his corporeal members, and to reverence creation as that which points beyond itself to the one true God or to enter into idolatrous worship of that creation.

Indeed, how radically free is human choice is manifest in Athanasius' belief that it was improper that what had once been created rational, having partaken of the divine Logos, should disregard God and fall back to non-existence. Improper though it was, Athanasius' God did not forbid it. The Alexandrian recognizes the risk that God took in allowing humans the capacity to shape their own futures. They are granted the full responsibility of making themselves and their world as they wish them to be within the conditions particular to their creatureliness. For Athanasius, possessing human freedom is of great value.

> If they remained good, they would enjoy the life of paradise, without sorrow, pain or care, in addition to their having the promise of immortality in heaven. (*D.I.* 3)

The price, however, to be paid for such a possession is the possible abuse of this creative freedom, with the ensuing harm.

> If they transgressed [the divine law] ... they would remain in death and corruption. (*D.I.* 3)

People are then truly self-shaping beings, permitted to live with the consequences of such freedom. If they choose to destroy themselves, they are allowed to have their choice and to live in accordance with their choice. Indeed, even when God becomes incarnate that people may be rescued from their self-inflicted wounds, God does not effect an enforced rescue. As we shall see, the Incarnation, for Athanasius, is the opening new possibilities for fallen humanity, which fallen individuals may seek either to realize or to resist.

Though graciously placed in a truly wholesome situation, people contemptuously exercised their free choice, and disregarded God. For this people alone were responsible. Clearly God was not responsible. He had made them free. He had also sought to safeguard them from abusing their freedom by granting them knowledge of God, by placing them in paradise and even by warning them of the dire consequences of turning from God. Nor was the Devil responsible. Athanasius does speak of the 'deceit which the Devil played upon man' (*D.I.* 6), and of people, 'by the Devil's counsel' (*D.I.* 5), turning towards things corruptible. Yet Athanasius still asserts that, 'men ... were themselves the cause of the corruption in death' (*D.I.* 5). They may have been counselled by the Devil; yet the Devil's counsel did not compel; and God, the Truth which has no time for deceit, had revealed himself to humans and thus given them the touchstone for exposing the Deceiver.

People alone were responsible. Never had God distanced himself from them, either by leaving himself invisible to them, or by revealing himself in but one exclusive way. God unveiled himself variously and appropriately. Should people choose to attend to the ever-knowable God, all might always do so. For all that, people freely and contemptuously chose to relinquish contemplating things divine and turned to things corruptible;

> and being unwilling to turn from things close at hand, they imprisoned their souls in the pleasures of their bodies, which had become disordered and defiled by all kinds of desires; and in the end they forgot the power [sc. to know God] which they had received from God in the beginning. (*C.G.* 3)

In contrast with the soul's created state, when it governed its body aright and when the soul was renewed by its desire for God, now the soul was governed by its body and was deadened through worldly desires.

Athanasius' Adam typically makes evident certain eternal truths. The Fall entails turning from contemplating God to forsake the knowledge of God, the Genesis account of Adam and Eve's realization of their nakedness being understood as want not of 'clothing' but of 'the contemplation of divine things' (*C.G.* 3). The Fall introduces 'shame', the hallmark of the breaking down of people's relationship with God, a shame the more marked given their having been initially created, '[their] mind fixed upon God in unembarrassed frankness' (*C.G.* 2).

People's turning from God amounted to more than a break in their relationship with God. For in turning from God, people relinquish the right perspective whereby to evaluate the world. Things which are good, but good in terms of their relationship to the only God, the source of all goodness, are then supposed to be good in themselves. This misevaluation leads to misuse, to things not being used to their divinely appointed ends. Hence, for example, as created,

> the body has eyes in order to view creation and through its harmonious order to recognize the Creator ... It possesses hearing in order to listen to the divine sayings and to the laws of God;

and it has hands too, in order to do necessary actions and to stretch them forth to God in prayer. (*C.G.* 4)

As fallen, people have turned

their ears to disobedience ... their tongues to blasphemies and abuse and perjury, instead of kind words; their hands ... to stealing and assaulting their fellow men. (*C.G.* 5)

Behind such there is the inversion of the soul's proper, critical governing relationship to its body and world. Now the body's desires are served by the soul, the soul delighting in its bodily passions, and so becoming its willing prisoner.

Indeed, bolstered by forgetfulness of God, and its pleasure now found in things of the moment, the human soul began to regard as significant those things near it. They and they alone became important for the body's desires and the soul's sense of 'fulfilment'. In time only visible phenomena were deemed to exist and only transitory things to be good.

Perverted then in nature, the human soul forgot that it had been created in God's image. No longer did it see the divine Logos. For

it had hidden in the complexity of fleshly desires the mirror it has, as it were, within it, through which alone it was able to see the Image of God. (*C.G.* 8)

So confused in its senses, the soul then represented the God which it had forgotten in tangible forms. In ever lower forms of matter the immaterial deity was represented: as heavenly bodies, as heroes, as mortal men, as women, 'whom it is not safe to receive in counsels on public affairs' (*C.G.*10), and as criminals, guilty 'of things forbidden even to ordinary men by the common laws of Rome' (*C.G.* 11), as irrational animals, inanimate wood and stones, and as pleasures and bodily passions. In short, they had become idolaters, 'having fashioned for themselves idols, considering non-existent things as real' (*C.G.*2). In the apostle Paul's words, used by Athanasius, they had 'exchanged the truth about God for a lie and worshipped and served the creature rather than the Creator' (Romans 1:25).

It is worth noting that, for Athanasius, such idolatry is not only 'making divine' those things over against the individual person, but also 'making divine' the individual person. In his anti-idolatry arguments Athanasius cites the tradition that 'those who make gods should themselves be gods; for the maker must be better than what he makes' (*C.G.* 9). Further, as good things have their 'type' in God, so evil things have theirs in fallen humanity, who, in their conceit, 'began to conceive of [evil] and to mould it in their own likeness' (*C.G.* 2). Whereas God created people from nothing in God's own image, people now were seeking to usurp God's place, fashioning idols in man's 'own image'. So they gave an improper value not only to matter but also to themselves, seeking, in the words of Genesis 3, to be 'as God'.

Closely related to this desire to be 'as God' is the matter of power. The soul, Athanasius notes, realized that it could move its bodily members away from God to worldly desire. This it then did, 'showing that it had that power' (*C.G.* 4). In exercising that power, there is the rejection of the humble dependency upon the one good God who begrudges none a full, whole and responsible life, and whence comes the soul's rightful oversight of its body and world. The authority graciously given of God is exchanged for power seized through conceit. This power is that exercised against God and others; and it effects consequences. Yet it is not a wholesome, creative and supportive power. It is anarchical and destructive.

This contorting what is good and the consequent evocation of life-threatening power is clearly seen in Athanasius' *De Fuga Sua* and *Ad Amoun*. In the former Athanasius cautions against those Christians who suffer death at their persecutors' hands and are supposed to have become martyrs for Christ. If, however, the time of their death and the 'hour' of death allocated them by the providential God do not coincide, their death is no martyrdom. It witnesses not to that providential God but to their cowardice, especially when the death is premature and those who die thus escape the greater trials whereby their souls might have been well fashioned by God. Christians, noting Isaiah's warning against putting 'bitter for sweet and sweet for bitter' (Isaiah 5:20), should not call 'suicide martyrdom'. In the letter to Amoun Athanasius warns against supposing that bodily excretions defile. The central concern here is not, however, that some monks have forgotten that, because the Creator of all is pure, natural bodily excretions do not defile; it is spiritual myopia, scrupulosity and even legalism. Under the show of concern for purity, the issue of whether bodily excretions are defiling is raised. The monks are then so distracted by this concern that they do not recognize the concern for what it has become, a deadening and not an enlivening concern. The concern has become a 'snare rather than a test', which it should be, establishing, testing and confirming virtue. It distracts, banishing from the monk the pacific 'salutary meditation', and causing disunity amongst the brethren. A right concern for purity has become an issue of scrupulosity: rather than liberating the person for God, it binds him to the law. The proper and serious service of God, 'with a pure heart', has been replaced by the legalistic keeping of scruples, with a troubled, frivolous mind. That which should confirm people in realizing God's claim upon them has become a legalistic point, whereby people seek to establish their claim upon God.

What is highlighted in precluding neither death at the persecutors' hands nor purity, but only their misinterpretation, is that when Athanasius speaks of the Fall being the turning from God to matter, he is not working with the premise that God and matter are necessarily incompatible. In contrast with the mind's fallen state is not the unfallen state in which the soul forsakes the world and contemplates God alone. For Athanasius' sense of the material world, of which even the soul is a part, witnessing to him upon whom it is dependent, and his sense of the Incarnation and of judgement, 'according to what one has done in the body, whether good or evil', suggest an awareness of the mind's penetration through the world to God, rather than withdrawal or separation from the world. This penetration through the world to God is, however, qualified by that withdrawal which is proper to the doctrine of God in his simplicity and perfection, to that of the created world in its dependency, to that of people created in the divine image, with the vision of God as their goal, and to that of the individual, immersed in the created world as the scene of obedience but having a relationship with God, who is both within and beyond time. Thus, the premise in the light of which the turning from God is assessed is that while there is ever involvement there is also detachment. Moreover, this detachment, whether in withdrawal or contemplation or ascetic discipline, is not only the negative discipline of not being ruled by this world's pressures and desires, but also the positive regime which is grounded in the truth that God is beyond, to be loved for himself as the source and goal of all existence. It is in the not remembering by God's children that their Father is to be loved above all the good gifts that he has freely given that the Fall occurs.

In its misvaluing creation, the soul did indeed harm itself, binding itself to things over which it ought to have had direction. Rather than moving, or controlling, things, it was moved by things. For its

57

turning from God to the pluriformity of matter amounted to its movement from simplicity to pluralism, abandoning the desire 'for the One, even Reality, . . . for the various and separate desires of the body' (*C.G.* 3). The idea of the difference between God and the material world as that between simplicity and plurality is extensively discussed in Plato's *Parmenides*, an important work for Neoplatonism, is common to thinking concerning the Fall through Origen's understanding of humanity's descent from unity to multiplicity (cf. *De Principiis* 2.1.1), and is important for Athanasius. For Athanasius thinks that the unfallen human soul, though contingent, is 'integral' in its contingency, through its unwavering desire for the one, unifying God. In turning from God to the various desires of the material world, however, the human soul deprives itself of the only Source of all unity, and consequently of its own integrity and unity. The soul nevertheless supposed that it yet preserved 'its own integrity' (*C.G.* 4). In that it still moved, it was persuaded that it was still free and in control. It 'thought that, provided it was in motion, it would preserve its own integrity and would not be at fault in exercising its capacities' (*C.G.* 4). Athanasius recognized that fallen people were indeed still free and mobile; they were still freely using their own abilities to satisfy the desires that they had invented. Yet Athanasius also recognized that these fallen people now no longer recognized the difference between the freedom resulting from a right choice of God and the slavery resulting from choosing self-interest. To illustrate this Athanasius employed the Platonic image of the charioteer (cf. *Timaeus* 69C). Like the charioteer who no longer directs his chariot but is content to be drawn hither and thither by his horses, so the soul no longer is in control but is contentedly carried along its course by its bodily members. Like this charioteer, who wrongly supposes that he is driving with purpose towards the winning post, the fallen soul in delusion believes that it is well; though it has turned from the road to God, it does not perceive 'that it has strayed from the road and missed the goal of truth' (*C.G.* 5). It has forgotten that the human soul was formed 'not just for movement but for movement towards the right objective' (*C.G.* 4); and its sincerity reinforces its forgetfulness. Indeed, Athanasius cites an incidence of such folly. The Greeks, he maintains, have turned their eyes from God's Logos; and though they are no longer purposefully striving towards the goal of Truth, they sincerely but wrongly suppose that they alone are wise and 'rational' and that the Christians, who have eyes alone for the Logos, God's Reason, are 'irrational' (*C.G.* 5).

There is in Athanasius' thinking a sense of the gradual, deepening fall into the abyss of ignorance, error and sin. People fall from worshipping God to worshipping the celestial world, thence the terrestrial, and therein firstly the rational and latterly the irrational.

> In their trespasses men had not stopped at the set limits, but gradually moving forward, at length advanced beyond all measure. In the beginning they had been inventors of evil and had called upon themselves death and incorruption; and in the end they turned to vice and exceeded all iniquity ... they became insatiable in sinning. (*D.I.* 5)

The most interesting portrayal of this descent into evil is perhaps found in the description of Adam and succeeding generations. Created in unembarrassed frankness, the fallen Adam, aware of his loss of divine knowledge, was ashamed. Subsequent generations, although having fallen, supposed themselves still to preserve their integrity. For them there was no shame, only mistaken self-justification. There was no realization of having fallen. They deceived themselves as to their state: their souls' motion, rather than their motion in the right direction, was viewed as evidence of health. Having fallen from delighting in matter as a 'sacramental' means to God to enjoying matter as an end in itself, they then began to fear the loss of that whence their immediate gratification came. Indeed, they not only feared its loss, but also desired it the more. Thence came injustice, theft and murder. People's selfishness, the resultant breakdown in mutual trust, and the inability of contingent matter to satisfy humanity's innate desire for the non-contingent, combined to pull all further and further into the bottomless pit into which each had fallen; and the more that people deluded themselves in thinking that their plight was no plight, the worse their plight became.

The Fall, then, is a movement from doing right to doing wrong, or more particularly, from a right and wholesome relationship to an ever more distant and impersonal one. This is true whether one looks at the breakdown of the relationship between God and people, between person and person, between human beings and the rest of creation, or even between the human soul and its body. Athanasius is aware that disorder at all levels has its roots in sin, where sin in its fundamental meaning is lack of God, separation from God, of which ignorance and disorder are symptoms. In contrast with the common idyllic life of paradise, lived in a holy community, the fallen life is one in which society is ever fragmenting, individuals living increasingly only for themselves. Confident, trustful communion, sharing in imitation of the never-jealous God, gives way to possessiveness, meanness and individualism. Ever seeking to satisfy their bodily desires, fallen individuals collect and steal and hoard; and increasingly they begin to fear the loss of that to which their voracious desires cling, lost either through another's rapacity or through each one's own death, the final separation from one's world. Anxiety and fear, undergirded by avarice and competitiveness, are the marks of people's ignoring God, and breaking their relationship with the enliving Truth.

Notes

1 Theophilus of Antioch, *Ad Autolycum* 1.2.

2 Plotinus, *Ennead* 1.6.5.

3 *Ad Autolycum* 1.2.

4 Clement of Alexandria, *Stromateis* 4.6.39.4–40.

5 Philo, *De migratione Abrahami* 190–191.

6 *Ennead* 1.6.5–9.

7 Ibid., 1.6.8–9.

8 Compare A. Louth, *The Origins of the Christian Mystical Tradition: From Plato to Denys* (Oxford, 1981), pp. 75–7 and J. Breckenridge, 'Julian and Athanasius: two approaches to creation and salvation', *Theology* 76 (1973), pp. 73–81.

9 See Louth, op. cit., pp. 75–6 for the idea that

> in *Contra Gentes* we see Athanasius, the young Origenist. The soul has fallen from the level of *nous* to the level of *psyche* — in straight Origenist fashion — and, as *psyche*, it is involved in the body. The soul can achieve union with God again by contemplation. Indeed, in his account of this, Athanasius is more Origenist than Origen, for the emphasis Origen puts on the soul's reliance on God's mercy in its return to God is lacking. But if we turn to *De Incarnatione*, the picture changes radically. The soul in *De Incarnatione* is created *ex nihilo*, is frail, and depends on God's grace even for steadfastness before the fall.

> See also A. Louth, 'The concept of the soul in Athanasius' *Contra Gentes–De Incarnatione*', *Studia Patristica* (*Texte und Untersuchungen* 116; 1974), pp. 227–31. For an alternative view see A. Pettersen, *Athanasius and the Human Body* (Bristol, 1990), pp. 5–6.

10 *De migratione Abrahami* 191.

11 Aristides, *Apologia* 1.1.

12 *Ad Autolycum* 1.7.

13 Irenaeus, *Adversus omnes Haereses* 2.8.1.

14 E. P. Meijering, *Orthodoxy and Platonism in Athanasius: Synthesis or Antithesis?* (Leiden, 1968) suggests that the levels through which God reveals himself include 'ideas' belonging to God (p. 13). This suggestion fits ill with Athanasius' strong sense of the simplicity of God and the radical distinction between Creator and creation.

15 J. Trouillard, *La Purification plotinienne* (Paris, 1955), p. 138.

16 Compare Christopher Wordsworth's hymn 'Songs of thankfulness and praise', and its reference to the 'great Epiphany' when all through grace shall see the Lord (*New English Hymnal* 56).

17 A. R. Peacocke, *Creation and the World of Science* (Oxford, 1979), p. 208.

3

Renewed in the knowledge of God

Serious as turning from God is, Athanasius is unwilling to view it as irreversible. The individual's situation is deteriorating but is not beyond repair. For all, even though fallen, through their free will, retain the power of choice, and hence the possibility of repentance, *metanoia*, the reorientation of their vision. Athanasius can therefore write of the charioteer who, though careering aimlessly hither and thither, may still look up, reorientate himself and make for the proper goal, and of Amoun's colleagues, examples of the fact that the Fall is still occurring, and occurring not only amidst simple Christians, who may turn from their legalistic keeping of scruples to an edifying use of law. The possibility of repentance comes of several ideas. There is no person who is totally turned from God. For to be totally turned from God is to be totally turned from Life, and so not to be, but to have returned to the 'nothing' whence all once was created. Insofar as people exist they have choice, and its concomitant, responsibility. Just as no one's culpability for ignoring God, and for any consequent sins, is removed by the exclusion of choice, so no one is wanting choice and has an excuse for continuing to ignore God and to remain in godlessness. All may have marred the image of God in them; yet each still has that image.

So let the Greeks who worship idols not make excuses, nor anyone else deceive himself that he knows no such road [to God] and therefore finds a pretext for his godlessness. For we all have stepped on that road and know it, even if we do not wish to follow it ... [This road] is each person's soul and the mind behind it. (*C.G.* 30)[1]

Nor may anyone find an excuse in God. For God never withdraws. His presence is ubiquitous and his self-revelation is uninterrupted by human folly.

Athanasius' sense of evil as neither natural nor proper to a person, nor inevitable, tallies with this. Like Plato,[2] Theophilus[3] and Irenaeus,[4] Athanasius believed that people invented evil.

> The soul of men, shutting the eye through which it could see God, imagined evil ... Thus evil's invention occurred to men and was formed from the beginning. (*C.G.* 7)

Athanasius' arguments supporting these beliefs are straightforward. Evil cannot originate in God, who is good and simple. For anyone who is good would not be good if he created evil. When, however, that good being is also simple, the very possibility of creating evil, even when that possibility is not realized, is precluded. For while a composite, mutable being, such as a human, may be able to do evil but may choose not to do so, a simple, immutable being will only and ever be able to do that consistent with its nature, which in the case of God is good. God does not even choose not to create evil; God is 'unable' to create evil. Nor does evil originate in a Demiurge, the inferior deity to whom Gnostics ascribed the origin of the material universe, distinguishing him from the Supreme God. For Athanasius believed that Scripture evidenced that there is only one God, any Demiurge being by definition denied. He further argued there could not reasonably be an evil Demiurge alongside the good God. In their antagonism one to another, they would have proved to be mutually destructive. Suggestions that evil either is self-existent, and thus exists even prior to the world's creation, the subsequent arena of evil's activity, or that it originates in matter Athanasius also dismissed. God created *all* things, and, as originally created, *all* these things were good.

While, however, evil does not originate in matter, it is not unrelated to things material. Evil 'enters' this world when people no longer fulfil their proper role in the divine scheme, and so cease to be what they are purposed to be, the worshippers of God alone and the responsible and rational stewards of creation. When then people no longer maintain their original state, and worship, for example, the sun rather than the sun's Creator, they forfeit a proportion of their original God-given worth. For they break their proper relationship with both God and the sun, in the latter case by turning a deaf ear to the sun's continuous crying 'Worship not me but him whom made us both'. This decrease in the goodness of any person's nature means that that person has to that extent become evil. Evil then does not originate in matter, even though it is parasitic upon matter.

Athanasius does write of evil being 'unreal' or 'non-existent' (*C.G.* 4). He means that it is unreal and non-existent in the primary sense of the words: it is not real and existent as the eternal God is. It is also unreal and non-existent in the secondary sense of the words: it is not real and existent as a virtue like goodness is, whose existence comes of participation in the non-contingent Source of all goodness. It is unreal and non-existent in the sense that a person, being a creature, cannot bequeath being to anything. For being contingent, a person cannot give life. That the giver of life must be superior to that given life is a tenet that Athanasius uses both to undermine the idolater's act of 'making gods' and to support the necessity of creation's Redeemer not being a creature but God. Evil is, however, *supposed* to be real. It is an invention of humans. Usurping God's place, they fashion for themselves idols, wrongly giving creaturely things divine worth. As such, evil 'exists' and may be as powerful and frightening as, for example, a nightmare. Indeed, it may be more subtle and more alluring, and therefore the more powerful. Matter is, in truth, good; it is harmonious, imaging the divine beauty; it is near and accessible and comprehensible even to the simple of mind. As such it rightly is revered and appreciated. It is but a small step from so valuing it to being possessive of it, to coveting it and therein idolizing it. The more one finds delight in this world, the more one is comforted in and through it, and so is unwilling to show that intellectual generosity of spirit which distinguishes the symbol from that symbolized, the creation from the Creator.

So evil is explained, and not simply out of theoretical concern. Athanasius stresses that everyone's failure to worship the one true God, with the consequent loss of true self-knowledge, of responsible living in community and of rightful respect of God's creation, is without excuse. Each failure is each's fault. The only proper response to this failure is repentance: a free, willing and responsible turning from the mind's idolatrous figments to seeing the world *from the divine perspective* and thereby recognizing again the one true God who reveals himself therein.

Reversible though a person's turning from God was, and much to be desired though the knowledge of God was, that person alone was responsible for the lack of appreciation and the ingratitude shown in foolishly declining the gift of knowing God. Faced with this, Athanasius ponders the question why God does not leave people to live with the consequences of their free actions. Since they have chosen to ignore God, while repentance should not be precluded, should not their free choice, with its full effects, however dire, be respected? For, if God is Truth, the consequences must stand. In a sense Athanasius allows them to stand. For his God must be true to his word. Hence as long as an individual continues to ignore God, that person lives with the consequences of their ignorance; and this is so no matter how long and however God seeks to tempt that person away from this ignorance, back to the enlivening appreciation of God. God is, however, not just Truth but also Goodness. No matter what a person does, no person qualifies God. God is God is God. As the Incarnation is not to God's benefit, humanity's fall is not to God's detriment. People may turn from God and yet God still remains infinitely good, never jealous of anyone's profitable and full existence in obedient knowledge of the Creator. God still wishes fallen humanity's full existence. He does not force existence; but he never denies humanity the possibility of existence. Thus God ever seeks to offer people not only the possibility of returning to know the Creator, but of returning to a secure knowledge of the Creator, whence they will not turn. Indeed, God's goodness and magnanimity is reflected in his offering not simply a return to the pre-lapsarian state of the original creation, from which people might again fall, but an entry to a 'new creation', wherein they may remain, blessed for ever.

To such arguments Athanasius adds others. If there was no need to renew humanity in God's image, there was no need for humans to have been made initially cognizant of God. For God is consistent and immutable. Thus, either they should have been created irrational and be permitted to continue living irrationally, or, having been created rational, should be rescued from the life of ignorance and irrationality to which they had slipped. The immutable, good God did create humans rational; and so reasonably God wishes to recreate them in rationality. People's renewal in the divine image stems therefore not from choice but from God's immutable and good nature.

Athanasius introduces a further argument, based upon the dignity owed to God. If God did not redeem people but left them worshipping not God but others, God would be interpreted, albeit wrongly, as having created them for some end other than himself. 'What obligation then would there be to God who made [them], or what glory would he have?' (*D.I.* 13). Similar thinking, loosely reflecting the parable of the vineyard, follows.

> A king who is a man does not permit the realms which he has founded to be handed over and become subject to others and to escape from his power. He reminds them with letters and frequently sends to them friends; and, if needs be, he himself finally goes to win them over with his presence, lest they become subjects to others and his work be in vain. Will then God not have much greater pity on his creatures, lest they stray from him and serve those who do not exist? (*D.I.* 13; compare Matthew 21:33ff. and parallels)

The arguments, it must be stressed, are not based in a possessiveness on God's part; through his goodness God wishes lost humanity's recovery, even as through his goodness he originally created humanity. Indeed, God created for *humanity*'s benefit; the service of 'those who do not exist' is to *humanity*'s detriment. God himself is not altered. Certainly, the dignity due to God is indeed compromised by people's ceasing to worship him: it is compromised in the same sense as a human monarch's dignity, which, even while the monarch remains monarch, is denigrated by the people's not recognizing that the monarch is monarch. Status and recognition of status are not the same, and the indignity to the monarch in fact rebounds to the people's and not the monarch's detriment. Kingship is not made the less by its not being recognized by the kingdom's subjects, but their citizenship is indeed made the less meaningful. Further, God's wishing humanity's recovery is for *humanity*'s benefit. Athanasius' concern in these arguments is therefore with the effect upon people of this indignity shown towards God. Ignoring God is to God's dishonour insofar as people who properly were created to live not only through God but for God now no longer live to God's glory; but it is to their ruin. What then looks like God's jealousy for himself is in fact God's jealousy for humanity's godly well-being.

In short, these themes, severally and together, leave but one possibility in the face of humanity's ignoring God, namely, 'that [God] should renew again that which was in his image, in order that through it mankind might be able once more to know him' (*D.I.*

13). So it is that while asserting strongly that the Incarnation was not for God's benefit, Athanasius also notes that it 'has not happened against the glory of his Godhead, but to the glory of God' (*C.Ar.* 1.42). That humanity, made and lost, should be left lost is not to the glory of him who is unchangeably good; that human beings, made and lost, should be found again and should become God's knowledgeable servants is indeed to the good of humanity and the glory of God, people's renewal in the divine image testifying to God's eternal goodness and mercy.

Given the impropriety of leaving people ignorant of God, Athanasius turns to the matter of how to correct this impropriety. Could they not be forgiven and restored to wisdom? Could they not be recreated in the image even as they were first created in the image, by divine *fiat*? Athanasius' response is a resounding 'No'. While forgiveness is essential, it but covers people's blameworthiness for turning from God. It neither treats that turning's consequences, nor provides a secure remedy. At best forgiveness would be 'ambulance work', mopping up blood, but neither treating the wound nor removing the wound's cause. Forgiveness would not be renewal in the divine image, but absolution of past errors; and it would not preclude subsequent error. The divine *fiat* would leave people, absolved of sin, in a world where God continuously reveals himself — reflected in the pure human soul, suggested by creation's harmony, and pronounced through the law and prophets — and yet where his people could still misunderstand or ignore the divine voice. Once again forgiveness might be needed. Creating people in God's image, placing them in paradise and surrounding them with the ring fence of divine warning against abuse were not originally sufficient: there is no reason to suppose that they will be sufficient later. God's jealousy for our continued well-being would not tolerate such uncertain renewal. Only the Father's Image could restore those who once were made in that image, and only sufficiently by his coming to this human realm. The problem was humanity's, and it needed to be met from within this realm.

As when a figure which has been painted on wood is spoilt by dirt, it is necessary for him whose portrait it is to come again so that the picture may be renewed in the same material; because of his portrait the material is not thrown away, but is redone in it. (*D.I.* 14)

Even so, when God's Image, impressed upon humanity in the creative act, is dulled by an individual's turning from the enlightening Truth of God, and is overshadowed by the deceit of demons, it is necessary for the same Divine Image to draw near again to that upon which it was initially stamped, that its image in humanity may be renewed.

Only the divine Logos could recreate humanity in his image, but not effectively and securely by any existing means. Creation was still the vehicle through which God revealed himself. Yet in the past it had not succeeded in safeguarding people in knowing God, and even now it had been rendered ineffective; people, foolishly misinterpreting its harmonious manifestation of God, madly were captivated by the worship of creation and not the Creator. Nor were the remarkable Old Testamental prophets sufficient. Ignoring God was a predicament which covered the whole world, and which was complicated by demonic deceit. The Old Testament prophets had spoken God's word; but being mere men they did not have the capacity to traverse the whole world to tackle this universal problem, and their voices were drowned out by the demonic counterfeit claims to truth. Moreover, all existing means of God's constant revelation were creaturely; and not being God's Image, they could not effect the re-imprinting of God's Image in people. Only the one, simple Logos, the Image of God, could do so. The only Saviour, God's very Image, therefore devised a new and appropriate means. He drew near. Not that he was previously distant. God was, it is true, unknown, but not for want of God's self-revelation. God's drawing near was his accommodating himself to the human situation. Hence he became man. As all now directed their attention not heavenwards but earthwards,

> as it was right for him to wish to be of help to man, he came as man and took to himself a body like theirs, of humble origin ... in order that [man] who [was] unwilling to know him by his providence and government of the universe, yet by the works done through his body might know the Logos of God who was in the body, and through him the Father. For as a good teacher, who cares for his pupils, always condescends to teach by simpler means those who cannot profit by more advanced things, so does the Logos of God. (*D.I.* 14–15)

The infinity of the Logos, whereby he is not contained by but contains the whole cosmos, is of significance here. His infinity precludes his being excluded from taking a body, even a humble body, whereby people might be gradually reintroduced to the simpler truths of God before being led on to the profounder truths; and it precludes his being limited by his body, so still permitting his ongoing self-revelatory activity in the world. The Incarnation, his coming to the human realm, to renew people in the image and knowledge of God, is therefore in accord with God's previous and continuing means of self-revelation: in the human soul, through creation's harmony, and by the word of the lawgivers and prophets. Each in turn focuses what was manifest but less obvious in what preceded it. Even as the whole creation has cried 'worship not me but him who made me', so the assumed body cried, but only the more audibly to those entrapped in idolatry by demonic deceit. The ubiquitous presence and the oneness of the Logos mean that he is not limited in his self-revelation. The content of the revelation, the one Logos, is the same, whether it comes through general revelation or through the Incarnation. The situation and the efficacy but not the contents change. Athanasius' theme that to live in and through the Logos incarnate is to live the natural life is particularly evidenced in that the divine Wisdom, who may be known through a person's contemplating the human soul, upon which the Logos has made his impress, may be more profoundly and more clearly known in and through the Incarnation. The one Logos, who is manifest in his imprint upon each one's soul, is made the more obvious in his taking to himself that very humanity, made in the divine impress (*C.Ar.* 2.81).

So the Logos offers us all the most appropriate entrance to the knowledge of God. If anyone does not recognize the truth in one place, not because the truth is not there but because that individual cannot appreciate it there, that person is turned to another place, where the truth may be more obvious to that person. One is again reminded of Athanasius' comparison of the work of the Logos with a teacher who teaches a pupil at the pupil's level, bringing him on from whatever the pupil's level is to a greater and more profound understanding of truth. Having then been met in the very area in which each was making his mistake, each is led firstly from his immediate error, and then further into the truth, until eventually each recognizes God in all, and no longer confuses God with all. Thus

the Lord touched all parts of creation and freed and undeceived everything of all error ... in order that no one might be able to err any more and might find everywhere the true Logos of God. So man henceforth, closed in on every side and seeing everywhere ... the divinity of the Logos extended over the world, is no longer mistaken about God but worships him only, and through him recognizes well the Father. (*D.I.* 45)

No longer has anyone an excuse for not worshipping the Logos, and through him his Father. Significantly, the individual is not condemned as being wrong, but is graciously shown right; repentance is invited. The merciful dimension of this correction is emphasized in Athanasius' statement that people are 'closed in on every side', seeing everywhere the divinity of the Logos. The phrase 'closed in on every side' reveals God's unwillingness to allow any to escape the knowledge of God. The Logos, as it were, casts his net widely, so as to hinder any escape to further ignorance.

So, while the Logos has ever been everywhere revealing his Father, now his revealing presence is recognized by all everywhere. So, in fulfilment of Isaiah 11:9, God fills the universe with the knowledge of himself. The alteration lies not in God and his relation to the world. For God is immutable. The alteration is in humanity's appreciation of God. Indeed, the revelation through a creaturely body reintroduces people to perceiving God in the words of the lawgivers and prophets, in creation's harmonious existence, and in their having souls made in the image of God. In a sense, if the Fall is a person's worshipping creation rather than the Creator, the divinity's coming in creation enables the reversal of a person's worship, to worship the Creator rather than creation.

The essential divinity of the Logos is highly significant here. Interpreting Hebrews 3:1–2, Athanasius stresses that the Logos is 'faithful' in the sense of 'trustworthy'; the Logos is one who has a claim upon people's faith, for he is Truth.

Being the Son of the true God, he is faithful and ought to be believed in all that he says and does, himself remaining unalterable and not changed in his human economy and fleshly presence. (*C.Ar.* 2.6)

Consequently those who have lost a full knowledge of God are not left without hope. They may still encounter the whole divine Truth in one like them, in Jesus. This is all the more significant when we remember that Arianism believed that while the Logos knew God as well as any creature could and shared his knowledge of God with others as much as any creature could, the Logos neither was very

Truth nor knew the very Truth in its fullness. 'For it is impossible for [the Son] to explore the Father who exists before him' (*Thalia* 35–36). For Athanasius, that people could look upon the face of God in Christ was the basis of much human hope.

The matter assumed is equally significant. Although people had turned from God, they thought they still knew God. For they had made matter their 'god'; and in this idolatrous relationship they remained, in sincerity although in error.

> Because men had turned away from the contemplation of God and were sunk, as it were, in an abyss, with their eyes cast down, and they were seeking for God in creation and in sensible things, and had set upon mortal men and demons as gods for themselves, the merciful and universal Saviour, the Logos of God, took to himself a body and lived as a man amongst men, and took the senses of all men, in order that those who supposed that God was in corporeal things might understand the truth from the works which the Lord did through the actions of his body, and through him might take cognizance of the Father ... Wherever they directed their senses ... they learnt the truth from all sides. (*D.I.* 15)

God stooped not only to the very level of creation which people were then worshipping, but also to the particular thing or person whom they then mistakenly worshipped. God entered not just the general state and general purview of people but graciously entered the *particular* situation which each mistook. God treated particular problems and not just general errors. The very particularity, the materiality, the historicity, the act and not just the word, are important, and underline the divine goodness and mercy. Instead of simply highlighting that a problem exists, the Logos highlights that this problem exists for this person. One who worshipped a contemporary was shown by Christ's incomparable power over all that amongst everyone Christ alone is God. The individual confused by demons is corrected by Christ's masterly exorcisms. The Greeks who divinized long-dead heroes are enlightened by Christ's resurrection: they still remain dead, while he died and alone has risen, victorious over death. So God graciously meets each one's particular state.

The 'becoming man', wherein God and people are intimately united, is most important for our renewal. Formerly, the Logos, God's Truth, whether mediated through creation's harmony, the law or the prophets, in a sense, lay over against them, to be accepted or rejected; and generally the Logos was rejected. When therefore the bequest of knowledge to people is from without, its receipt by them is neither certain nor secure. When, however, the Logos became man, the Truth became man. The externality of the previous dispensation is replaced by the intimacy of the new dispensation. For the Logos, God's Truth, reveals himself to the humanity which he has become; he reveals himself to himself, as God to himself as man; and as man he will not reject the Truth that as God he graciously reveals. It is in the light of such that the later Athanasian statements concerning both the Logos' becoming man, not merely coming upon a man, as formerly upon the prophets, and the Lukan account of Jesus' growth in wisdom through the ever-increasing self-revelation of the divine Logos to his assumed humanity are to be viewed. Yet, in securing the gift of knowledge to himself, the Logos is at the same time securing the gift of knowledge to mankind. For the Logos reveals himself to the humanity which he has become, and that humanity is one with us. The security of our renewal in the knowledge of God therefore lies in the security of the Logos as God bequeathing that knowledge to himself as man, as we are: the giver has become the recipient. So secured, God's revelation is not, however, forced upon mankind. In their obstinacy people may yet not perceive God. Revelation is a gift, originating in God's goodness, which may be rejected and whose rejection will be judged.

Central to Athanasius' thinking concerning humanity's renewal in the knowledge of God is the accommodating of revelation to people's capabilities. The truth is manifest in all parts of creation. When a person mistakes God's revelation here, God, as it were, graciously calls for that person's attention from elsewhere. Thus when people no longer see God in the mirror of their creaturely souls, God calls for men to see him through creation; and when they begin to worship creation, rather than its Creator, God called to them through the prophets; and when even this failed, God took upon himself a part of that whole creation which they had idolatrously worshipped. Even then, that part of creation is not any part, but a lowly human form. Of all creation, Athanasius maintained, only humans were in error concerning God. Hence God sought that

from a likeness they might be able to understand and see him. For, because they were men, they would be able to know his

Father more quickly and more closely through the body corresponding to theirs and through the divine works effected through it, as they considered that the works done by it were not human but God's. (*D.I.* 43)

The likeness of Christ's body to theirs and the unlikeness of his works to theirs readily opened their eyes. An example is then given. The Logos is very Life. Yet Athanasius asks 'how would the Lord have been shown to be Life unless he had given life to what was mortal?' (*D.I.* 44). Being Life, he does give life to all, holding all things in being. Yet it is in his giving life to the crucified body that people especially realize who the Logos ever is. In defeating death the Logos is recognized as him in whom all things live and move and have their being. The divine voice is heard more clearly when it speaks in the human language of incarnation.

Even after the Ascension, God is so gracious. The Church has been graciously renewed in the imprint of the divine Wisdom. Thus through their peers living a godly life, darkened minds are brought to the divine Light. So Athanasius understands Matthew 10:40, 'he who receives you, receives me'. Within this context Athanasius uses the traditional contrast between the supposed wisdom of the Greeks and their clear failure to persuade, and the simple oratory of Christ and Christians and their obvious success in winning converts. Echoing a tradition found, for example, in Justin Martyr's comparison of Socrates, the 'Christian before Christ', with Christ,[5] Athanasius writes,

> wise men amongst the Greeks have written so much, yet have been unable to persuade even a few from the nearby places about immortality and lives of virtue [while] Christ alone, by means of simple words and through men unskilled in speaking, has persuaded crowded congregations throughout the world to despise death and think of things immortal, to turn from things temporal and consider things eternal, to take no thought of earthly glory but to seek immortality. (*D.I.* 47)

The simplicity of both Christ and his disciples highlights all the more the divinity's majesty. The possibility of mistaking the true agent of the work is reduced. Such great works cannot have their ultimate source in such humble humanity, even though they are effected through it. Clearly this tallies well with Athanasius' sense of the true dependence and receptivity of humanity upon God, of the essential distinction between Creator and creature, and of God the Logos, being unknowable in himself and knowable only through his works.

Hence it is that whichever way and however low people turned their gaze, God met their gaze, that they might recognize the only God. Nothing would stand between God and his wish to turn their attention back to a proper appreciation of the law and prophets, witnessing to their Lord, of creation's adoration of its Maker and of the human soul's imaging the divine Impress.

In accommodating his self-revelation to man's condition, God is not altered in himself. He whom people see even in and through the assumed body is the all-glorious Logos. That revelation is special in that though people see the all-glorious Logos, they are yet not dazzled by his glory. They see the glory as 'in a mirror dimly'. The darkened glass shields the viewer, while not altering that viewed in itself. Revelation is not therefore the parading of God's glory before everyone, as if in self-congratulation. Rather, all is done not for God's but people's benefit, driven by that divine goodness which ever wants to woo them back to fullness of life.

This conception of the Logos veiling himself for human benefit is highlighted in *De Incarnatione*. Working with the premises that God who is invisible by nature is knowable though his works, and that people have turned from knowing God, Athanasius asks why the Logos did not seek to renew their knowledge of God 'through other, better parts of creation' (*D.I.* 43) such as the sun or moon or stars, rather than through a mortal and corruptible body. Athanasius' reply is that the Logos did not come to overwhelm others but to heal and teach suffering people.

> For it is the task of one who is revealed only to appear and to astonish those who see him; but it is the task of a healer and a teacher not simply to come, but to be of service to those in need and to appear in a way that they could bear, lest by his superiority he trouble the needy and the coming of God be of no help to them. (*D.I.* 43)

Athanasius' point is not to deny divine revelation through celestial bodies but to stress the requirement not to dazzle and blind the needy. God's will is to appear in a manner tolerable to people in their self-inflicted handicap.[6] By revealing himself 'through such simple things' (*D.I.* 54) God mercifully concentrates a person's mind. By drawing attention from universal providence to the particularity of the Incarnation he transfers each one's attention from the general to the particular, and teaches what all may confirm in the general. The specific focuses the general. In short, when anyone was confused by the wider canvas, that person was enabled to retain an understanding by focusing upon the detail of the canvas.

This unveiling the divine glory has two important consequences. By appearing through such a degrading humanity, greater witness to the divinity is borne. The glorious divinity is all the more remarkable when seen against the backcloth of a humbled body. Further, poor phrases and humble humanity reduce the chances of idolatry such as may originate through failure to distinguish the glorious celestial bodies and their glorious Creator Lord. Secondly, by not being compelled or startled into recognition of the Logos, the nature of each person's response and subsequent relationship with God is recognized. The desired response is not simply that of marvel but the open acceptance as one's own of God's Truth. An intimate relationship, as portrayed in the narrative of the garden of Eden, and as evidenced in the relation of a child to a loving Father, and not simply that of the audience to a stage performer, an admirer before a Magician, is to be effected.

A variant explanation of God's accommodating self-revelation occurs in an explanation of Proverbs 8:22. The Son is like a son who,

> when [his] servants were lost and in the hands of the enemy by their own carelessness, and need was urgent, was sent by his father to succour and recover them; and, on setting out, were to put over him like dress with them, and should fashion himself as they, lest the capturers, recognizing him as the master, should take flight and prevent his descending to those who were hidden under the earth by them. (*C.Ar.* 2.52, echoing Luke 20:9ff. and parallels)

Generally Athanasius follows the Origenistic line that the Light of God must not dazzle weak human eyes, lest the enabling a person to see and appreciate the truth be hampered. Here there is a sense of needing to come upon the Devil and his demons unnoticed in order to effect the *coup de grâce*. This idea is different in emphasis rather than content from that which surrounds the theme of God's accommodating himself to mankind's state. For human renewal in the knowledge of God is at the same time the destruction of the ignorance and deceit which binds any in subjection to the Devil. Moreover, when particular incarnational aspects of God's accommodation are considered, ideas very like that of *C.Ar.* 2.52 are found. So, for example, unassumingly Christ draws near to the worst possible death. Death does not, as it were, recognize him as Life; it does not flee and so deprive him, who cannot bring death upon himself, of revealing himself the Lord even of death. Indeed, the more ordinary the humanity with which the Logos is 'dressed', the more effective both the exposure of the devilish deceit that death is the End and the opening of all eyes to God's Resurrection Life.

Closely allied with the awareness that in goodness God seeks not to dazzle those to whom he reveals himself is the Alexandrian's understanding of Christians' ignorance of when the end-time shall be. The signs of its imminent advent, but not the time of its advent, have been revealed (*C.Ar.* 3.42ff., referring to Mark 13). 'For who, knowing the day of the End, will not be dilatory with the interval? But, if ignorant, who shall not be ready day by day?' (*C.Ar.* 3.49). This ignorance is then further evidence of God's goodness, a goodness which is anything but shortsighted. 'The Lord, knowing what is good for us beyond ourselves, thus secures the disciples' (*C.Ar.* 3.50). Both God's toleration and Christ's acceptance of this ignorance sanction our humble acceptance of our ignorance of the end-time and secure us in godly discipline. Again, like the good teacher, the Logos does not give people that knowledge which may be to their detriment. There is a realistic and kindly assessment not only of where God should begin a person's education but also where he should limit it.

Given this sense of God's accommodating his self-revelation to a person's particular state, what are we to make of Athanasius' treatment of Christ's miracles? Do these not blind rather than heal a person's poor sight? On reflection, it would seem that for Athanasius the miracles are not an obstacle but an encouragement to faith. Properly viewed, they are not to be seen as ends in themselves but signs which manifest God. So, fashioning a body of a Virgin, healing diseases, walking on water and the feeding of the five thousand constitute signs which point to Christ as Lord of creation. These miracles do, however, witness to more than that the Logos is divine. They suggest a particular type of divinity. They testify to saving Power in action, removing devilish deceit; they point to a gracious divinity and no wholly transcendent, alien deity, a point underlined when Athanasius remarks that Christ's works 'proved him God, that [people] might both worship the goodness of the Father and admire the Son's economy for our sake' (*De Decret.* 1). The goodness of the Father which prompts the Son's saving miracles precludes an untouched and untouchable God.

Nor do these miracles differ entirely from the rest of creation. The miracles' pointing beyond themselves to God is similar to all creation's existence and harmony in witnessing to the Creator; the miracles only differ in their heightened witness. Equally both creation generally and the miracles in particular seek to evoke people's acknowledgement of God as their God. To that extent, whether the miracles are pointing to Christ being the promised Messiah, for only at Christ's coming did 'the blind see, the lame walk, the deaf hear and the tongue of the stammerer [was] loosed' (*D.I.* 38, referring to Isaiah 35:3–6), or to Christ's Lordship over nature, that 'he was not merely a man but God and the Logos and the Wisdom of the true God' (*D.I.* 16), all, severally and together, call for everyone's response.

Even, however, if these miracles are consistent with God's general revelation, there is the question of whether or not an individual's response is forced. Does not the fact that the 'impossible' has happened so surprise people as to startle them into involuntary belief? Athanasius' implied answer is 'no'. The miracles do not dazzle and hence neither preclude nor compel belief. People have sunk to such ignorance of God that they need to be 'shocked' into awareness of their error. Rather like an alarm clock which needs to be loud enough to penetrate sleep, so these miracles have to be obvious enough to penetrate people's darkness. Only by Christ's changing water into wine could the Egyptians who so venerated water be awoken to the Creator and Lord of water (compare John 2:1ff.; Irenaeus, *Adversus omnes Haereses* 3.2.9). Moreover, although the miracles are a manifestation of God, they are not overpowering, in that they are seen alongside other miracles accredited to others. In a sense, Christ's miracles are then but some amongst others. Yet that is their very purpose. Even as when people began to worship the creation rather than the Creator, the Logos took upon himself a creaturely body that people might mend their ways, so here, when people began to worship long-dead heroes and demons, the Logos graciously worked miracles, to highlight the emptiness of these people's worship and to turn them back to the worship of the one and only true God. Even Christ's miracles, which seem so contrary to history, are thus seen as taking seriously the particular errors of particular people and seeking to correct these errors. The Logos incarnate thus showed through his own works the weakness of the many that were supposed to be divine and the strength of the one who is God. 'For wherever men were attracted, [the incarnate Logos] lifted them up and taught them his true Father' (*D.I.* 15).

For all the taking particular errors of particular people seriously, there is yet some sense in which any miracle subverts matter and history. For, almost by definition, miracles run 'contrary' to history. Yet two things must be remembered. People have improperly turned their attention from God to matter. The purpose of miracles is to rectify this situation: hence its primary emphasis is upon divinity rather than matter. Secondly, the revelation so effected is to enable people to adopt a right attitude to matter, God's creation. In this sense the miracles are not opposed to matter, but to people's incorrect attitude to matter. They seek to transform their attitude, that they may worship the Creator and not creation.

Even then we must remember that Athanasius does not think that miracles compel belief. They may be clear evidence of God alone being God. Nevertheless each must respond to the revelation through the miracles; the miracles in themselves do not overcome an individual's estrangement from the Truth. People behold the miracles and are then called to react to the miracle worker. Through comparison with those of others, people are invited to pass beyond seeing Christ's miracles as but some amongst many miracles, to knowing them as the true works of God, and other miracles as but counterfeits, to recognizing and acknowledging him who works God's works to be their God.

Christ's miracles are then not seen as inconsistent with the general picture of God's self-disclosure. The miracles are part of God's graciousness, who not only reveals himself but reveals himself in a comprehensible form, and to particular individuals, however lowly their level. Like nature itself the miracles point beyond to the Creator. So the miracles fit Athanasius' understanding of the Incarnation as the humble advent of a hidden God, markedly contrasting with the glorious and public second coming of the Logos. Through creation, through his miracles and through both creation's outcry at his death and his triumphing over the worst death that his enemies could devise, the Logos revealed himself as the everlasting, unchanging and irreplaceable Lord of creation, and so warned against the central error of idolatry, the transference of sovereignty from the Lord of creation to creation.

Before such an incarnation, thankfulness is the only proper response.

Central to Athanasius' thinking concerning the Incarnation is the thought that while the divine Logos reveals himself, neither he, nor his Father, who is known through the Logos, are yet comprehended or 'contained' in themselves. As the Logos

is invisible, yet is known by the works of creation, so, having become man, although [himself] not being visible in a body, it would be known from his works that it was . . . the Logos who was performing them. (*D.I.* 18)

God is other than his creation, although in it all, sustaining it by his power. This idea, which is part of the long tradition that asserts that God can be known in his gracious relation to the world but not in himself, looks forward to the idea which will surface in the thinking of the Cappadocian theologian Gregory of Nyssa (*c.* 330–*c.* 395), that the Christian life is always a hopeful journey into the infinite, divine nature, and never the possessing or comprehending of God. Herein faith is always faith, and knowing God is always an appreciation directed away from itself towards a deity to which no one will ever be adequate. The knowledge of God so revealed is then very different from that which, it is supposed, enables the recipient of the revelation to lay claim upon the revealed God. Here the revealed knowledge is that which ensures that the divine claim is laid upon man, whose nature is ever to look forward to the 'other' God.

It is then not surprising to find that Athanasius affirms that every individual is contemplative. Even the 'unlettered' Antony contemplates. For contemplation is a part of being truly human. Equally, it is no surprise to note that contemplation is a form of reconciliation, and not the *means* to reconciliation. Contemplation is the response to the self-revelation of the invisible deity, who claims the Christian for himself; it is not, as for Gnosticism, part of the armoury employed to establish one's position with God.

Interestingly, this sense of every Christian engaged in a pilgrimage of faith towards the boundless Truth, the End without end, revealed especially in the Incarnation, ties in with the fact that a person's renewal in the knowledge of God involves the putting aside of all that is sub-rational, and resisting the belief that rational faith is a form of Hellenistic 'intellectualism'. Being renewed in the image of the divine Logos, Reason and Wisdom, the Christian is renewed in reason and wisdom. Yet in such renewal no ultimate privilege is granted to the renewed mind. Created by God, the mind is as creaturely as the body which it now wisely governs; as such it is as much in need of sustenance, enlightenment and transformation as its creaturely body, which naturally would tend towards evil, darkness and death. Indeed, this absence of privilege for the mind is manifest in that, as it is renewed, it realizes that the divine nature, in contradistinction with the divine action, is 'invisible and indiscernible' (*D.I.* 16). There is no renewal which will make the human mind capable of seeing God. The only understanding of which the renewed human mind is ultimately capable is to know that he who revealed himself to be the 'Son of God and the Logos of the Father, Leader and King of the universe' (*D.I.* 16) is unknowable in himself. Our renewal in the knowledge of God is then humble acceptance, solely in faith, of the mind's incapacity to comprehend God, whose divine nature is beyond all rational comprehension.

This idea is most important for Athanasius. For it reverses the hierarchy of the Fall, wherein people become 'as gods' and know that which they wrongly worship. Now they are renewed in awareness of their own contingency and inability to know the truly non-contingent, incomprehensible God. Further, it distances Athanasius from particular contemporary Hellenistic thinking, which assumed that the human intellect, when truly purified, returned from the multiplicity of things to pure simplicity. The mind, renewed, gravitated back to its proper home in the Transcendent One (cf. *Ennead* 6.9.11). Plotinus would thus write of the 'ecstasy' in which the mind was freed from its limited and complex existence to the simple life in the divine One. Athanasius, however, writes of the renewed mind not being mystically absorbed into divinity but being alerted to the fact that it encounters the 'invisible and indiscernible one'. God, even when he has become flesh, is revealed to the mind as ever the increate Lord who is yet on the far side of the essential distinction of Creator and creature. Renewal in God's image does not then place the human mind in a Platonic security of mystical union with the One. Athanasius agrees with people such as Plato and Plotinus who variously suppose that the mind cannot *express* God in word or concept. Athanasius does, however, go further than them in grounding this incapacity in the metaphysical distinction of the increate God from the human mind, created from nothing. Moreover since, for Athanasius, God's nature is unknowable, knowing God amounts to knowing the divine works, God's willing, philanthropic relation to the world, and this knowing God is expressed in a life lived in accord with such works. Hence there is the connection between knowing God and a holy life; and hence at the last judgement all shall be judged not simply according to their knowledge but according to their works, whether good or bad, well-advised or foolish. Indeed, given this connection between knowing God and living a godly life, hypocrisy is precluded, and practising what one preaches is sought. 'Knowing God' is then not so very different from 'being faithful to God', a faithfulness which is shown by a person who is body and soul, and who relates both as one who thinks and one who acts. Even then it must not be assumed that orthodoxy necessarily and always precedes orthopraxis. Rather, the two chase one another, like a serpent chasing its tail. For true knowledge of God leads to correct behaviour; and 'a good life and a pure soul' (*D.I.* 57) are necessary for the appreciation of a true understanding of God. The same point, but emphasizing the corporate aspect of the life lived in the knowledge of God, is made when Athanasius writes that only in

> being included in [the saints'] company, through the manner of his life, may [the lover of Christ] understand those things which have been revealed to them by God. (*D.I.* 57)

This holy life involves adopting a new attitude to matter and to God. People begin to treat themselves critically, no longer allowing their bodies to enslave their souls, but requiring their soul to be true to their created role of governing the body. They also begin to view matter generally from the divine perspective. Therein they no longer are possessive of it, hoarding it to others' detriment. They begin again to see creation as orderly, recognizing its harmonious being as witnessing to its Creator and Sustainer. The holy life is then personal; but it is not private. As the Logos revealed his heavenly Father through the temple of his assumed humanity, so Christians

> have become God's temple, and in consequence are made God's sons, so that even in [them] the Lord is worshipped and beholders report that God is of a truth in them (*C.Ar.* 1.43)

Our renewal in the knowledge of God is not therefore solely for our own benefit, but for that of the wider world. A missionary dimension is not optional: knowing God and witnessing to God are two sides of the one coin. Knowing God involves the service of God in the drawing of others to God that the world may be filled with the knowledge of God 'as the waters cover the sea'. Knowing God is then an aspect of being both the faithful child and the minister of God; and the renewed state is, in a qualified sense, a 'continuation' of the Incarnation.

The renewal of humankind in the image of God is then their being made glorious. They become the glory of God, not on their own account but on account of the True Glory of God who, through becoming incarnate, bestowed his glory upon mankind. So glorified, people again know their true nature as faithful creatures of God, and wisely witness to their true Glory, their Master and Sustainer.

Notes

1 Cf. Irenaeus, *Adversus omnes Haereses* 4.37 and 39; Origen, *De Principiis* 1.84.

2 Plato, *Republic* 508C ff.

3 Theophilus of Antioch, *Ad Autolycum* 12.

4 *Adversus omnes Haereses* 4.64.3.

5 Justin Martyr, *Apologia* 2.10: 'no one trusted in Socrates so as to die for this doctrine, but in Christ ... not only philosophers and scholars believed, but also artisans and people entirely uneducated, despising both glory and fear and death; since he is a power of the ineffable Father and not the mere instrument of human reason.'

6 Compare *Adversus omnes Haereses* 4.62.

4

From godly life to death and corruption, and back

TO DEATH AND CORRUPTION

Central to Athanasius' thinking regarding creation is the Johannine belief that all things were made by God and that without him nothing would continue to be. Alongside this is his belief that death and corruption are natural to everything drawn from the 'nothing' whence God creates and sustains. Consequently people are because they are made and sustained by God; they may suffer death and corruption because they are made from nothing. Yet their suffering death and corruption is not inevitable. For while people by nature are corruptible, 'by the grace of participation in the Logos they could have escaped the consequences of their nature' (*D.I.* 5). Death then is seen as an ever-present, potent threat, even while it does not lord it over creation.

The degree to which Athanasius understood death to be ever present, threatening to drag the orderly back to the orderless 'nothing', must not be underestimated. The ancient world of Graeco-Roman civilization may have been cultured. Yet it was also frequently without hope. The thought of the future often struck chill: old age was dreaded as the threshold leading out into cold darkness; death ruined the enjoyment of the present with the intruding thought of the dark future, so that life might appear as a gift little worth receiving. When such is remembered, Athanasius' sense of creation ever in danger of returning to the 'nothing' whence the divine Creator ever preserves it, and his belief that naturally mortal humanity, 'had it kept [its likeness to God] ...

83

would have blunted its natural corruption . . . and would have lived henceforth as God' (*D.I.* 4) seem the more poignant. Even the ancient image of the sword of Damocles, hanging by a fine thread over the heads of the revellers, does not do justice to Athanasius' thinking on death. For that sword may threaten, but it does not press against the revellers' flesh. For Athanasius, death continuously must be resisted. It is not sufficient even to pray that the sword's thread may not break. Each must continuously wear the protection of the Logos of God, lest death's point, even now pressing against human flesh, punctures it. Athanasius' picture is not static. It is of relentless conflict and of adversaries actually at grips.

All that is required for death to move from threat to actuality is for individuals to turn from their divine defence. Thereby they would deprive themselves of eternal life, which 'means that when they perished, they would remain in death and corruption' (*D.I.* 4).

People did turn from God, and freely brought upon themselves that great impropriety wherein 'what had once been rational and had partaken of the Logos should perish and return again to non-existence through corruption' (*D.I.* 6). Yet God would not deny the legitimate, even if inappropriate, sway that death now had over people. God had warned them that the consequence of turning from him would be death and corruption. When then they turned from God, death established through God's warning its strong hold over them. Through an unholy alliance with God's true word, death usurped God's benign lordship over each one's future. Hence all who turned from the only Source of life 'received the condemnation of death which had been previously threatened' (*D.I.* 4).

The use of terms like 'threaten' and 'condemn' initially seem to sit uneasily alongside Athanasius' good God, wishing all to live the true, felicitous life of Paradise (*D.I.* 3). Yet it is not God who plans people's death; rather, people upset God's good purpose for their vitality, and bring death upon themselves through freely turning from the only Source of life and incorruption. Indeed, when they deprive themselves of life, God, who envies none existence, is placed in an awkward position: what he has created and wishes to be is passing from existence. What then may be made of the 'threats'? These refer to the ordinance to Adam in Eden that if he broke God's word, he would die, and be banished from Paradise (*D.I.* 3, referring to Genesis 2:16–17). God's word, it must be remembered, is a ring fence against people's abusing the faculty of free will. Its purpose is good, to secure the grace of their true life in paradise; only incidentally does it result in judgement, condemnation and death. What it 'threatens' is what God will find 'improper', his creatures passing to non-existence. We would be better to allow our thinking to be coloured by a simple analogy. My young son, in his eagerness to watch a procession in the street below, leans out of the window of my first-floor study; I cry 'If you do that, you will fall and kill yourself'. These words are not a threat, but a warning of possible consequences. Similarly we may view God's 'threats'. God's ordinance is a warning, the consequences of not heeding being dire; and his desire is that these dire consequences will not occur. Nor need the term 'condemnation' alter the above suggestion. The 'condemnation of death' has as its opposite the 'idyllic life of Eden'. The latter is God's wish for everyone, and the former is God's elaboration of the inevitable consequence of turning from the only Source of life. The latter is a person's lot who remains faithful to the life-giving God, and the former an individual's lot who turns their back on the gift of life, ever offered but never forced. In a sense, those who remain open to God and receptive to his good gifts escape condemnation; and those who are unfaithful and turn from God, by those very acts bring condemnation upon themselves. They condemn themselves. The language of 'condemnation' describes people's turning from God, which calls down condemnation, or better, is itself the relational aspect of condemnation. This is the corollary of the fact that only in the one God does anything exist. There is no neutral ground between life and death; they are absolute alternatives. Hence God is judge and, in a sense, the Law. He does not judge in accordance with an independent, self-existent law. Those who trust in God and are faithful to the Life which he is escape condemnation, while those who are unfaithful, by that very fact sentence themselves. The process of judgement and condemnation is an inseparable concomitant of salvation. There is then no real contradiction involved when Athanasius writes that God both wills all to live and threatens condemnation.

Death is an absence of life; dying, meanwhile, is a process, the ongoing result of turning from the life-giving relationship with God. When then people turn from God, they renounce their proper role in the divine order and begin to cease to be what they were created to be. They forfeit a proportion of the life with which God endowed them. This decrease in well-being or increase in the corruption of human nature means that a person has to that extent died. Significantly, Athanasius will then speak of the harmonious union of the governing human soul and governed body in Eden, the tension of soul and body, even the soul's captivity by its body, in fallen existence, and the separation of the soul from the body in death. Having then died, a person *remains* dead. For God knows the rightness of a fallen person's death; and people, being creatures, have not the capacity to hold themselves in life against the continuous pull of the 'nothing', let alone the ability to bring themselves back from death. This *remaining* dead is further significant in that death thus would seem to mount a challenge to God who willed people to *remain* in Paradise; so death becomes potent and would seem to be victorious.

Given death's emptiness, one wonders why people turned from life. This is the more interesting a question, given that originally there was no evil, that they were placed in Paradise as a security against falling and were given knowledge of God as a ring fence against turning from God, and that they were warned of the fatal consequences of breaking with God's beneficent order. Certainly God took every precaution lest any fall.

The Fall's possibility existed from the very outset, as is implied in God's desire that the newly created Adam 'might never abandon his concept of God nor leave the saints' company' (*C.G.* 2).[1] This possibility lay in human materiality. Whereas Platonists regarded human materiality as the mark of the Fall, Athanasius saw such as granting its possibility. Being made 'from nothing', people were inherently weak, insecure beings. They had a natural tendency to gravitate from the unifying, stabilizing God, who alone graciously holds all matter in being, to disorder, death and the 'nothing'.

This contingent being God called into existence. Yet God did not hold any in existence perforce. From the very outset mutability and choice were part of a creature's definition.

Having established people's capacity to fall, Athanasius hints at why Adam chose to abandon the paradisial good. Adam was deceived as to his own interests, supposing that he was better off cleaving to the lesser good of matter than the greater good of the Creator of matter, who had already in fact given him that lesser good. Adam was mistaken as to human nature. He did not recognize that to choose that contrary to God's philanthropic will was not only to abuse the power of choice but also to alienate the soul from the Source of its freedom. He misunderstood freedom, failing to distinguish 'freedom' in dependence upon God and 'freedom' in independence from God, which actually is no freedom but subjection to the material world and ultimately to the 'nothing' whence it came. For there is no 'ground' to be occupied by man between the one God in whom all may fully exist and the 'nothing'. Adam imagined that his God-given integrity might be preserved by exercising mere choice, not noting the inalienable connection between integrity and right choice. These are symptomatic of a great misunderstanding concerning status and power. As a creature, Adam was bound to creation, to enjoy it as God's work. He was to be critical, viewing all through God's eyes. At the Serpent's urging, though not compulsion, Adam chose to abandon God. He believed that now his status and power were as God's, knowing good and evil. In fact, he placed himself in subjection to an imprisoning selfishness, in the power of transient matter, and ultimately of corruptible mortality. A desire for status and power, irreconcilable with God's will for contingent humanity's wholesome obedience, led to Adam forsaking his God-given status and power as a creature made in the image and likeness of God.

For all these hints, Athanasius explicitly follows the traditional 'free will' explanation. He insists that although people foolishly acted in accordance with 'the devil's counsel' (*D.I.* 5, echoing Genesis 3) 'they were themselves the cause of their corruption in death' (*D.I.* 5).

FROM DEATH TO LIFE

People alone are therefore responsible for their foolish turning from God and their gradual but certain dying. God alone, meanwhile, is responsible for their salvation from their self-inflicted mortal wound. People's predicament certainly occasioned this salvation. People were its stage. God's goodness, however, prompted it. For God's nature is everlastingly and unavoidably good. Accordingly, God, through his Logos, created people. This natural goodness, being unalterable and illimitable, is never frustrated by even the grossest folly. Hence the same good God, who originally envied nothing its existence, even now begrudged not fallen humanity existence. Thus, through the same creative Logos, the same merciful and good God sought to draw people back from corrupt mortality to new life. In a sense God cannot but redeem people. Yet this is not tantamount to saying that God is forced to redeem. For what God so does, he does willingly. For his will is a voluntary expression of his being, whose character is unbegrudging goodness. Thus, his nature is ever to allow people's existence; and this existence he thus ever wills, his being and his will being one; and people's existence God wills to continue, even in the face of the Adamic disobedience, God's natural goodness knowing neither bounds nor change. In short, humanity's salvation was then in accordance with neither an arbitrary, mutable will, reacting benignly to an *ad hoc* need, nor external compulsion, but was both freely and naturally God's desire.

God the Creator and God the Redeemer are therefore one. It is as if

> a king had constructed a house or a city and brigands attacked it through its inhabitants' negligence; he in no wise abandons it but avenges and rescues it as his own work, having regard not for its inhabitants' negligence, but for what is fitting for himself. So, all the more, when the human race, which had been created by himself, descended to corruption, God the Logos of the all good Father did not neglect it, but effaced death which had fallen upon it ... and reformed all people's estate by his own power. (*D.I.* 10)

The analogy's point is God's rightness in rescuing his own creation, a rightness defined by and in God's very goodness, even though the need for rescue came of humanity's own fault. Who God is and not what people do defines God's acts.

The goodness of God, an idea partly drawn from Plato's *Timaeus*, accounts for Athanasius' understanding of not only why but also how God redeems. For humanity's salvation from mortal corruption God's *fiat* is inappropriate. The Arians, it seems, held that God could release people from sin by simple *fiat*. Athanasius restates the Irenaean position. God could have but spoken, 'and so the curse could have been undone' (*C.Ar.* 2.68).[2] Yet God's goodness demands not what was possible for God but what was expedient for humanity's long-term existence. Whatever else, God's *fiat* would not have secured people's long-term existence. Divine absolution would but return them to their prelapsarian state, their condition still being that from which they might fall again. It would not guard against human history being but a sorry succession of sin and absolution. Indeed, in addition to not bringing individuals to a secure, radical transformation of humanity, God's *fiat* might even bring them to a more sorry state than that in which they were first created. For a person returned to the prelapsarian state by divine *fiat* would be one 'who had learned to trespass'

(*C.Ar.* 2.68). No longer innocent, people having once sinned would be weaker in their resistance to the Serpent's continuing seduction. This would especially be so, given that a *fiat* could not free people from their fleshly weakness, namely the natural affinity for that nearby and the innate tendency to return to the 'nothing' whence all originated. The divine *fiat* would leave all forgiven, but with the possibility, if not the probability, of sinning again, and again needing forgiveness. Athanasius' argument is not Paul's argument against sinning the more that grace may abound the more. Rather, it stems from God's goodness which wills humanity's existence to be firm and steadfast (*C.Ar.* 2.73) and not fearsomely precarious. Further, the *fiat* would never free people either from the Law which threatens death to the disobedient (cf. *C.Ar.* 2.68) or from the mortal corruption resulting from disobedience, which 'would not be abolished in any way except by everyone dying' (*D.I.* 9) or by the Logos dying for all. For the Law, given by God whose word is unchangeably true, was not to be waived but to be fulfilled; and death could not be forgiven, as disobedience, its introducer, could.

> Hence, in his goodness the Logos 'came at the fullness of the ages', and when sought said, I am he. For what he does, that is profitable for man and was not fitting in any other way. (*C.Ar.* 2.68, referring to Hebrews 1:2 and John 18:8)

Indeed, God's goodness makes possible incarnation, the expedient means of salvation. The Arian God is characterized by his otherness; he is sublimely remote and simple. Although termed a 'framing energy', their God, Athanasius believes, is 'not fruitful, but barren ... as a light that lightens not, and as a dry fountain' (*C.Ar.* 2.2). This belief he finds confirmed in that while 'human nature is prone to pity and sympathizes with the poor, [the worshippers of the Arian God] have lost even the common sentiments of humanity' (*Hist. Ar.* 62). With utmost difficulty the Arian deity shares himself with creatures. In contrast Athanasius' God is not abstract, distant nor solitary. Naturally the Father begets and the Son is begotten. His nature is conceived as an eternal relationship of mutual love, goodness and generosity, perfectly expressed and existing for its own sake; and this is the basis of God's drawing near to his creation. Not in untempered splendour, but in a humility driven by the Father's goodness, the Logos supports all created things; and in the same humility, but this time effected in and through the Incarnation, the same Logos makes mankind children of the one heavenly Father (*C.Ar.* 2.63–64). God's goodness drives his will to see humanity securely saved, and allows the very means necessary to effect such. Indeed, the degree to which God's approachability to creaturely people even in their need is made possible by the divine, natural goodness is seen in Athanasius' strong assertion that the Logos did not merely come upon man, but became man. Mortal and corrupt humanity he made his very own.

God's goodness naturally 'demands' and makes possible humanity's salvation. Yet this goodness is not unaccompanied by conditions. For while God cannot but offer the possibility of salvation, God can only render that possibility actual if and when the consequences of the breaking of God's word are met. The divine word's truthfulness is as important as the divine goodness. God's goodness wills that people should not perish; his divine word, broken by humanity, meanwhile requires that, having died, all should 'remain in death and corruption' (*D.I.* 3). Not to act in accordance with the Law, and its consequences for the disobedient, would be to be unfaithful to himself, from whom to turn is to deprive oneself of life. Accordingly, it was appropriate to meet the consequences for humanity of disobeying the Law, and so, fulfilling the Law's demands, to fulfil the Law's purpose, the continuing expression of God's goodness and the wholesome existence of all people.

Goodness therefore is no mere toleration. It would have been all too easy to see God's goodness waiving the consequences of human trespass, God being viewed as giving unlimited benefits and never exacting dues. *Dieu pardonnera: c'est son métier*; God will forgive: it is his business. Athanasius' deity is not so. He is a sovereign, demanding God. Goodness and truthfulness are one. Hence his inability to waive his law's consequences; and so the Logos undertakes the Incarnation as suffering love. It is against such a background that grace is truly to be understood as the unmerited and incomprehensible activity of the one, true and good God. Unless Athanasius' sense of God's sovereignty and of his rightful demands upon dependent humanity is understood, Athanasius' sense of the grace involved in the Logos of the good God becoming man will not be appreciated.

Given people's mortal and corrupt condition, it is imperative that the Saviour is very God. For those who deify should themselves be god; for the maker must be greater than what he makes ... and the giver has to bestow what is in his possession. (*C.G.* 9)

Creatures, being created from nothing, are naturally mortal and open to corruption, and so do not have the wherewithal to grant life. Indeed, even were the saviour that most sublime of creatures, the Arian Logos, people would be left as pawns, ever fought over by two *creatures*, the Logos and the Devil. To neither could final victory be guaranteed. People, 'being between the two, would have been ever in peril of death, wanting him in and through whom [they] might be joined to God' (*C.Ar.* 2.70). Not only, however, are all creatures naturally mortal, but all have fallen.

What help then can creatures derive from a creature that itself needs salvation? ... A creature could never be saved by a creature any more than the creatures were created by a creature. (*Ad Adelph.* 8; cf. *C.Ar.* 2.67)

Not being God, a creaturely saviour could not join a work to the Creator; and being 'under the sentence of death' (*Ad Max.* 3), 'how ... had he power to undo God's sentence and remit sin?' (*C.Ar.* 2.67).

Being naturally, powerfully and eternally immortal and incorruptible, God the Logos is capable of ever bestowing that which is lacking to dying individuals; and being the never exhaustible source of life, he is he in whom all may be brought to 'abide ever immortal and incorruptible' (*C.Ar.* 3.33). Further, being above everyone (*D. I.* 7), 'he alone is able ... to suffer for all and is competent to be an advocate on behalf of all before the Father' (*D.I.* 7). His infinity, which knows no bounds, will permit no exceptions. He can relate to and act for all. Not one of those liable to mortal corruption is beyond the purview of the Highest. Thus it is fitting that he who initially created and 'at the beginning sentenced' and condemned things originate, should 'alone remit sins' (*C.Ar.* 2.67) and recreate man; the Creator recreates.

That only very God may securely effect humanity's salvation is stressed even in reference to God's raising people from the deeds of darkness to a godly life. Originate humanity is mutable. This all shows not only in being liable to sin but also in sinning. For their salvation people therefore needed one who did not succumb to sin. Such a one another mere human may not be. A mere human, however saintly, being naturally mutable, is ever liable to sin; and it often happens that he, who is now good, afterwards alters and becomes different, so that one who was even but now righteous soon is found unrighteous. (*C.Ar.* 1.51)

People's being redeemed from sinning by even the most holy creature would thus not be secure. Indeed, were the Logos but a mutable creature, no matter how august a mutable creature, and were he righteous, whether from being subject to laws, or from being bound towards righteousness, or from hating iniquity through fear of falling away, he would yet be naturally alterable, and so open to conceding before the Devil's next attack. That needed was an immutable one. Hence the unalterable Logos, the eternal Image and Type of righteousness, who was not merely a just judge and lover of virtue, but the very dispenser of virtue, just and holy by nature, became humanity's secure Saviour.

Equally necessary for people's salvation was a human body. The broken divine Law demanded the suffering death and corruption. For it was absurd to annul the Law before it was fulfilled; the disobedient's penalty of death could be overlooked or waived only at the expense of God being untruthful to himself. Yet this death was to be countered. This mortal corruptibility, however, existed neither on its own nor was it an abstraction. Nor was it incidental to a person. For 'the corruption which had occurred was not outside the body but was involved with it' (*D.I.* 44). Death's Saviour was not therefore to be external to the assumed mortal body. 'It was necessary that instead of corruption Life should adhere to [the body], so that as death had been in the body so might Life also be in it' (*D.I.* 44). So the incorruptible and immortal Logos took to be his own 'a body like ours, since all were liable to the corruption of death' (*D.I.* 8). This he did because the divine Logos, who alone could give humanity the much required resurrection life, being very Life, could not himself die, because the death required was not the Logos' but humanity's, and because it was necessary to meet death and oust it from where it currently held sway. The thesis of Gregory of Nazianzus, the contemplative theologian (329–389), that 'what is not assumed is not redeemed' (*Epist.* 101 *Ad Cledonium*), is here anticipated. This assumed mortal body was then surrendered to death on all's behalf. So death was truly encountered and killed, and Life combined itself intimately, fully and securely with humanity. Indeed, it combined itself with particular people. For Athanasius understands death as this man or this woman's death, as is evidenced in the particularity of this man or this woman or even this young child suffering a martyr's death. Through this death for all, the Law's demanding of disobedient individuals the penalty of death was met in full; and the penalty fully paid, the Law's power was rendered void.

Full divinity and true humanity are then central to Athanasius' understanding of secure salvation. So too is the Logos 'drawing near' in assuming a mortal body, the realm where mortal corruptibility then held sway. Thereby there is the transference of human mortal corruptibility to God. Only through a real and intimate union of the Logos and of the body born of Mary was the Logos able to transfer

> our origins to himself [so that] we may no longer, as mere earth, return to the earth, but as being knit into the Logos from heaven, might be carried to heaven by him. (*C.Ar.* 3.33)

Only by his having truly become man, and not by his having 'drawn near' by coming upon a man, as he did upon the prophets, would salvation be truly secured. Only by the immortal Logos giving the grace of immortality to his assumed mortal humanity, which died for all, was his assumed humanity, and therefore humanity, securely raised from death.

This point applies equally to God's raising people from the deeds of darkness. The immutable Logos became mutable man and meets the Devil in the very arena where the Devil sought to deceive all people. Through his mutable flesh the immutable Logos met the Devil's temptation to sin and securely defeated him. So the greater strength which the unalterable Logos graciously gave his mutable flesh was made available to all.

Once therefore very God had assumed a human body, which was essentially ours, and so met and destroyed human weaknesses,

> men henceforth no longer remained sinners and dead according to their proper affections, but, having risen according to the power of the Logos, abode ever immortal and incorruptible. (*C.Ar.* 3.33)

Alongside this explanation of salvation, Athanasius employs several traditional motifs. He uses a sacrificial motif: the body taken of Mary is pure and spotless; it is offered for all to the Father. Indeed, the sacrificial motif extends itself in *C.Ar.* 2.7, where the Logos incarnate is described as the everlasting high priest of our confession. For after offering himself for us ... [now] he himself brings near and offers to the Father those who in faith approach him, redeeming all and for all expiating God. (*C.Ar.* 2.7)

This motif, relying heavily on Hebrews 7:24–25, seems more to echo the scriptural passage than to be making a conscious theological point. Certainly Athanasius' Father is he whose goodness is jealous for even fallen man's existence, rather than one whose wrath needs assuaging. Legal motifs abound: the Logos summons death and proves it to be dead (*D.I.* 23); by offering his assumed body to death for all, the divine Logos paid, and paid in full the penalty or 'debt' for breaking the law. Certainly there is no room in his thinking for legal fiction or caprice, the guilty being treated as innocent or having their full and just penalty waived. Rather, he rendered 'all guiltless and free from the first transgression' (*D.I.* 20). Within this legal context there is the idea of reconciliation. This reconciliation is not, however, that of either God with himself or God with the Law. Certainly God cannot waive the consequences of people's turning from God's goodness which envies none existence; and God cannot waive his goodness which does not begrudge even the fallen their existence. Yet this does not amount to an internal dilemma within God which required reconciling. It is but the outcome of the truth that God is ever the sole source of life. He ever offers all life; and all live only insofar as they do not turn from him in whom alone they may move and have their being. Nor does the above constitute conflict between God and the Law. For that Law was given to safeguard life in God. Whatever the consequences of a person's disobedience, the Law itself was an expression of God's good will. The real tension was between God's gracious longing for humanity's continuing well-being and people's ingratitude and self-inflicted death. The need for reconciliation was between dying humanity and the life-giving God. Even then, a person's death is not owed to God. For death was due as the consequence of turning from God who alone gives life; and it is 'owed' as a penalty for disobedience only in the sense that the Law describes the con-sequences of a person's being faithless to, or turning from God. Legal motifs are used, but not woodenly, of the *relation* of God to humanity and humanity to God.

The Pauline motif of Christ as the Second Adam is common. Becoming man, the Logos took 'earthly flesh, having Mary for the mother of his body, as if from virgin earth' (*C.Ar.* 2.7). In line with Irenaean thinking, and not contrary to Athanasius' insistence that only an unalterable, divine Logos may secure a person's moral development, salvation is portrayed as that established through the second Adam, born of the virgin Mary, who was tested even as the first Adam, drawn from the virgin earth, was tried, but now without sin. Indeed, continuing the Adamic imagery, Athanasius elaborates this sinlessness when considering the Christian's being brought to live under God's rule. The unalterable Logos took upon himself alterable human flesh, 'condemned sin in it, secured [the flesh's] freedom and its ability henceforth to fulfil the righteousness of the law' (*C.Ar.* 1.51). Having effected such in himself, the Devil's power over all was annulled. Henceforth

should the Serpent again make an assault, even the Serpent's deceit might be baffled, and the Lord, being unalterable and unchangeable, the Serpent might become powerless in his assaults against all. (*C.Ar.* 1.51)

By the second Adam's unalterability as God, and his having made his naturally alterable flesh unalterable by grace, the Christ grants all a secure, righteous life. Athanasius then sees the whole saving act as the complete reversal of the Fall. Prelapsarian man, though hedged about with the safeguards of divine grace, was right to fear death and the Devil. Redeemed man rightly does not fear either. For the Devil was brought to naught in his assault upon the Logos incarnate.

Thus [the Devil] is cast out of Paradise into the eternal fire. Nor shall [men] have to watch against women beguiling [them *sc.* as Adam was beguiled through Eve] ... in Christ [humanity] shall be a new creation, and neither male nor female. (*C.Ar.* 2.69)

So the types and anti-types are employed: Adam and Christ; Eve and Mary; Adam's expulsion from Paradise and the Devil's exile to hell; and the passions of the flesh, leading to sin and death, and the Christians' high morality, resulting from man's redemption and witnessing to the acknowledged Lordship of the Creator.

As Christ is seen in contradistinction with the first Adam, so the effects of his resurrection are seen in contradistinction with those of the Fall. As a result of the Fall, there was a loss of knowledge of God, the repudiation of things heavenly, idolatrous deification of the creaturely, and the grasping and selfish hoarding of things by means of law-breaking. In line with Justin's thinking[3] the resurrection effected the reversal of these. 'All irrational desires cease and everyone raises his eyes from earth to heaven' (*D.I.* 31). Henceforth people cease impiety, relinquish idolatry, resist demonic deceit and begin to live virtuously, to desire heavenly things and to know the Father. Such is evidence that Christ was in very truth raised from death to life. Indeed, it reveals not only that 'Christ is alive, but rather, that he is Life' (*D.I.* 30), a qualification which lies behind Athanasius' belief, much used in his anti-Arian arguments, that God, and God alone, can destroy corruption and give life, and can unravel demonic deceits and lead each into all righteousness.

It must be stressed that even this salvation from unrighteousness is wholly an act of grace. The movement is from the unwanting, self-existing divine Logos to the needy, contingent world; and this movement, however genuine the Incarnation, is in no sense to the detriment or benefit of the Logos, but solely to humanity's good. Through his goodness the Logos becomes man and dies for all, not to establish his goodness, but to secure humanity's righteous being; through his magnanimity he accepts the form and duration of death which befits people's needs, in terms both of re-opening the way to heaven through being crucified in the air, the temporary domain of the Devil, and of safeguarding all from either doubting that the death had ever occurred or forgetting that the death had once occurred, by staying dead for three days, neither so short a time as to permit people to suppose that death had not occurred, nor too long for people to have forgotten that the raised Christ formerly had died. Even his victory over death's power is coloured by his desire to be the good teacher who stoops to the level of even the most obtuse pupil: he shows to his most cruel enemies his power over their most ignobly contrived death, their ignoble acts but highlighting his noble act, an act ever for their salvation. All this is done because of who the Logos eternally is; that done does reveal who and what he eternally is, but does not establish who and what he is. There is therefore a substantial difference between Athanasius' sense of the salvation from mortality and the Neoplatonic understanding of the soul's 'return' to the One. While, like Plotinus, Athanasius does not think that God is either bettered or worsened by his relationship with matter, Athanasius, unlike Plotinus, does assert God's graciousness: his God is concerned for matter; he extends himself in care for it. Philanthropy and providence, rather than a distant, transcendent solitude, are the hallmark of Athanasius' divine Creator and Redeemer.

Christ's resurrection is understood both in an individual and a communal sense: Christ is indeed raised from death to life, but that resurrection is also an earnest for all. Hence Christ is titled both 'true Life' and 'Life Giver'. Christ effects death's destruction, and Christians are the recipients of the grace of Christ's resurrection. This however needs qualification. For there is a sense in which Christians are more than recipients of Christ's grace. The death of God in Christ does uniquely give meaning to the Christian's death. Yet the Christian's death also gives meaning to Christ's. As R. D. Williams notes in regard to a similar situation,

> there is a circle of interpretation: the martyr finds God in his suffering because he is assured that his Christian identity as a child of the Father, as a redeemed person, is the fruit of Christ's cross; and the 'content' of Christ's crucifixion, the nature of what was there endured and enacted, is filled out by the present experience of the martyr.[4]

There is this circle of interpretation, but it does not render the two events equal. The one flows from the other: God 'shows everyday victories over [death] through his disciples' (*D.I.* 29) while the disciples follow Christ's pattern.

This following Christ's pattern constitutes not an escape from this world but a transformation of this world. A result, as we have noted, of Christ's resurrection is that people begin to live virtuously. To this end people engage in spiritual exercises which prepare them to despise this present life and to welcome death. This despising the world is not, however, to be understood as an anti-worldly, escapist stance, nor as a quasi-Hellenistic salvation of a person from the world of matter to that of spirit; nor is death welcomed as freeing the essential self from the material world. To despise this world is to reject the abusing of God's world, by whatever means. This is manifest in at least two ways. Firstly, Christians prefer martyrdom to apostasy, where apostasy is not simply the denying particular credal statements, but turning from right faith in practice. Apostasy is qualifying or refusing the worship of the one and only God, evidenced, for example, in deifying the celestial bodies, as in astrology, or in sacrificing to the emperor. To despise the world is then not a rejection of God's creation, wherein his providential care is patent, but the dramatic assertion that the Christian will live for the Truth and, if necessary, die for it. Secondly, Athanasius recognizes a close connection between the Christian's everyday spiritual exercises and his death in Christ.

Spiritual maturity is learnt through individual histories. For the historical world stands within the purpose of God; it is the anvil upon which the Christian virtues are to be forged. Hence the religious impetus is not to escape from the temporal and the particular and the fleshly but to see and to realize human experience in its entirety as the arena of God's saving activity. The individual, as Athanasius' *Festal Letters* and *Life of Antony* suggest, is to be brought to maturity, to be completed and perfected. Hence, even individual human acts are significant. Indeed, there is a seriousness about the particular individual's experience of conflict, persecution and tragedy. They are not seen, as in Gnosticism, as signs of spiritual immaturity, but as that wanting reconciliation and integration and healing in and through God incarnate. Given such, the martyr's embracing death is no isolated event in his life, but is, *if it occurs*, the natural culmination of that far more prosaic process of dying daily for the Truth. It is the climax in Christian living, but the climax to that lifelong process in which each learns to live under the sovereign Truth. The Christian, the servant of this Truth, thus daily despises his body and its world. Yet this service is not realized in withdrawal from the body and the life in this world, but in freedom from egocentricity and idolatry and in liberation into that generosity of spirit which results in both the service of everyone in their need and the proper respect of God's creation, and which ends in the worship of God. The life then which is marked by service and compassion for the whole world and by the sole worship of God is the life which so despises this world. Thus the martyr's death and the life which rightly uses God's world are inseparable.

This transformation of the self, exchanging a view of the world as an end in itself for understanding it under the divine purview, stands in contrast with the Neoplatonic thinking of Porphyry (274–c. 305). In his *Sententiae ad intelligibilia ducentes* Porphyry teaches detachment from the material world for the sake of contemplation and the purgation of the soul, which leads to that freedom which makes the soul like God. This is withdrawal from the world, and not Athanasius' withdrawal from a misevaluation of the world that it may be rightly revered. Athanasius' concern is resurrection and not simply immortality; and this resurrection is the transformation and not the relinquishing of matter.

There is another sense in which Athanasius views the resurrection life as maturation and not withdrawal. The Christian life is one in which communal life is not necessarily inferior to the solitary. The religious life does not necessarily entail withdrawal from

society. The monk Dracontius had been elected Bishop of Hermopolis Parva, in the north-west of the Nile delta. This prompted
concern lest Dracontius, leaving his monastery's tranquillity, might
be unable to live a full and honest Christian life. Certainly a
Platonist would find living the true life in this world difficult.
Athanasius' thinking is different. It is coloured by his view of the
Incarnation: God the Logos lived a life faithful to God in the very
midst of this world, and lived this life for others. Christ's disciples
can do the same. In consequence Athanasius cites examples to
show that remaining in the monastery is no guarantee of a saintly
life, and that living in this world is not necessarily deleterious to the
true life in God. He mentions

> bishops who fast and monks who eat ... bishops who drink no
> wine, as well as monks who do ... bishops who work wonders, as
> well as monks who do not. Many ... of the bishops have not even
> married, while monks have been fathers of children, and con-
> versely ... bishops who are fathers of children and monks of the
> highest kind. (*Ad Drac.* 9)

Further, alluding to John 17:12–13, Athanasius warns Christians to
be Christlike in being concerned for those entrusted to them by
God. For 'each shall give account [on the day of judgement] for
those entrusted to his hands' (*Ad Drac.* 6). Should then the newly
elected bishop not come to Hermopolis Parva but continue in his
monastery, he would not show responsibility for his fellow Christians and be unfaithful to God. For it was God's will that he should
lead and feed them. By not coming forth from his monastery, he
would not bring to fruition the conversion of those many even now
on the point of turning from their heathen ways; and rather than
feeding his flock with instruction from Scripture, he would furnish
them with a pretext for not standing firm in the Truth in this world,
whatever their situation and whatever the cost.

Yet Athanasius still holds a very high view of asceticism. Hence
he delights in those bishops who are also monks who have persuaded 'a damsel to live as a virgin and a young man ... in
continence' (*Ad Drac.* 7). Ideally, this asceticism involves fasting
and celibacy. Eating and drinking wines in moderation, and pro-
creating within marriage, are good but seemingly not the greatest
good. This seems corroborated in the near-contemporary letter to
Amoun, where Athanasius notes that there are certain acts which
are not always right or wrong, their propriety depending upon the

circumstances in which they are performed. Thus, for example, while generally it is not right to kill, 'in war it is lawful and praiseworthy to destroy the enemy' (*Ad Amoun*). Marriage is another such act. Marriage and begetting within it are good, when the alternative is licentious adultery. So, 'if a man chooses the way of the world, namely marriage, he is not indeed to blame' (*Ad Amoun*). Yet Athanasius continues, 'he will not however receive such great gifts as the [celibate]' (*Ad Amoun*). For whereas marriage is 'the more moderate and ordinary', virginity is 'angelic and unsurpassed' (*Ad Amoun*).

> If a man embraces the holy and unearthly way, even though, as compared with [marriage], it is rugged and hard to accomplish, yet it has the more wonderful gifts. For it grows the perfect fruit, namely an hundred fold. (*Ad Amoun*)

It is most noteworthy that practising the higher form of Christian life is not limited to those who withdraw from society; it may be embraced within society. Indeed, Athanasius writes, Dracontius may even be able to live this life 'better' in society than withdrawn from the world in his monastery. This is the same idea as that found in the *De Fuga*, where Athanasius advises the persecuted not to seek death at the persecutors' hands as an escape from the harsher but beatific life of flight. In his letter to Dracontius Athanasius advises not seeking to stay in the monastery, escaping the harsher, God-fearing life in society.

Noteworthy also is that this higher form of Christian living, though appearing individualistic, is not. It is concerned with the individual; for each individual is responsible for their own life before God. Yet it is not individualistic. For each individual, in being responsible before God, is also responsible for their neighbour. This Athanasius poignantly emphasizes when he tells Dracontius that a bishop may fast and abstain from wine, not only in faithfulness to God but also in responsibility for his neighbour, 'in order that thus fasting . . . [he] may feast others with [his] words, and whilst thirsting for lack of water, water others by teaching' (*Ad Drac.* 9).

Another consequence of the saving act of the Logos is a person's liberation from the domination of the fleshly passions. For,

> while [the Logos] himself, being impassible by nature, remains as he is, not harmed by those [human] affections, but rather obliterating and destroying them, [people], their passions as if changed

and abolished in the Impassible One, henceforth become themselves impassible and free from them forever. (*C.Ar.* 3.34)

This being freed from human passions for ever may mean exactly that, but only in reference to our *post mortem* existence, when there shall be no more 'crying nor pain'. Our redemption to 'impassibility', it would seem, is not so conceived this side of the grave. For Athanasius is no docetist: in this life even Christians suffer. Christians' present freedom from pain, it appears, is the freedom of their 'being no more abandoned to their service' (*C.Ar.* 3.34). Trust in the life-giving Logos means that Christ's disciples need no longer fear suffering; passions need not deter them any longer from right acts. The non-Christian fears want and so hoards all that is near; when persecuted he flees; and when faced with death, she is cowardly. Once saved by Christ, he no longer covets that nearby, but trusts God to supply his need; no longer does she shrink before her persecutor, but stands firm for the truth, and whether in life or death, convicts the persecutor of the error of so attempting to suppress the Truth; and no longer does any fear death, imagining it to be the separation from all those things whence meaning comes. Knowing that all are who and what they are in and through God alone, Christians courageously and trustfully commit themselves into the hands of God. Of such impassibility within this passible world both Christ and Christian martyrs are evidence.

This trustful and pacific acceptance of suffering Athanasius clearly sees as possible only in the strength of Christ. On their own people are not so, as is evidenced in the ever-increasing covetousness, antagonism and fear of death of those turned from God. Though he does not cite the dominical words, 'where your treasure is, there will your heart be also' (Matthew 6:21; cf. Luke 12:34), he knows this idea. When one holds mammon dear, asceticism and death are difficult; and when one worships God alone, one's attitude to this world is free and generous.

Only in the general resurrection will this salvation to impassibility find its completion, when each, ethically and physically, will know wholly the grace of being freed from passions for ever. Now there is a certain temporal dualism, the Christian knowing this grace in the sphere of ethics and still awaiting it in that of nature.

This same temporal dualism seems to exist in Athanasius' treatment of humanity's redemption from death and corruption. Athanasius writes in vaguely Pauline clauses of 'all dying in him' (cf. Romans 6:8) and of the incarnate Logos having 'by the grace of the resurrection rid [people] of death' (*D.I.* 8). Yet he is not supposing that this salvation is immediately and comprehensively effective. Athanasius is realistic: whatever Christ achieved, men and women still die, although they now die with the hope of the resurrection. For Christ's body, raised incorrupt from death suffered on behalf of all, is the 'first fruit of the universal resurrection' (*D.I.* 20). Athanasius is therefore content to maintain that

> by the incarnation of God the Logos were effected the overthrow of death and the resurrection of life ... no longer as condemned do we die; but as those who will rise again we await the general resurrection of all, which God 'in his own time will reveal'. (*D.I.* 10, quoting 1 Timothy 6:15; Titus 1:3)

Athanasius elaborates upon this. Employing the Pauline imagery of seeds sown in the ground, to rise to a greater existence (cf. 1 Corinthians 15:36ff.), Athanasius suggests that each dies and remains dead, but

> only for the time which God has set for each, in order that we may be able to obtain a 'better resurrection'. We do not perish when we are dissolved, but we rise again. (*D.I.* 21, referring to Hebrews 11:35)

Certainly Athanasius uses the language of triumph. Christ 'has shown triumphs and victories over death and ... has rendered it powerless' (*D.I.* 28). Yet the Alexandrian does not see Christ's resurrection as the cancelling out of the cross and death. He does not replace a theology of the cross with one of glory. For there is no way to resurrection but through the cross; and resurrection does not make things easy, but gives the grace and strength to undertake the difficult. It is not arrogant and complacent, superficially believing that all will turn out well in the end. Equally, however, it is not the pessimistic acceptance that the world is a sorry scheme of things without final meaning. It rather speaks of a belief that when Christians fall, and even when the worst happens, and martyrs are made, the world's end is not met. For the divine Logos, the world's Creator and Recreator, is ahead, having opened new possibilities for all though his life, death and resurrection. Certainly Athanasius recognizes that it is for each to seize that possibility and so know its realization. For it is he who 'puts on the faith of the cross' (*D.I.* 28) who meets death and, through the divine Life, knows resurrection

Indeed, the final seizing of that possibility — freedom both of and through the cross — is continuous with the daily seizing of that possibility — the mundane perfecting of human life. Therein monks like Antony, who had long practised ascesis, the dying to self, show the impassibility of resurrection even on their death beds; and 'not only men, but women and children prepare for [death with spiritual exercises]' (*D.I.* 27). God then is seen as opening the way in and through Christ, and people are seen as those whose decision it is whether or not to set foot upon it. For resurrection is not a possession or a state, but a new life, a new future to be constructed daily. There is no automatic progress. Resurrection means not that in spite of all that a person does, all will turn out for the best; it means rather that God in Christ, dying and living, is with each and is ahead of all, opening the way in which any may choose responsibly to follow.

Athanasius' point then is that Christ's death does not effect the triumphalistic cancelling out of death, but the complete annihilation of death's threat and power. By offering his assumed humanity, the Logos 'delivered all, who by fear of death were all their lives subject to death' (*De Decret.* 14). The condemnation rightly earned through the Adamic transgression is removed, the law's demands fully met. People still die, for as creatures they are still weak by nature. Yet even as the Christ, through his human body, was unable not to die, and yet was 'unable to remain dead because [his body] had become the temple of Life' (*D.I.* 31), so Christians in Christ, though dying, are raised, no longer remaining dead under the earth (*C.Ar.* 1.43–44). What Christ counters is the power of death. Hence people no longer fear it; they die but no longer *remain* dead. Now death 'never again [had] influence over those who were like him' (*D.I.* 8). Death's power, which lay in fallen individuals' not only dying but remaining in death, was thus exposed by resurrection's strength, those who died and rose again in Christ now remaining incorruptible (*D.I.* 9). The sovereignty of the divine Life was again appropriately known.

There is indeed a sense in which Christ counters that power of death which undermined the propriety, dictated by God's creative goodness, of people's existing, and existing in and for God: Christ brings it under God's control. For Athanasius hints at death now being that which God uses to effect for each 'a better resurrection'. This is not to imply that previously death was entirely outside God's control. For it was he who authorized its possibility, a consequence if and when people turned from him who is Life. In a sense death then was God's 'punishment'. Now it is transfigured, death now having a remedial purpose, promoting a sinner's reformation.

For Athanasius there is then no way to resurrection except through death. It may even be said that resurrection is freedom from the power of death and corruption, the consequences of breaking the divine law; it is a freedom born of the cross. Resurrection then is continuous with what has been before, the perfecting of dying humanity, through the birth, life and death of Christ. It is also continuous, on the grander scale, with humanity's creation from nothing, and fall; for it is its completion. Thus the drama of God's goodness, his concern and his loving kindness for creation, is all of one piece.

Such a secure salvation of the whole person, body and soul (*Tome* 7), was not the returning of a person to the prelapsarian state, wherein each would still be faced with the possibility of breaking the divine law and thereby coming again under its mortifying influence. It was the promotion of the person to a better state. The Law had been fulfilled, and death's power had been met.

> As when a great king has entered some great city and dwelt in one of the houses in it, ... and no longer does any enemy or bandit come against [the city], but rather it is treated with regard because of the king who has taken up residence in one of its houses. So also it is in the case of the king of all. Since he has come to our realm and has dwelt in a body similar to ours, now every machination of the enemy against mankind has ceased and the corruption of death, which formerly had power over them, has been destroyed. (*D.I.* 9)

In short, when a person is perfected in and through Christ, that person is 'restored, as [he] was made at the beginning, nay, with greater grace' (*C.Ar.* 2.67). Salvation to a better state, it must be emphasized, is not to be understood as suggesting the absence of continuing and sustaining grace to prelapsarian humanity and its presence to redeemed humanity. The superiority of the redeemed state lies in that state's security. It is in the Bestower of the Spirit, sanctifying himself as man that all may be sanctified in truth (*C.Ar.* 1.46), in giving what he ever and unalterably had as God to himself as man, and for humanity, people in their need receive permanently and securely (*C.Ar.* 1.45–48). The permanence of the giving and the security of the receiving, in which the one and same gives and receives, albeit in two economies, establishes a security of humanity's God-given existence such as never was before the Incarnation and hence in the prelapsarian state. Without the unalterable Logos of God becoming man, people, in accordance with their originate nature, would remain alterable, and so still open to error, it being the nature of the alterable to be able to err. Salvation through incarnation is then not simply the renewal of the former creation, which had fallen, but the preservation of the new, which had come into being through the Christ.

Salvation from sin and death does not then deliver people to a neutral position. A person is either enslaved to sin or a servant of the living God; each may be either to a greater or lesser extent a slave to sin, or a more or less faithful servant of God. None, however, is in a third position alongside these two spheres of existence. Salvation thus delivers people from sin to 'participation' in God, to deification. For the Logos 'became man that we might be deified' (*D.I.* 54; cf. *Ad Adelph.* 4). This deification belongs to the realm of dogmatics rather than contemplation. For it describes the consequences of Christ's saving work, and neither a mystical state enjoyed by a contemplative nor the consequences of the human soul being either naturally divine or even made in the image and likeness of God. Deification owes nothing to humans, considered in their own being. At most it owes something to them in that it comes about through the divine humanity of Christ; by being incorporated into his body through baptism — for deification is an ecclesiastical process in that it takes place within the communion of the Church, to which admission is by baptism — people are joined to divinity through the assumed humanity. The theological datum therefore is Christ. The philosophical conception, that of participation by people in God, who is both Being and the Source of all being, clearly is related to Hellenistic thought. Yet it also differs significantly. Porphyry, for example, denied the grace of incarnation and for that reason saw deification as a state to be achieved by a philosopher's own efforts. For Athanasius, however, deification was made possible solely by divine initiative. The Christocentricity is integral to Athanasius' thinking here, Christ being the means and guarantor of this grace.

A motif closely related to people's being deified is their adoption as children of God.

From the beginning we were creatures by nature, and God is our Creator through the Logos; but afterwards we were made sons;

and henceforth God the Creator becomes our Father too. (*C.Ar.* 2.59)

The qualification of people's relationship is the result of a response to unforced divine kindness. By receiving 'the Spirit of the natural and true Son' (*C.Ar.* 2.59), whereby God's creatures are graciously introduced into the divine Son's relation to his Father, we receive power to become God's children and cry 'Abba, Father'. Therein, through the assumption of a common humanity by the Logos, people were securely made one with the Son in his unity with the Father; what the Son eternally is, that people by grace are now made. Importantly for their creaturely salvation, rather than salvation from creatureliness, people as people are not naturally changed in being so drawn into a filial relationship with the Father. 'When, according to grace, they are said to be begotten as sons, still no less than before are men "works" according to nature' (*C.Ar.* 2.59). Athanasius almost thinks in a chiastic way; the Logos is Son of God by nature, and graciously becomes man. People are creatures by nature and are graciously made sons of the Father (*C.Ar.* 1.37–38). The givenness of the essential difference between God and creature, so prominent in Athanasius' doctrine of creation, is staunchly maintained in his understanding of salvation. However much people participate in God, they remain essentially creatures, transfigured creatures, but creatures nevertheless. For 'a work could never be Son or Logos; nor could the Son be a work' (*C.Ar.* 2.5). Deification is rather our being brought into a holy communion, with one another and with God, through the grace made secure in and through Christ's assumption of humanity. It is that process in which people, creatures of the Creator and fellow creatures of all creation, are transformed, a process begun in baptism, continued throughout this life and fulfilled in the life to come. For the godly life to be lived here and now, within the baptized community, is an earnest of that future, resurrected, divine life in God.

There are passages where Athanasius initially seems to understand deification in a universalistic way. The Logos assumed our originate, human body, that, having deified it, he might 'introduce us all into the kingdom of heaven after his likeness' (*C.Ar.* 2.70). The same Logos is described, in an allusion to Romans 8:21, not as one who groans or needs freedom, but as he who gives sonship and freedom to all (*C.Ar.* 2.72). Yet alongside such are statements to the effect that 'he judges, but each of all things originate is bound to give account to him' (*C.Ar.* 2.72). The point here is that all originate things are dependent for their well-being upon their Creator and Sustainer; such being so, all owe him responsibility. Thus, though the divine Logos both wills that all may be saved, and, remaining very God, became man as all are human that all may be brought near God — for otherwise we should have had nothing 'common' with what was 'foreign', namely God — each yet will be judged in accordance with whether that person has allowed this divine, life-giving will to be realized, and realized not just generally in humanity, but in that particular person's humanity. The particularity of the response of each individual to Christ's work for all, whether or not 'each ... has faith and wears the sign of the cross' (*D. I.* 29), suggests that Athanasius does not maintain that

> when the Logos assumed [human nature] and suffused it with his divinity, the divinizing force would be communicated to all mankind, and the Incarnation would in effect be the Redemption.[5]

Deification is then not simply the result of Athanasius' optimism. It may be hopeful, but it is not brash optimism either that, come what may, good will result or that hurt and evil have been totally eliminated. For Christ experiences the divine life through willing submission to death; he is exalted through self-denial; he is given worth through humbly receiving God's grace and does not achieve status by self-concerned, egotistical activities. His sanctification is a lifelong practice, begun and ended in God. Like the First-begotten from the dead, the child of God lives and dies and is raised to new life. He is the martyr, the 'witness', who takes up his cross and follows Christ, to death if necessary, but always to God the Father.

Notes

1 To consider the view that the portrayal of the fall from life to death is different from that of the fall from knowledge to ignorance, the Adamic figure in the former being an historical figure, and in the latter non-historical, see A. Louth, 'The concept of the soul in Athanasius' *Contra Gentes–De Incarnatione', Texte und Untersuchungen* 116 (Berlin, 1974), pp. 227–31; A. Pettersen, *Athanasius and the Human Body* (Bristol, 1990), pp. 9ff. Whether or not the differences are of emphasis or substance, and explicable or not by the two works' different purposes, both portraits centre the fall upon people's abusing their free choice in turning from the life-giving Truth of God.

2 In *De Incarnatione* 9 Athanasius seems to suggest that the divine word of forgiveness was not possible. For such would render untrue God's word that the Adamic breaking of the divine law would result in death and corruption.

3 Justin Martyr, *Apologia* 1.14.2–3.

4 R. D. Williams, *The Wound of Knowledge: Christian Spirituality from the New Testament to St John of the Cross* (London, 1979), p. 15.

5 J. N. D. Kelly, *Early Christian Doctrines* (4th edn; London, 1968), p. 378.

5

The Incarnation

Athanasius treats the Incarnation, at times, almost in passing, in that his main interest is God's wholly gracious salvation of humanity, secured through the Incarnation; and, at other times, he is seemingly uncritical, accepting points as 'givens' of the received ecclesiastical tradition. Further, he considers the Son's being fully and immutably God, and his becoming man, against the background of those then thinking that the Logos was creaturely and became divine. There are therefore certain consequences. Athanasius is not primarily concerned with the anthropology of the Incarnation; his interest is the 'why' rather than the 'what' of Christ's humanity. Athanasius stresses the divinity of the Logos even when at times it may seem that his becoming man is thereby undermined. He emphasizes that Jesus, who is ignorant and grows in wisdom, who suffers and dies, as God is immutably Wisdom and Life. Athanasius will so stress the miracles, necessary to rouse people from the sleep of ignorance to the wakefulness of knowing God, that Christ's humanity at times may appear qualitatively other than ours, if not somewhat docetic. There is then an absence of stress on the humanity; but it is not underplayed. For what occurs here is a focus upon one aspect of the 'God became man' and not on others, and not the assertion of one while denying the others. Polemical reasons apart, this is due partly to Athanasius' thinking that human nature is properly passive, the receptive instrument of the life-giving Logos, and his consequent recognition that Christ's humanity is 'uniquely responsive to the ultimate ground of being . . . the Logos'.[1]

In language reminiscent of Romans 1:3, Athanasius maintained that

> The Lord, who proceeded from Mary, whilst God's Son by essence and nature, is of David's seed according to the flesh, and of holy Mary's flesh. (*Ad Epict.* 2)

Clearly he held that the Incarnation was a central part of the Christian tradition. Yet Athanasius still felt the need to defend its propriety. For not only non-Christian Hellenists denied the propriety of God's presence in a material body. Gnostics, who though rejected by Catholics as non-Christians saw themselves as not only Christians, but enlightened Christians, allowed God's 'incarnation' in his revealing himself through words, but not historically conditioned words, and certainly not acts and events. To all intents and purposes they rejected the substantial, material and historical incarnation of Athanasian theology. Arians, dedicated theological conservatives,[2] meanwhile subscribed to a deity whose transcendent majesty precluded his drawing near. Athanasius' defence therefore begins with the belief that the Logos is infinite, and hence neither limited to nor excluded from this world. Matter establishes no 'no-go' areas. The Logos transcends the limited body and the world of which it is a part, and consequently is not handicapped by it; and yet he is immanent in it, his transcendence not precluding his ubiquitous presence in the finite world. The Hellenists, Athanasius noted, had partially grasped these truths: they allowed that the Logos was involved in the world, providentially illuminating and moving it. However, they wrongly denied that the same Logos could fittingly be involved in a creaturely body. Hence Athanasius asks these people, who had so adopted a Stoic understanding of the creative Logos:

> If God's Logos is in the world, which is a body, and he has passed ... into every part of it, ... what is unfitting in our saying that he came in a human body? (*D.I.* 41)

Athanasius, however, is sufficiently astute to realize that his argument holds only if there is commonality between the whole and the part. Hence he seeks to counter the Middle Platonic view that the divine Logos might properly be seen to illuminate the whole cosmos but not a particular body, held on the grounds that the cosmos here is the *Kosmos noētos*, which is identified with God's

Logos,[3] while the body is not so identified, being created from nothing. Athanasius' response is to assert a radical and comprehensive creation from nothing: all is formed from nothing. The divine Logos then should be either excluded from all, both the cosmos and the particular body, or recognized as fittingly involved in everything created from nothing. 'Whatever they suppose about the whole, they must also think similarly about the part' (*D.I.* 42).

To Athanasius' mind his critics are hoisted upon their own petard. They allow that the divine Logos is active in and through all creation. It, as is the body which is a part of this whole creation, is created from nothing. Thus they should reasonably and consistently allow that 'it is not unseemly that the Logos should be in a man and that by him and through him the universe should have light, movement and life' (*D.I.* 42). Athanasius then drives home his point with a simple analogy.

> If anyone were to say that it is unfitting that a man's strength should also be in his toe, he would be considered mad, because he admits that a man penetrates through and acts in the whole body, but does not allow him to be also in a part of it; so he, who admits and believes that God's divine Logos is in all and that everything is illumined and moved by him, would not think it unseemly that a human body also should be moved and illumined by him. (*D.I.* 42)

For Athanasius a homely truth highlights a greater principle.

Athanasius' concern is to distinguish condescension from impropriety. Certainly the Logos, who is 'above all', assumed a mortal body. For the Hellenists a deity's incarnation was 'improper', there being an essential incompatibility between the spiritual and the material, between God and body. Not so for Athanasius: God is the Creator of the material; and whilst there is an essential distinction between the Creator and the created, there is no antithesis. Rather, there is a proper concern of the good Creator for the creation which he has made. Thus, for Athanasius, God's assumption of a body, driven by fitting concern for matter, is neither 'improper' (*D.I.* 6) nor 'unfitting' (*D.I.* 41). Indeed, it would have been 'improper' had God's good Logos not assumed a body for the world's salvation. The Incarnation is then not *to alogon*, 'that contrary to reason', as the Hellenists maintained, but *to eulogon*, 'that according with reason' where *to eulogon* is defined in relation to *ho Logos*, God's good Logos or Reason; the renewing Incarnation is seemly as it accords with the very nature of its subject, the divine Creator Logos. Almost imperceptibly Athanasius moves from denying the impropriety of the Creator assuming a creaturely body to asserting its propriety. God's goodness is not limited; he is no divine Maker who creates and then leaves his creatures untended and at the mercy of their own actions. Rather, through condescension, he raised his creation again to God.

Just as the infinity of the Logos did not preclude the Incarnation, so it did not preclude the continuing activity of the incarnate Logos throughout the whole cosmos. Indeed, it enabled him properly and fitly both to be present immediately to this world which needs healing through a creaturely body, and yet to remain true to his healing self, the eternal and unaltered Enlivener and Sustainer, providentially active everywhere and at all times.

When the Logos made himself present immediately to this world he 'did not dwell in a holy man at the consummation of the ages as he had come upon the prophets, but ... the Logos himself became flesh' (*Tome* 7; cf. *Ad Epict.* 2.). For the advent of the Logos through individual prophets and saints was noticeably different from that in Christ. 'When they were begotten, it was not said that [the Logos] had become man, nor when they suffered was it said that he himself suffered' (*C.Ar.* 3.31). Only when he was born of Mary at the end of the ages 'was it said that he took flesh and became man, and in that flesh suffered for us' (*C.Ar.* 3.31; *Ad Epict.* 11); and, unlike those who have yet to rise from the dead, he alone has already risen. Further, Athanasius notes that Jesus' contemporaries found him extraordinary. If the Logos had come upon the man Jesus as he had upon the Old Testamental prophets,

those who saw him [would not have] been startled, saying, 'Whence is he?' and 'Wherefore dost thou, being a man, make thyself God?' For they were familiar with the idea [sc. of the Logos coming upon a man], from the words 'and God's Logos came' to this or to that prophet. (*C.Ar.* 3.30, referring to John 9:29; 10:33; Ezekiel 27:1 and the like)

Something consistent with but different from the coming of the Logos upon the prophets and saints was happening in and through the Incarnation. In it he who was ever God and who had hallowed all upon whom he formerly had come now had become man.

Athanasius finds theological corroboration for his scriptural exegesis. Those who suppose that the Logos descended upon, rather than became, the man Jesus, separate the Logos from the assumed humanity. They may assert what is proper to the distinct divine and human natures of the Logos, but at the expense of denying that all done is done 'by one' (*C.Ar.* 3.35), and so they set 'at naught the grace given us by him' (*Ad Adelph.* 8). For what was necessary for mortality's complete exclusion from humanity was not simply the Giver of all life, nor a body, wherein death was possible, but the Logos become man.

> If the Logos had been outside the body and not in it, ... [death's] attendant corruption would have remained in the body. For this reason the Saviour rightly put on a body in order that the body, being joined to Life, might no longer remain as mortal in death, but having put on immortality, might then rise up and remain immortal. For once it had put on corruption, it would not have risen unless it had put on Life. (*D.I.* 44)

Athanasius therefore asserts a union in which the two distinct natures are maintained. The subject in the Christ is the Logos, in both his divine and human economies. Without the union of the two distinct natures the divine Logos may not assume what is naturally humanity's, mutability, passibility and mortality, and, doing away with such, invest people with what is natural to the Logos, immutability, impassibility and immortality. This union, indeed, qualifies what may appear to be a rather wooden reading of the Gospels. The Arians suggested that the creaturely passions recorded there established that the Logos was a creature. In response Athanasius allocated passions and miracles to the human and divine economies respectively. For it is necessary to recognize 'what is proper to each' (*C.Ar.* 3.35). Yet Athanasius' anti-Arian exegesis is not quite as wooden as first impressions suggest. For, at the same time as recognizing what is proper to each economy, it is also proper to note that 'both these things and those are done by one' (*C.Ar.* 3.35). Hence Athanasius keenly suggests that while passions naturally belong to the assumed humanity, they are yet the assuming Logos'; and he eagerly maintains that while grace comes from God the Logos, it is yet securely mediated through the assumed humanity. The passions which *are* of the flesh *are said to be* the Logos'; and the divine works which *are* of the Logos *are wrought* through the body, which the divine Logos has assumed as his instrument of grace and salvation. Thus, there are two natures, but not two independently existing natures; there are two economies of the one divine Logos; and there are human passions, which properly belong to the assumed flesh, but which are not left alone, isolated from the impassible divinity of the Logos, but are brought into an enlivening contact with God, that these passions may be relieved.

It was not long before Athanasius had to explain his understanding of the clause 'become' flesh (John 1:14). He thought it signified neither the divine essence of the Logos nor his natural generation of the Father but his 'descent to mankind and high priesthood, which did "become"' (*C.Ar.* 2.7). Athanasius found a shadow of this 'becoming': Aaron was not born a high priest but a man.

> In the process of time, when God willed, he became a high priest; and he became so, not simply, nor as betoken by his ordinary garments, but by putting over them the ephod, the breastplate and the robe ... and going in them into the holy place, he offered the sacrifice for the people; and in them, as it were, mediated between the vision of God and the sacrifices of men. (*C.Ar.* 2.7)

Similarly, the Logos was ever with God; but when the Father willed the ransom of all,

> then, as Aaron his robe, so the Logos truly took earthly flesh ... that as high priest ... he might offer himself to the Father and cleanse us all from sins. (*C.Ar.* 2.7)

So, on taking flesh, the Logos

> did not become other than himself ... but, being the same as before, was robed in [flesh]. The expressions 'he became' and 'he was made' must not be understood as if the Logos, considered as the Logos, were made, but that the Logos, being Framer of all things, afterwards was made high priest by putting on a body which was 'of the world of becoming' and 'was made', and was such as he can offer for us. (*C.Ar.* 2.8)

This thinking is closely related to that concerning ministeries of beneficence. Athanasius refers to images of God and of people 'becoming' an assistance to another. Such 'becoming' does not indicate the original becoming or the essence of the [benefactor] but the beneficence coming to [the needy]. So, when the saints say concerning God, 'he became . . .', they do not denote any originate becoming, for God is without beginning, but the salvation which is made to be unto man from him. (*C.Ar.* 1.63)

The ministry of the Logos of beneficence, or of salvation, to the needy equally only came into being when the Logos, he who is, entered the world of 'becoming' by 'becoming man'.

The intimacy of this Logos with the man whom he became is highlighted in two discussions. The one concerns the one subject in Christ and the other the worship of Christ. The Arian backcloth to Athanasius' writing encouraged him clearly to draw the distinctions between the two economies. Hence, for example, the Logos stretched forth his hand humanly to heal Peter's wife's mother, but stopped the illness divinely; in the case of the man born blind, human was the spittle which he used to make the clay, but divinity opened the eyes upon whose lids the clay was put; and as man he called Lazarus, but divinely he raised him from death (*C.Ar.* 3.32). Yet 'the same' (*Tome* 7) both asked where Lazarus was buried and raised him up, both applied the clay and healed the blind, and both suffered and yet opened the tomb and raised the dead. The Logos worked 'as God' through the humanity which he had become, and that same humanity qualified the Logos, so that he truly acted 'as man'; and the two economies find their unity in the one Logos. These observations are not possible if the Logos simply came upon a person. The reality of this 'becoming' is made yet more manifest in Athanasius' countering the opinion that Christians worship a creature. Christians, he states, rather worship the *Logos incarnate*.

If the flesh . . . is in itself a part of the created world, yet it has become God's body. And we neither divide the body, being such, from the Logos, and worship it by itself, nor when we wish to worship the Logos do we set him apart from the flesh, but knowing . . . that the Logos has become flesh, we recognize him as God also, after having come in the flesh. (*Ad Adelph.* 3)

The assumed humanity cannot in fact be separated from its Logos (*Ad Adelph.* 5). For it was brought into being by the Logos, exists in and through the Logos and cannot exist apart from the Logos. Hence, once the Logos has become incarnate Christians can only worship 'the Creator who has put on the created body' (*Ad Adelph.* 6). The intimacy of this 'becoming man' is the more obvious when we compare it with the coming of the Logos upon the prophets. In those cases, the prophets could be separated from the divine Logos and the divine Logos could properly be worshipped apart.

Various other biblical and non-biblical expressions are used to describe the Incarnation. Athanasius will use the Johannine motif of the body being the divine temple, and will then assert its indwelling by the Logos. He will maintain that God 'assumed a body', language common to the ecclesiastical tradition that maintained to varying degrees that essential distinction between the eternal Godhead and the temporal humanity. He will note that 'the incorporeal Logos made his own the body's properties, as being his own body' (*Ad Epict.* 6) Such a statement describes the Logos who is not distant from the world in which he becomes incarnate, and so does not, as it were, draw near to it, but who yet identified himself particularly and peculiarly with a certain part of creation, while not thereby divorcing himself from the rest of creation. Indeed, by making 'his own' the passible body, God is able to identify with not only creation, but also its particular aspects, its particular tests, temptations and passions. For Athanasius is concerned with particularity as well as generality. God knows, for instance, that humanity is mortal; but he also appreciates that this particular man or woman will die. The paradigm of 'making his own' is the Father's relation to the Son and the Son's to the Father, each being the other's own, while yet retaining their own integrity. As the Logos is the Father's, so, insofar as a creaturely body, with all its passions, can be God's, this body belongs to the divine Logos.

Such identification of the Logos with humanity lies behind the paradox that the Logos was

> he who suffered and yet suffered not: suffered because his own body suffered and he was in it ... and thus suffered, and suffered not because the Logos, being by nature God, is impassible. (*Ad Epict.* 6)

This paradox may seem on the edge of slipping into contradiction. Yet Athanasius will not have this. Arguing elsewhere concerning the title 'first born of creation' Athanasius remarks that 'the same cannot be both "only begotten" and "first born" ' (*C.Ar.* 2.62), except in different relations. Yet the Logos is both 'only begotten' and 'first born' and hence must be such in different relations, as

God and as man respectively. Without the acknowledgement of these two relations the two epithets are 'inconsistent with each other' (*C.Ar.* 2.62). So it is that the Logos as God is impassible, the only begotten, wise, and the like, and as man is passible, the firstborn, ignorant, and the like. As the Logos truly became flesh, the Logos as man is passible; and as the Logos did not cease to be very God in becoming man, the Logos as God remains impassible. In short, neither contradicts the other: 'man' and 'God' are not the same and so not mutually exclusive. Moreover, the true natures of both in one must be retained if there is to be very God, who alone can save, becoming very man, where salvation must be fully and finally wrought.

Athanasius casts further light upon this when referring to the Pauline statement that Christ became 'a curse for us' (Galatians 3:13). 'He has not himself become a curse, but is said to have done so because he took upon himself the curse on our behalf' (*Ad Epict.* 8). This is, as it were, another example of the intimacy of Logos and flesh, wherein the respective natures are retained. Even as the flesh is truly worshipped because of the Logos who assumed it, so the Logos is accursed because of the flesh which he became. What is significant here is that the curse, and the suffering, properly and naturally belong to the flesh, whose distinct nature the Logos respected even while making it his very own. Equally significant, however, is his distinct, natural immutability and impassibility. For 'to whom the affections are ascribed, of him too is the triumph and grace (*C.Ar.* 3.33). We should also note the distinction made in the *De Decretis* and *De Synodis* between 'being' and 'being called' in the debate concerning the relationship of 'Sonship' and 'divine essence': the Son not only 'is called' but 'is' God. Similarly, the curse and the passions are the assumed humanity's. It is in this sense that the divine Logos 'is called and in fact is' blessed and impassible, while he truly 'is called' accursed and passible, through becoming flesh which 'is called and truly is' accursed and passible. The same point is made differently when Athanasius expands upon the belief that creaturely attributes are not natural to but assumed by the Logos: in that sense 'the Logos partook of none of the body's attributes' (*D.I.* 43) but 'suffered because his own body suffered and he was in it and thus suffered' (*Ad Epict.* 6). Athanasius here almost anticipates Gregory of Nyssa's argument in *Contra Eunomium* 2 that God is not bound by definitions. When therefore the Logos is known in suffering flesh, he is not to be deemed to be either only vulnerable, as the Arians suppose, or only impassible, as

Docetists imagine, but is to be appreciated as him who in goodness is mightily able to make himself weak and suffering, through identifying himself with a passible nature not his own. His condescension in making suffering flesh his own then becomes evidence of his sovereign goodness, not limited even by a conceptual framework which finds possible contradictions in God becoming man and the impassible One suffering.

This conforms with the belief that although the Logos became very man, he himself is not altered. Even as the sun is true to its very nature and is neither polluted by its shining upon terrestrial objects nor overcome by darkness, so the divine Light is not compromised in its bringing light to those who live in darkness. Accordingly, the divine Logos was neither damaged by human passions nor improved by the receipt of charismata. He is ever Son and Lord, and never in himself is made such, as the unlearned might conclude from an illegitimate reading of texts such as Proverbs 8:22, Acts 2:36 and Hebrews 3:1–2. He is ever the Giver of grace and never the simple recipient of such, as Matthew 28:18 might suggest. Being eternal Wisdom, he does not advance in Wisdom (Luke 2:52) nor is he ignorant (Mark 13:32; cf. Matthew 16:13; John 11:11ff.); and being eternally the providential Life of God, he was not fearful (Matthew 26:39; John 12:17). Not surprisingly then, when Athanasius alludes to Philippians 2:6–11, he maintains that in becoming man the Logos did not empty himself of divinity. Rather, while assuming the form of a servant, for humanity's succour, the Logos yet remained Lord, 'the Creator coming in a creature' (*Ad Adelph.* 8). Just as the divine Logos remains very God, unaltered by his general activity in creation, so he remains unimpaired by his specific involvement in the humanity born of Mary.

Athanasius looks beyond philosophical assumptions to 'proofs', from both Scriptures and the Christian life, that the Logos remained God even when incarnate. In reference to 1 Peter 3:19 Athanasius argues that had the Logos changed into the assumed body, there would not have been need of a tomb. For that body would itself have gone to preach to the departed. Yet tomb and preaching in Hades there were (*Ad Epict.* 6). John 20 concerns Thomas's seeing the nail prints in the risen Christ's hands. The hands, Athanasius argues, were not the Logos but those of the Logos. An Old Testament analogy also is used: the Jerusalem Temple is a 'shadow' of the Lord's humanity; he 'is in the flesh as in a temple' (*Ad Adelph.* 7). Neither the Temple nor the assumed body are to be confused with God indwelling them. Perhaps, however, Athanasius' most compelling image draws upon Christians' own experience of God's working in them.

> As we, by receiving the Spirit, do not lose our own proper substance, so the Lord, when he became man for us, ... was no less God. For he was not lessened by being enveloped in a body, but rather deified it and redeemed it immortal. (*De Decret.* 14)

A corollary of this is that the Logos was not contained by his body; nor was the universe thereby deprived of 'his action and providence' (*D.I.* 17). He is unlike the human soul which, while being able to proceed beyond its body's bounds to consider things afar, is unable to act upon or affect the things considered. The Logos is not a concerned but helpless bystander. Rather, he 'lived as a man, and as the Logos gave life to everything, and as the Son was with the Father' (*D.I.* 17). Nothing was deprived of his divinity. For while yet enlivening and controlling his body, he also still enlivens and controls the creation of which it is a part.

The infinity of the Logos therefore is understood neither abstractly nor impersonally. He is within all 'according to his goodness and power and yet without all in his proper nature' (*De Decret.* 11). This gains significance when viewed against Athanasius' portrayal of the Arian God as 'powerful' but alien and distant, rather than powerful and concerned. Here power is closely linked with creativity, providence and incarnation. Rather than separating, power here links God with his whole fragile world. In contrast, Athanasius maintains, the Arians argued that 'the Father alone wrought with his own hand the Son alone, and that all other things were brought to be by the Son as by a servant' (*De Decret.* 7). For nothing originate can tolerate the Unoriginate's absolute and powerful hand, which brings into being as a creative intermediary the Logos, who shields the delicate creation from God's awesomeness. Athanasius' God is not so.

> [He] goes down with Jacob to Egypt, ... speaks face to face with Moses ... He it is who through his Logos made all things, great and small; and we may not [*sc.* as the Arians would to safeguard the Father's power and transcendence] divide the creation and say that this is the Father's and this the Son's, but they are all of one God, who uses his proper Logos as a hand, and in him does all things. (*De Decret.* 7)

119

For Athanasius God's goodness 'softens', as it were, his power so that all things originate may stand confidently before the High and Mighty One; for each is sustained by the High and Mighty One.

Athanasius repeatedly stresses the similarity of nature of Christ's humanity with ours (*D.I.* 34; *C.Ar.* 2.61; *Ad Epict.* 5); it is of a 'common substance with all bodies' (*D.I.* 20). Formerly Athanasius was content to confirm this by referring to both John 1:14, which he read as signifying the Logos becoming *man*, it being Scripture's custom to call man 'by the name of "flesh" ' (*C.Ar.* 3.30, referring to Bel and the Dragon 5, Joel 2.20), and to Hebrews 2.17, 'he had to be made like his brethren in every respect'.

With time, Athanasius' confirmation became more elaborate. In Corinth, where Epictetus was bishop, some believed that Christ's body must be co-essential with the divine Logos. Then, even after its assumption,

> the Triad remains a Triad; for then the Logos imports no foreign element into it. But if [one] admits that the body derived from Mary is human, it follows, since the body is foreign in essence, and the Logos is in it, that the addition of the body results in a Tetrad rather than a Triad. (*Ad Epict.* 8)

Athanasius disagreed. Initially Athanasius had simply asserted that the Logos fashioned for himself in a pure and spotless virgin a body, 'and that not foreign to our own' (*D.I.* 8). It was a temple, in which to dwell, be known and die. The beliefs of those Corinthians forced Athanasius to elaborate upon his simple assertions. She from whom the body was taken was really a human being. She was 'betrothed' to a man; she 'brought forth' a son, whom she wrapped in swaddling bands; him she suckled. Mary clearly was fully and truly human. Athanasius then remarks that the angel Gabriel spoke not of 'what is born in thee' but 'of thee', that what was born might be believed to be not induced extraneously upon Mary but naturally of her. That naturally of the creaturely Mary is indeed a creaturely humanity. For

> nature clearly shows that it is impossible for a virgin to produce milk unless she has given birth, and impossible for a body to be nourished with milk and wrapped in swaddling bands unless it has previously been brought forth. (*Ad Epict.* 5)

Indeed, veneration of Mary herself required acknowledgement of Christ's humanity. Were Christ's humanity co-essential with the

Logos, it itself would be eternal and not need the obedient Mary for its coming into being; the creaturely humanity's denial would render Marian devotion superfluous. Further, were Christ's humanity not truly creaturely, his being circumcised, taken into Simeon's arms, his maturing and arriving at adulthood, his hungering, thirsting and tiring, his hiding himself from hostile pursuers before his hour was come, and his crucifixion would make no sense. The immutable Logos could not be their subject; nor could a flesh, co-essential and co-eternal with that Logos. If the biblical descriptions are to be given full weight, their subject must be mutable, passible and creaturely flesh, born of a genuine mother, namely Mary.

This creaturely body's assumption did not, however, cause the Trinity's expansion, as the Corinthians feared. For the Triad, properly understood, is 'true, really perfect and indivisible ... and not accessible to addition ... or diminution' (*Ad Epict.* 8–9). The eternally simple God is then neither enlarged nor bettered through the body's assumption. Rather, it is the assumed flesh which is bettered as a result of its fellowship and union with the enlivening Logos.

Certain passages do raise questions as to whether Athanasius wholeheartedly and consistently admitted Christ's true humanity. He mentioned the virgin birth; he believed that the Logos 'imitated' our condition (*C.Ar.* 3.57); he referred to the assumption of 'an imperfect body' (*C.Ar.* 2.66); he treated Christ's passions in what has been called a psychologically docetic manner; and only late in his career did he expressly acknowledge Christ's human soul's presence, although maybe not its functions.

That Christ's body was from a pure and unspotted woman, ignorant of a man (*D.I.* 8), appears not to undermine the body's reality, but to reveal the divinity of him who formerly worked the virgin earth in the act of creation (*C.Ar.* 2.7) and now was born of a virgin. Indeed that the virgin birth did not belie texts like Hebrews 2:17 seems evidenced by Athanasius' treatment of our relation to Adam. Unlike us who have human parents, Adam 'was created alone by God alone through the Logos' (*De Decret.* 8). Nevertheless, Adam

> came of the earth, as other men, and the hand which then fashioned Adam is also both now and ever fashioning and giving entire consistence to those who come after ... Therefore in respect of nature, he differs nothing from us, though he precedes

us in time, so long as all consist and are created by the same hand. (*De Decret.* 9)

Similarly, the humanity fashioned of the virgin Mary by the creative hand of the Logos differs nothing from us though he too precedes us in time, each and all being created and consisting by the same hand.

That the Logos 'imitated' our condition does not necessarily imply that our human condition is not truly and wholly assumed. For imitation in itself does not necessarily imply unreality, as is evidenced in Christians' imitating Christ. Equally, references to the Lord's 'having been found in the fashion of a man', and to his being like the vineyard owner's son, who put over him 'like dress' with the servants captured by the tenants, and fashioned himself like them (*C.Ar.* 2.52; cf. Luke 20:9–19), do not question the humanity's genuineness. Their point seems to be to distinguish a human individual's relation to human passibility from that of the Logos: it is naturally man's; it is 'imitated' in the Logos, in that, though real, it is not natural to the very Logos. This indeed tallies with Christians' 'imitating' God: Christians' immortality and incorruption are real, but are theirs by grace and not by nature.

The 'imperfect body' is not an acceptance of docetism, but the acknowledgement that that assumed is not the prelapsarian, 'perfect' humanity, but the post-lapsarian, which has become imperfect in lacking immortality and the way to paradise (*C.Ar.* 2.66). Only by assuming such an imperfect body could the perfect Logos identify with fallen humanity, meet their very imperfections and needs and perfect them 'by healing [their] wounds and [vouchsafe to them] the resurrection from the dead' (*C.Ar.* 2.67). 'Perfection' here refers to humanity's gracious sharing in God's immortal Logos, and 'imperfection' to its falling from that gracious sharing.

Athanasius treats Christ's passions largely as a result of debate concerning the interpretation of such biblical texts as Mark 13:32 ('of that day or that hour no one knows, not even ... the Son') and Luke 2:52 ('Jesus increased in wisdom'). These the Arians saw as proving that the Son was mutable and passible and hence not very God. Athanasius disagreed: ignorance, increase in wisdom and the like referred not to the Logos as God but the Logos *as man*. Yet Athanasius' interpretation of these texts cannot be reduced simply to the theological issue of whether or not the Logos is very God, and its corollary, in what sense God is Father. There is also the soteriological dimension. The passions are, for Athanasius, an integral part of the Incarnation, which was undertaken for our salvation. Hence, Christ's passions must be real passions: otherwise people's real passions will not be met. The divinity of the Logos must be genuine: otherwise he will not be a sufficient healer of the real passions he meets. There must be a real union of the Healer with the passible humanity needing healing, and not simply the Healer's coming *upon* a passible person: otherwise the salvation will not be secured. The treatment of these texts, which suggest Christ's passions, is therefore regulated by assertions of the inalienable impassibility of the divine Logos, of the passions' reality, and of the impassible Logos incarnate's saving humanity from these passions. Within this exegetical framework, neither the distinction of psychological from physical passions, nor the issue of the human soul are central. Hence Athanasius will exhort the reader of the Gospels,

> though things human are to be ascribed to the Saviour in the Gospels ... impute them not to the Godhead of the Logos but to his manhood ... To the flesh are the affections proper; and although the flesh is possessed by God in the Logos, yet to the Logos belong the grace and power. (*C.Ar.* 3.41)

Accordingly Athanasius explains Christ's advance in wisdom. In Luke 2:52 the Logos 'humanly here is ... said to advance, since advance belongs to man' (*C.Ar.* 3.52). This advance occurred as the assumed humanity advanced in the divine Wisdom which made it his own. 'As the Godhead was more and more revealed, by so much more did his grace as man increase before all' (*C.Ar.* 3.52). This advancing in Wisdom is real; it is not to the detriment of the divine Logos and it is to the humanity's benefit, Christ's humanity gradually becoming 'to all the organ of Wisdom for the operation and the shining forth of the Godhead' (*C.Ar.* 3.53). As Christ's advance was for the sake of all, the consequence of such was that people then advanced; and their advance was then 'none other than [their] renouncing things sensible and coming to the Logos himself' (*C.Ar.* 3.52). There is, as it were, the gradual and constant burnishing of humanity, that it may the more reflect God's Wisdom in its own human sphere. The increase in wisdom is seen as ever-widening witness to the ever and only wise God. Yet while this growth in wisdom is essentially the service of God, it is also humanity's deification. For, being contingent, made for the worship and service of God, people find their fulfilment and perfection in their laying themselves open to their perfecting Lord and fulfilling Creator. Nor is this 'transcending of human nature by degrees' (*C.Ar.* 3.53) a subtle, incipient docetism. Human nature, when it so advances, does not become less, but more human. In its newly found wisdom it relinquishes any possessive and mortifying slavery to matter for generous and enlivening service of God.

The obverse of this advance in wisdom is that the same Logos 'as man, by reason of the flesh' (*C.Ar.* 3.43), whose property it is to be ignorant, especially of the hour of the end of all things (cf. Mark 13:32), is ignorant. This ignorance's reality Athanasius underlines through both his determination to defend the divine Logos from being called its unqualified subject, and his assertion that it demonstrates that Christ's humanity is genuine. 'As, on becoming man, he hungers and thirsts and suffers with man, so with men, as man, he knows not' (*C.Ar.* 3.46). This classification of ignorance with hunger and thirst does not, however, fight shy of this psychological passion, but stresses *this* psychological passion's reality: even as the Christ truly hungered and thirsted, even so he was ignorant of the end-time, truly sharing even in this aspect of mankind's ignorance.

Athanasius' treatment of John 11:11–12, the account of Lazarus' dying and being raised, has been seen to undermine his willingness to acknowledge the ignorance of the Logos. Athanasius knew that Arians used this Johannine passage as proof that the Logos was ignorant and so a creature; his opponents might have expected him to have responded in his traditional manner, acknowledging the ignorance, but centring it in the assumed humanity. Yet Athanasius maintained in regard to the question of John 11:34 that 'one does not for certain ask questions from ignorance. For it is possible for one who knows still to ask concerning what he knows' (*C.Ar.* 3.37); and he understood the question to Mary and Martha, as to where their brother Lazarus lay, as evidence not of Christ's ignorance, but his testing the sisters. Perhaps however this is not a fighting shy of acknowledging Christ's ignorance. Athanasius is clearly treating not the general issue of Christ's ignorance, but a particular passage which the Arians employed to establish the creatureliness of the Logos. He therefore points out that this passage establishes not that the Logos is a creature, but rather that he is God. He recalls situations such as Caesarea Philippi (Mark 8) and the feeding of the five thousand (John 6) where Christ asks questions not out of ignorance but to allow those questioned to realize that the questioner is 'the Christ' (Mark 8:29), and 'the prophet who is to come into the world' (John 6:14). In the instance of Lazarus, Christ's question allows the sisters to articulate that Lazarus is indeed dead, a fact which Christ plainly knew, as Athanasius notes through referring to John 11:14, where Christ is reported as informing his disciples so; and his question further prepares the ground for the right interpretation by the audience, the sisters included, of Christ's subsequent act. For, to quote two Johannine texts:

> Jesus told them plainly, Lazarus is dead; and for [his disciples'] sake [he] was glad that [he] was not there, so that [his disciples] might believe. (John 11:14–15)

and 'many therefore of the Jews which came to Mary and beheld that which [Jesus] did believed on him' (John 11:45). Christ's searching question permits his audience to recognize that Lazarus, who now is alive, was formerly truly dead; it also allows them to reappraise who Christ is: not a mere creature, but very Life. So the Christ, although not ignorant in this instance, *carried* the sisters' ignorance, replacing it with knowledge as to who Christ truly is; and through this whole instance, he so carried

> our ignorance that he might vouchsafe to us the knowledge of his own, only and true Father, and of himself, sent because of us for the salvation of all. (*C.Ar.* 3.38)

Athanasius' treatment of this particular Johannine passage recognizes that another person's ignorance may be abolished otherwise than by Christ's assuming that ignorance: a well-placed question may as easily open a person's eye. Such exegesis, driven by the Johannine text and not by fear of admitting Christ's ignorance, does not therefore undermine Athanasius' acknowledgement of Christ's ignorance; but it does undermine the Arian belief that this text established the creatureliness of the Logos.

The Logos also was subject to passions of suffering, weeping and fear, but only in and through his assumed humanity. 'When [he] became flesh and had become man, then it is written that he said [sc. that he feared], that is, humanly' (*C.Ar.* 3.55, referring to Matthew 26:39; John 12:17). Again, this stressing that this fear both is not attributable to the very Logos and is proof that 'though impassible, [the Logos] had taken a passible flesh' (*C.Ar.* 3.55) would seem to underline the fear's genuineness.[4]

Athanasius not only admits these passions which he denies to the divine Logos, but also recognizes that they are blunted and countered by the divine Logos in the assumed body. He admits these passions. Yet he is not content to rest with this admission. For he believed that Christ's passions were suffered that all might be saved from them. Hence a potentially static view gives way to a dynamic view. Ignorance, fear, suffering and death are admitted, but only to be alleviated. In his dispelling ignorance, lightening suffering and conquering death, there is the divinizing of everyone in Christ. What superficially may appear to be inchoate docetism is in fact pervasive soteriology.

As the good teacher, Christ's questions avail Peter and Mary and Martha, and through them readers of the Gospels, of the opportunity to make their own the Truth which the Father through his own Logos ever reveals. Although questions are asked, they do not subvert but establish the eternal Wisdom. Athanasius equally seeks to demonstrate that Christ's ignorance, when admitted, is not an embarrassment to God but is for people's benefit. It is proper to the flesh; and this ignorant flesh the Logos has assumed both willingly and out of love for ignorant humanity. Even as the good teacher rightly condescends to the level of the pupil, so the divine Logos graciously stoops to that of ignorant people. Yet even as the good teacher so condescends, but is not content, for the pupil's sake, to remain ever at the low level to which he has condescended, so the Logos, for ignorant people's sake, is eager that his flesh shall advance from ignorance to Wisdom.

Athanasius is, however, also aware that while the truth is given, and so ignorance dispelled, not the whole truth is now given. In his treatment of Mark 13 in *C.Ar.* 3 and *Ad Serap.* 2 Athanasius notes that Christ alerts all to the signs of the end-time's advent. Being thus forewarned, people will not be startled nor scared when its signs appear, but readied for the End which they sign (*C.Ar.* 3.48). Yet the exact time of the end-time the Logos did not reveal, lest Christians

> might become negligent of the time between, awaiting the days near the End. For they will argue that only then must they attend to themselves. (*C.Ar.* 3.49)

The limited dispelling of ignorance is still related to people's salvation, that each 'may advance day by day, as if summoned, reaching forward to the things before and forgetting the things behind' (*C.Ar.* 3.49). Through both the knowledge revealed and that deliberately withheld people are put on their mettle, that all may wisely live in and for God.

For Athanasius, the divine Logos therefore not only becomes man but a man like all others, at once knowing and ignorant. As very man it is right and proper that he not only recognizes God but also seeks to enable others to know him; thus his use of the testing questions of Peter, Philip, Mary and Martha. Further, as very man, it is fitting that he both is ignorant of when the end-time shall be and, rather than speculating, should humbly accept this ignorance; hence his statement, 'no, not even the Son'. What the Christ knows and does not know is typical of a creaturely being, even if maybe qualitatively different; and his responsible attitude to that knowledge and ignorance is typical of a godly human being, of one who is a paradigm of full and wholesome human existence.

Initially Athanasius' treatment of Christ's questions and ignorance of the end-time may seem rather *ad hoc*, driven at best by such an overwhelming desire to protect the divinity of the Logos as to allow almost any exegesis which effects this protection. On reflection, however, the themes of human reliance upon God's gracious self-unveiling for any advance in wisdom, of God's goodness and mercy, of our limited knowledge and of the propriety of living in accordance with the truth revealed all colour Athanasius' interpretation. Even the seemingly arbitrary reading of 'the Son' in 'of that day or that hour no one knows, not even ... the Son' (Mark 13:32) as referring to the 'Son of man' and not the 'Son of God' appears less arbitrary, given Athanasius' relating ignorance of when the end-time shall be to God's merciful withholding of knowledge which might prove too powerful a temptation to laxity and indiscipline.

So, by testing questions and by the advance in wisdom of assumed ignorant flesh, human ignorance is dispelled, as and where appropriate.

Equally the Logos incarnate endured fear and suffering 'that he might lighten these sufferings of the flesh and free it from them' (*C.Ar.* 3.56); by dying, he destroyed death, showing himself the Lord of all. Yet none of these saving acts undermine the reality of either Christ's or Christians' humanity. People were fearful, suffering and dying; but they were created to live a pacific life in God. Hence Christ lightened their suffering. Nor does this 'lightening' Christians' suffering amount to a quasi-docetic attitude. Christians still are, Athanasius all too readily admits, treated dreadfully. Yet, he also readily admits, they now face this treatment confidently and calmly. For contumacy is now impotent against those who now are sealed with Christ and have the promise of resurrection; insolent behaviour now no longer prevails in tempting Christians to respond in kind.

This point is explained more fully when, writing of Matthew 26:39, Athanasius remarks that

> for the sake of this [fearful] flesh [the Logos] combined his own will with human weakness, that destroying this affection he might in turn make man undaunted in the face of death. (*C.Ar.* 3.57)

The assumed human will is transformed by the assuming divine will, with the result that people now wish what God wills for them. The human and divine will coincide, the humanity which wills remaining human and the divinity which wills remaining ever wholly divine. For, in becoming man, God does not cease to be God; and the humanity is not weakened, but, in and through God, is fulfilled. Athanasius understands Matthew 26:39 as suggesting the replacement of the human will in the sense not of its elimination, but of its transformation: through being assumed into God the man Jesus is transformed in his putting aside an improper fear of death through his recognizing the propriety of trusting in God even in death. The Saviour God so elicits faith in his enlivening self that he destroys his human affection of fear before his death: not as man, whom the Logos became, does the Christ will, but as God the Logos wills. This, however, is not the end of the story. Athanasius cannot leave aside the belief that the Logos did not become man for his own sake, but humanity's. Hence his frequent assertion that 'he made man undaunted in the face of death' (*C.Ar.* 3.57), as is witnessed in the early apostles' and martyrs' contempt for death. There, there is no denial either of the human will, or of the reality of the apostle or martyr who wills. Even women and children now, though not formerly, willingly go to death rather than betray Christ. Formerly they wished to hoard things, all of which necessarily were lost through death. Now they see all such from the divine perspective; they now know that they live and move and have their being in God, who died and rose for them, and that, good though this life and its comforts are, they are as nothing when compared with their Creator. Hence they fully find themselves in willing fidelity to God, even when that obedience leads to preferring God to this mortal life. What is denied is the presence of any willing which is contrary to God's. Athanasius further cites the instance of the apostle Peter, whose will patently was transformed. Formerly, when Peter reacted negatively to Jesus' disclosure that Jesus should suffer and die, Peter was castigated, 'You are not on God's side, but men's' (*C.Ar.* 3.57, quoting Matthew 16:23). Latterly, as an apostle, Peter responded to the high priest's strictures not to preach Jesus in Jerusalem by saying 'We must obey God rather than men' (*C.Ar.* 3.57, quoting Acts 5:29). God is understood not to remove sufferings but to transform the human will, rendering it now undaunted and deathless. Again, in reference to a temptation resisted, it is recorded that 'this was Antony's first contest against the devil, or rather, this was in Antony the Saviour's success' (*Vita Ant.* 7).

The Logos seeks to expose the assumed selfish, fearful human will to the generous, confident divine will. In trust the human will shall then deny not itself but what is contrary to the divine will and ruinous both to its humanity and to the world and society of which it is a part. It shall find itself in making the divine will its own. This transformation is then the disowning of not just one's sins, but one's idolatrous self-centredness. It is something much more radical than any mere ascetic exercise or trivial self-denial: it is to deny that not willed by God, and consequently to affirm oneself in that which the good God, who envies none a glorious and blessed existence, wills, the divine service wherein perfect human freedom is found.

It seems therefore that when writing of the two economies of the Logos, Athanasius puts real flesh upon the belief that

> it was consistent that when [the Logos] had taken a body, he should exhibit what was proper to it; ... again it was consistent that when he went about in the body, he should not hide what belonged to the Godhead. (*Ad Max.* 3)

Different as the economies are, neither precludes the other. Otherwise their saving unity would be threatened. Yet, in all these acts, there is a certain asymmetry to be acknowledged: the divine initiates and the human responds, though in the manner of neither the puppeteer to the puppet nor the bully to the victim. Indeed, the humanity, though responsive, is yet the decisive place where God makes his appearance. Through human words and acts God speaks in the language that everyone understands; and by working his divine works in a fragile humanity he highlights his divinity and heals the humanity.

It is a commonly received opinion of scholarship that before AD 362 Athanasius did not allow a human soul in Christ and that after 362, if a soul was admitted, it was given no theological function. This received opinion is based upon various observations: the Logos seems to relate to the assumed body as a human soul does to its body; psychological passions are referred to the 'body' of the Logos; in death the Logos is separated from its body even as a human soul is from its body; though the Arians denied Christ's human soul, Athanasius is not recognized as asserting it; and when he may assert it in the *Tome* of 362 he does so in a manner which yet allowed Apollinarius' representatives, who though anti-Arian yet denied Christ's soul, to subscribe to the *Tome*'s content.

The Arians did deny Christ's human soul, suggesting that the Logos had taken its place. Certainly prior to 362 Athanasius did not show his rejection of their view by asserting that 'Christ had a human soul'. Yet that was not the only way then of rejecting that view. The Arians seem not to have made a major theological issue of this denial. Yet it seems to have been a point sufficiently significant that the ecumenical creed of Nicaea noted, over against the Arian view that 'the Logos became flesh', that the divine Logos 'having become flesh, became man', the added clause possibly amounting to the rejection of the Arian view that the Logos assumed only flesh.[5] Athanasius had a great preference for reiterating Nicene clauses, even where their meaning was not very clear, lest he provided a pretext for others to rewrite the faith and its credal formulae (*Tome* 5). Athanasius also tended throughout his writings to describe the Incarnation by variants upon the form, 'the Logos became flesh and became man'. This may be no more than a semi-automatic use of the Nicene formula. Yet this semi-automatic use may amount to a rejection, in Nicene language, of the Arian belief that Christ had no human soul.

By 362 Athanasius gave formal approval to Christ having a human soul, even if maybe he made no particular theological use of such an approval. Then he admitted that 'the Saviour did not have a body without a soul' (*Tome* 7), the negative form being explained, not by hesitancy, but by a rebuttal of the Arian contention that the assumed body was 'without a soul'. Indeed, it is to be noted that this Logos incarnate's salvation is that of both a man's soul and his body (*Tome* 7). This may indeed suggest the later principle, 'what is not assumed is not redeemed';[6] and if this is so, there may be a hint here that Christ's soul, so admitted, *is* of some theological importance.

If Athanasius is then very much an Alexandrian of his time, countering the Arian denial of Christ's human soul in forms consistent with the view that Nicaea was the only reliable anti-Arian weapon, we possibly should reinterpret the issues which have led to the *commonly received opinion*. One must consider whether the 'body' which the Logos enlivens and controls, to which passions, both psychological and physiological, are attributed, and from which the Logos is loosed in death is indeed a 'body', as opposed to a soul, or whether it is the assumed, creaturely humanity, in contrast with the incorporeal, Creator God. For the terminology may originate from Scripture and tradition, and not from anthropological debate. One must ask whether the Logos who enlivens and controls and withdraws himself from the assumed body is its governing principle, as each soul is to its body, thus allowing the thesis that for Athanasius the Logos has replaced the soul in the assumed humanity; or is he *its Creator and Sustainer*, as he is to all contingent things, which live and move and have their being in and through the divine Logos alone? One must reflect upon whether Christ's death, in which the Logos is loosed from its body, is to be interpreted anthropologically, akin to a person's, in which the soul is separated from its body, or theologically, akin to a person's whose death, evidenced in the soul's separation from the body, occurs through the withdrawal of the life-giving Logos, his no longer holding that person in unified being upon this earth. In regard to this, it is worth recalling the allusion to 1 Peter 3:19 in *Ad Epict.* 5, only two chapters before Athanasius makes an implied reference to Christ's human soul.

> The body it was that was laid in a grave, whence the Logos departed from it, yet was not parted from it, to preach ... to the spirits in prison.

In theological shorthand Athanasius seems to be suggesting that the divine Logos has broken his union with his mortal humanity, in order to allow its dying for all, yet has not entirely broken this union, lest it should pass away completely and not then rise again for all.

Possibly the commonly received opinion is then more a mirage than actuality. That Apollinarius' deacons were ready to subscribe to this *Tome* may be explained: the overarching problem which both Athanasius and Apollinarius were tackling was the Arian denial of the essential unity of the Logos with his Father, and any soteriological consequences. They saw the answer to this as the safeguarding the essential, immutable divinity of the Logos of the Father through referring the various properties, divine and human, to the appropriate economies. A common concern for safeguarding the essential divinity of the Logos and thus securing man's salvation, and a certain ambiguity which allows the term *apsychon* to be interpreted by Athanasius as 'without a soul' and by Apollinarius' deacons as 'without life' allowed their making common cause against Arianism.

Athanasius' Christ is a representative and not a collective figure. This recognition allows Athanasius to do justice to both the close bond between Christ and all people and his standing over against everyone, working the salvation of all, calling for repentance and ultimately judging. The representative Christ who stands with all is manifest both in the assumed humanity having the common substance of all, and in, for example, the common Saviour's death, 'the death of all [being] fulfilled in the Lord's body' (*D.I.* 20). Meanwhile, the representative Christ, who stands over against all, is manifest in his offering on our behalf as his own that which he has made his own of Mary, and in his rising, wherein he became the first fruit of the general resurrection, which others yet to die may graciously enjoy.

> His flesh before all others was saved and liberated, as being the body of the Logos; and henceforth we, being of one body with it, are saved after its pattern. (*C.Ar.* 2.61)

Indeed, this distinction but not division of Christ from others is underlined by the fact that the enjoyment of Christ's work is found not in every human being but in the 'faithful in Christ' (*D.I.* 21). What is generously made available in Christ must be appropriated by each.

There is then no division but a certain distinction between Christ and all others such as allows both communion with all through a common humanity, and action on their behalf. It is in the light of such clearly stated views that we should interpret such passages as:

> He is founded for our sakes, taking on him what is ours, that we, as incorporated and compacted and bound together in him through the likeness of flesh, may attain unto a perfect man and abide immortal and incorruptible. (*C.Ar.* 2.74; cf *C.Ar.* 2.61)

The emphasis is upon both the similarity of Christ's humanity, without which no one would be grafted into Christ, and people's dependency upon the divine Logos who assumed like humanity for the sake of their abiding immortal and incorruptible. Closer examination confirms this. Explaining the 'he created me' of Proverbs 8:22, Athanasius quotes 1 Corinthians 3:10–11 and notes that there is but one foundation upon which people are to be built, Jesus Christ. He accepts the premise that 'the foundation should be such as the things built upon it, that they may admit of being well compacted together' (*C.Ar.* 2.74). The divine Logos cannot be this foundation. For being the only begotten, there is none like him who 'may be compacted with him' (*C.Ar.* 2.74). Therefore the Logos became man; and in doing so 'he has the like of him, namely those the like of whose flesh he put on' (*C.Ar.* 2.74). Therefore, in regard to his humanity he is 'founded', that

> we, as precious stones, may admit of building upon him, and may become a temple of the Holy Spirit, who dwells in us. As he is a foundation and we stones built upon him, so again he is a vine and we knit to him as branches . . . according to his humanity. For the branches must be like the vine since we are like him according to the flesh. (*C.Ar.* 2.74)

Christ's humanity is not corporate but like. The superstructure is of like substance with its foundation, but is not the foundation, even as the branches are of the vine stock, but are not the vine stock. Any assumption that Christ's humanity is a universal humanity begins to wilt.[7]

It comes as no surprise that Athanasius views the Incarnation as the humble appearance of the Logos. This humiliation is the more marked, given the view of the second coming as God's glorious appearing. This coincides with tradition, which contrasts the cross with the coming in glory. It also ties in with the idea that the time of the Incarnation, though the end-time, is not the second coming. Now is 'the consummation of the ages' (*Tome* 7; *Ad Max.* 1; cf. Hebrews 1:1–2). For in Christ the truth dawns, a dawning which begins to reveal things for what they are. Now not only the Christ is worshipped as God, and through him the Father, but also the Greeks' seeming wisdom is exposed as folly. Yet, Athanasius will not write finality here: for a degree of provisionality still exists. Athanasius, it is true, does argue for Christ's divinity on the grounds both that, when God's true Wisdom revealed himself on earth, the Hellenists' wisdom was found to be wanting, and that different local cults were replaced by a ubiquitous monotheism in which 'only Christ is worshipped by all as one and everywhere the same' (*D.I.* 26). Yet the certainty of these arguments, born of polemic, is qualified by the provisionality found in Athanasius' sense that people are only gradually coming to an awareness of the Truth which has dawned.

> When the Saviour came, idolatry no longer increased, but even that which existed is diminishing and gradually ceasing. No longer does the wisdom of the Greeks prosper, but even that which does exist is now disappearing ... See how the Saviour's teaching increases everywhere, while all idolatry and all opposition to the faith in Christ diminishes day by day and weakens and falls. (*D.I.* 55)

The Truth has become incarnate; its victory is assured; error is declining, albeit gradually. In contrast, Christ's second coming will be

> a truly divine manifestation to us, when he will come no more in simplicity but in his own glory, no more with humility but in his own greatness, no more to suffer but henceforth to bestow the fruits of his own cross upon all, the resurrection and incorruption, no more judged but judging all. (*D.I.* 56)

The contrast then is not so much in terms of the very Logos, but his manner of appearing and the extent of his being honoured. Then God's glory shall be patent: he shall be worshipped for what he is in himself and for what he has effected for us. Now God's glory is not absent, only veiled and for all people's sake.

In the Incarnation therefore the divine Logos, who is Son by nature, becomes servant, in his loving service of humanity,

> that we, being servants by nature, and receiving the Spirit of the Son, might have confidence to call him by grace 'Father', who is by nature 'our Lord'. (*C.Ar.* 2.51)

This memorable reference expands the equally memorable

> He became man that man might be divinized ... He himself was harmed in no respect, as he is impassible, incorruptible and the

very Logos and God, but he cared for and saved suffering men. (*D.I.* 54)

Notes

1 F. M. Young, 'A reconsideration of Alexandrian Christology', *Journal of Ecclesiastical History* 22, no. 2 (April 1971), p. 114.

2 Cf. R. D. Williams, *Arius: Heresy and Tradition* (London, 1987).

3 Cf. Philo, *De Opificio Mundi* 17ff.; 24.

4 A. L. Pettersen, 'Did Athanasius deny Christ's fear?', *Scottish Journal of Theology* 39 (1986), pp. 327–40, especially on *te nomizomenē deilia*.

5 T. H. Bindley, *The Oecumenical Documents of the Faith* (2nd edn; London, 1906), pp. 38–9.

6 Cf. Gregory of Nazianzus, *Epistola* 101, *ad Cledonium*.

7 Cf. J. N. D. Kelly, *Early Christian Doctrines* (4th edn; London, 1968), p. 378. For a wider treatment see A. L. Pettersen, *Athanasius and the Human Body* (Bristol, 1990).

6

Trinity, terms, tribulations and truths

Athanasius was no exception to those Alexandrian theologians who, when treating the subject of the Godhead, looked beyond all creaturely categories of sensation and thought to an unutterably other God. Both in early and later works, he asserted that frail human nature 'was not capable by itself of knowing the Creator or of forming any idea of God at all' (*D.I.* 11). Yet Athanasius also maintained that naming God 'Father' amounts to making 'intimations of his incomprehensible essence itself ' (*De Decret.* 22). This complex of beliefs is part of the tradition which, in one form or another, goes back at least as far as Philo. Philo exceeded Plato's thesis that 'to discover this universe's maker and father is indeed a hard task' (*Timaeus* 28 C). For Philo believed that man's creaturely state prevented knowledge of what God in essence is. Athanasius' sharing in this tradition was a helpful tool in maintaining divine transcendence, an important consideration in his understanding of God. Yet Athanasius was not simply anticipating the fourteenth-century Archbishop of Thessalonika Gregory Palamas' metaphysic wherein God subsists in three modes, 'persons', 'substance' and 'acts'; knowing God is participating in his acts, which flow from his three divine persons, who alone share the eternally transcendent, incommunicable and incomprehensible divine substance. Athanasius' assertion seems more imprecise, being closely bound to the tradition which differentiated between conceptual and moral or relational knowledge of God. Philo's God addressed Moses thus,

I freely bestow what is in accordance with the recipient ...

Therefore to him who is worthy of my grace I extend all the boons which he is capable of receiving. Yet the apprehension of me is something more than human nature ... will be able to contain. Know yourself then, and do not be led away by impulses and desires beyond your capacity, nor let yearnings for the unattainable uplift and carry you off your feet; for of the obtainable nothing shall be denied you. (*De Specialibus Legibus* 1.43ff.)

Athanasius' thinking is consistent with Philo's beliefs both that in himself God is incomprehensible as a result of God's simplicity and humanity's creatureliness, and that God graciously reveals himself according to the human mind's humility and purity. Athanasius' thinking is also constant with Philo's belief that no one is to yield to improper desires for the unattainable. According to Athanasius, the faithful recognize the impossibility of speaking adequately about ineffable things; they therefore limit themselves to the Tradition, 'without inventing anything extraneous to it' (*Ad Serap.* 1.33). The unfaithful, meanwhile, whose unfaithfulness manifests itself not as 'disbelief' but 'false belief', fail to recognize that apprehending God is beyond human nature; their overweening spirit therefore asks how particular things can be, 'as though nothing can be unless they understand it' (*Ad Serap.* 2.1).

Athanasius' thinking allowed for genuine human participation in the one, holy, communion of the Father, Son and Spirit, while yet maintaining the Creator's transcendence over all creaturely knowledge. This proved an important bulwark against the Arians, whom he believed to be a destructively rationalistic party within the Church. Their principal wish was to protect the Deity's unique ingenerateness. For them God was single, the First Principle, indivisible, above all limitations. He was absolutely free, the unconstrained source of all that exists. Indeed, God's freedom was so radical that, while he freely expressed himself as every creature's Father, the notion that God was free not so to express himself was also conceivable. In consequence, the Arians felt compelled to reject any idea of a communion of divine being, of any eternal correlativity of the Father and Son. The acceptance of the Father and Son's co-eternity would suggest two 'ingenerates' and destroy the primary belief in the Father's unique ingeneracy. The Arians found support for their belief that there was 'one God, alone unbegotten, alone eternal, alone unbegun, alone true' (Arius, *Letter to Alexander of Alexandria*) in contemporary philosophy.

The Greeks assumed that the whole system of numbers originated from the simple number 'one'; their arithmetic lacked a 'nought'. Mathematically minded philosophers thus supposed that the source of all rational order in the universe was the indivisible One. Philosophically minded theologians were then often prompted to believe that God must be completely simple and 'ingenerate' and strictly immutable, the one defining uncaused Cause of all multiplicity wherever, whether within the material or spiritual realms. Were there two distinct, co-eternal 'ingenerates', there then must be a third which accounts for and distinguishes these two ingenerates. This third must also be eternal and ingenerate. These three co-eternal 'ingenerates' in turn require a fourth to account for them, and so on, *ad infinitum*. Any supposed class of ingenerates was thus thought to be a conceptual nonsense. God is then not to be understood as a generic term, the name of a substance in which the Father and Son share equally. There cannot be any substantial participation between them. Arians thus found support for the idea that there is no room for another eternal self-existent, even if he is the Son. Necessarily there is only one, ingenerate, First Principle, self-identical and without any contingent attributes; God is self-defining, being what God is necessarily and eternally.

Such thinking led the Arians to interpret the Father and Son's relationship in terms of not any substantial continuity but 'Creator' and 'creature'. 'Father' and 'Son' then become titles which refer to two distinct and unique substances which do not share substantial attributes and properties. The epithets do not mutually define each other. 'Fatherhood' is not then part of the essential definition of God as God, it being possible and quite proper to speak of God without speaking of him as 'Father'. Indeed, although paternity may be seen as an inalienable characteristic of God, it must be recognized as a title, the result of a punctilinear act of free will, whereby God's Son is created. For Arians God *is* God; and he *becomes* and is *called* rather than *is* Father. Nor is 'Sonship' an essential part of God's definition. For since God is wholly self-sufficient, he must 'beget' through his free, gratuitous love. Eternal generation thus rejected, the freely created Son is a cosmological principle, connecting God with his creation. Indeed, the title 'Son' reveals not something about God's nature but his relationship with that beyond himself. It manifests how God chooses to reveal himself to his whole creation and tells much concerning the ideal relationship of God with his creatures and they with him, of fatherly love and childlike trust respectively. However, whatever revelatory or soteriological efficacy this Son may have, this Son does not unveil anything directly about the divine nature; being a creature, he cannot bring anyone to an intimate and enduring, even though not fully comprehensive, knowledge of God.

This consistent picture of the simple God the Arians believed Alexandrian trinitarianism threatened. Such a coherent picture the Alexandrians meanwhile saw as a threat to the Son as very God, to God as immutable Father and to the nature of divinity itself as a generous community in which the Father, Son and Spirit are eternal correlatives. For Athanasius Arian thinking created a wholly improper understanding of God, which cut across the heart of Christian spirituality, prayer and worship, and which flew in the face of the dominical injunction that 'when you pray, say, Father, hallowed be thy name' (Luke 11:2). The issue therefore was not just soteriological, nor even only Christological. It was also theological. For in defending the Son's divinity Athanasius was defending God's eternal Fatherhood and a particular understanding of divine oneness.

Athanasius shares with the Arians the belief that God is not composite but is true, simple existence. Consequently Athanasius immediately excludes any form of polytheism. He rejects, for example, the Gnostic suggestion that there are two deities, the Father of Jesus Christ and the 'unbegotten maker and author of evil, creation's demiurge' (*C.G.* 6). Rather than introducing two divine principles, such excludes both from the realm of divinity. For there must be a separating agent of these two incompatible and dissimilar beings, 'which will derive from a third source, and itself will be God' (*C.G.* 7).[1] Athanasius' God, being simple, is not open to being defined by reference to any separating principle. The self-defining One who defines all others is Athanasius' One God: otherwise he is 'limited' in himself. Athanasius also rejects the thesis that God can only be if and as a person understands him (cf. *Ad Serap.* 2.1). Human reason or understanding, most valued capacities, but created nevertheless, are not the touchstone for a right appreciation of God. Hence, for example, divine paternity is to define human fatherhood, and not vice versa; the Image's begetting is self-defining; and the Logos is not a creature of time, as the Arians supposed, thereby allowing 'time [to be] the measure of the Godhead's Image and Form' (*C.Ar.* 1.20). Further, Athanasius rejects the view that the Creator is defined by his creation. Creation is good, but its having been so created is defined by the good Creator. There is no sense of creation being good in itself, or that its harmony and well-being are ends in themselves. There is but one End, as there is one Source, God the Creator and Sustainer, to whom creation's very existence, goodness and harmony all witness. Nor does God's enforcing the Law unto death against the disobedient Adam undermine God's oneness. God's conforming, albeit reluctantly, with the Law's demands, initially appears to question God's simplicity through the seeming rehearsal of the old Greek belief that beyond and behind the gods there operates Themis, a more ultimate and more powerful principle of justice.[2] Indeed, the Law's challenge to God's simplicity seems yet more pronounced when Athanasius' thinking about rival deities is recalled. Were there rival deities, there would be no pre-eminence nor superiority. For their strengths and weaknesses would be equal, both strong

> because they overcome each other's will by their existence, ... both weak as events occur without their will and contrary to their intention. (*C.G.* 6).

Similarly, the Law appears to challenge not only God's simplicity but his sovereignty. Yet, initial impressions are incorrect, and God's simplicity and sovereignty are preserved. The point of the account of the Fall is the demonstration that a simple, immutable God is in charge of the situation. The Law is given by a good God, its motive being philanthropic and its purpose to safeguard humanity in the blessed prelapsarian state. Only incidentally does the Law result in life's inseparable concomitant, death, to which those not observing the Law thereby sentence themselves. This is but the working out of Athanasius' strict divine simplicity. The Law's charge regarding death and corruption is but the making explicit what may be inferred from Athanasius' wider theology: there is only ever one God. He alone is Life, and only those who remain turned towards him have life. Those who separate themselves from God and concentrate upon themselves separate themselves from the sole source of all life. They bring upon themselves judgement and death, the inevitable corollaries of there being only one God, in whom alone is life, and of there being no neutral ground between the absolute alternatives, life and death. So it is that, being simple, self-consistent, God cannot revoke the Law. 'For God would not have been truthful if, after he had said that we would die, man had not died' (*D.I.* 6). Revoking the Law would have amounted to denying that God alone was the Source of all life. In short, God's not breaking the Law was God's being true to himself, of whom the Law was a forthtelling, and was not God's being bound by the Law. Indeed, that Athanasius' God is not limited by such a Law is manifest in that God not only allowed the Law its course but also met and fulfilled its demands in his becoming incarnate. Athanasius gives no satisfactory grounds for the altogether too superficial view of God's simplicity being limited by law. For Athanasius then God is simply God; he is not defined by nor subject to anything, that 'anything' otherwise becoming God's 'god'. Divine simplicity precludes any form of idolatry.

Such assertions of God's simplicity tally with the sense not only of his being other than the world but also of his not being excluded from creation by his transcendence. Thus, 'the one true God fills everything comprehended in heaven and earth' (*C.G.* 6). To dualists like the Gnostics the title 'one, true God' implied so simple a God that they were prone to imagine a 'bridge of beings', who effected the transition from the simple deity's pure immateriality to the pluriform world of matter; each being was progressively more material, less divine, more remote from perfection than its predecessor. Followers of the second-century Gnostic theologian Valentinus used the term 'fullness' to describe the region inhabited by this contingent of intermediate beings. For Athanasius the one, true, simple God is he in whom all, even this 'fullness', in so far as it exists, find completeness. God's Logos, through whom all are filled, needs no intermediaries and is not contained but is only at rest and is complete in everything in his divine Father (*D.I.* 17). Thus the simple God himself creates and is providentially present to all. Indeed, given the Hellenistic tendency to relate the divine to the spiritual and reasonable in this world, Athanasius' sense of the extent of God's containing and enclosing all things within himself is remarkable: his list of that comprehended ranges from the celestial to the terrestrial, the invisible to the visible, the special to the mundane. He mentions things on earth, in heaven, in the sea and the great oceans, all dry land and the verdure with which it is covered (*C.G.* 44).

Athanasius' one God is limited neither by another deity nor by principalities and powers nor by creation. God is not 'in a place' (*C.Ar.* 1.23); nothing is far from him (*De Decret.* 11). In his infinity and simple transcendence, he is self-defining, being in essence outside the universe, and present to all by his power, defining all.

It is against this background of the one God in communion that a number of Athanasius' terms must be viewed. To describe God's oneness in communion Athanasius employs terms like 'form', 'like', and 'proper', *homoousios* and *hypostasis*.

'FORM'

The term 'form' is used, but not in a particularly technical sense. Thus, 'there is but one form (*eidos*) of the Godhead, which is also in the Logos' (*C.Ar.* 3.15). Athanasius is here explaining the Son's being in the Father by reference to 'the Son's whole nature [being] proper to the Father's essence, as radiance is to light and stream to fountain' (*C.Ar.* 3.3). Radiance is not a second light, nor does it 'participate' in the light. It *is* light's proper, whole offspring (*C.Ar.* 3.3). The sun and radiance are two, but there is one light, the sun in radiance enlightening the universe. This imagery resurfaces when Athanasius asserts that

> we do not introduce three 'beginnings' or three fathers ... since we have not suggested the image of three suns, but suns and radiance. And one is the light from the sun in the radiance; and so we know of but one Origin; and the all-framing Logos we profess to have no other manner of Godhead than that of the only God, because he is born from him. (*C.Ar.* 3.15)

In contrast the Arians' Son is 'external' to God, a creature by nature and divine by the grace of participation. Athanasius will not tolerate this variableness and difference within the Godhead. Hence he stresses that

> there is but *one form* (*hen eidos*) of Godhead, which is also in the Logos, and one God, the Father, existing as himself according as he is above all, and appearing in the Son according as he pervades all things, and in the Spirit, according as in him he acts in all things through the Logos. For thus we confess God to be one through the Triad; and we say that it is much more religious to entertain a belief in the one Godhead in Triad than in the godhead of the heretics with *its many forms* (*polyeidous*) *and many parts*. (*C.Ar.* 3.15)[3]

'Form' is synonymous with 'nature'; and the 'one form' stands in marked contrast with the 'many forms'. Athanasius' understanding of God's oneness allows the Father and Son to have essential consistency; Arius' sense of divine simplicity requires God to be the lone god, the Logos therefore being essentially other than the Father. Thus, while the Arians' godhead has 'its many forms' or natures, one very God and his Son, although divine by grace, yet still essentially a creature, Athanasius asserts the essential continuity and consistency in God, the Father, Son and Spirit, one nature which unites them, without precluding their personal identities.

'LIKE'

Athanasius makes two assumptions when using this term. God is self-consistent in being and act; for the Triad is not 'unlike itself and diverse in nature' (*Ad Serap.* 1.20). Secondly, God is unlike creation. For 'what is the likeness of what is out of nothing to him who brought what was nothing into being?' (*Ad Serap.* 1.21; cf. 1.9). Creatures once were not and were brought into existence, while God eternally is. These assumptions combine in the beliefs that the Spirit proceeds from the Father and is given through the Son to the disciples (*Ad Serap.* 1.2), that grace is 'from the Father, through the Son and in the Spirit' (*Ad Serap.* 1.20), and that the Son is imaged in the Spirit, even as the Father is in the Son (*Ad Serap.* 1.20). Given such co-ordination and oneness, the letter writer asks 'who can separate either the Son from the Father or the Spirit from the Son or from the Father himself?' (*Ad Serap.* 1.20). Confirmation that this co-ordination and oneness lie not just in the moral but in the essential field Athanasius finds in Matthew 28:19, where the Spirit is named with the Son and Father. Given that the Son and Father are very God, the Spirit cannot be but a creature, who happens to be morally like God. For Athanasius thinks it 'absurd to name together things that are by nature unlike' (*Ad Serap.* 1.9). Who therefore, Athanasius wonders, will dare to suggest that 'the Son is other in essence from the Father, or the Spirit alien from the Son' (*Ad Serap.* 1.20)?

Thus, when responding to the Arian claim that the Logos, being a creature, is 'unlike' the Father in nature, Athanasius asserts that the Logos is 'like and proper' to the Father (*C.Ar.* 1.9): the Logos is in the Father and 'like the Father in all things' (*C.Ar.* 1.40). For the Logos is not a creature; and he therefore is 'different in kind and different in essence from things originate, and ... is proper to the Father's essence and of the same nature as him' (*C.Ar.* 1.58). For, since there are no other categories than God and all that is created, if the Logos is 'different in essence from things originate', he is 'of the same nature' as God.

Significantly, since the likeness is 'the Son's *natural* likeness and propriety towards the Father' (*C.Ar.* 3.36; cf. 3.11), the Son is like the Father in his sharing the Father's essential properties.

> The Father is eternal, immortal, powerful, light, king, sovereign, God, Lord, Creator and Maker. These must be in the Image to make it true that 'he who hath seen the Son hath seen the Father'. (*C.Ar.* 1.21)

Here Athanasius' Logos differs importantly from the Arians'. The latters' Logos being a creature, becomes eternal, immortal, and so on, and becomes such by grace. The former's is eternal and immortal, and is so by nature. This Athanasius stresses when he notes that the divine Son has no 'likeness' even to those who 'have been called "gods"' (*Ad Serap.* 2.4). For these latter have come into being, are called gods and are divine 'by participation in the Son' (*Ad Serap.* 2.4). The Son, meanwhile, is eternally divine. His divinity is indefectible, whereas creatures' divinity may be relinquished if any chooses to turn from participating in the Son's essential divinity. The assertion that the Son shares the Father's eternal properties does not, however, extend to sharing paternity. Working from a human paradigm, the Arians are portrayed as maintaining that 'if the Son is an Offspring of the Father and is like in all things to the Father, then he begets and he too becomes a father of a son' (*C.Ar.* 1.21). Athanasius rejects both the human paradigm and the Arian conclusion. For him, fatherhood and sonship in a divine being are perfectly, eternally and immutably expressed. While therefore the Son is in essence like the Father, he, as the eternally and only begotten Son, may not be like the only Father in becoming a father and begetting a son. The Son is like the Father in essence, sharing that one nature's common properties; but he alone is the Son, even as the Father alone is the Father. Athanasius' rejection of the suggestion that if the Son is like the Father in all things, he too may beget, is the result not of his picking and choosing on an *ad hoc* basis, but of his clear recognition of the eternal, immutable distinctions of the Father, Son and Spirit and the indivisible oneness of God's nature. The eternal, divine nature of the Son, who, as Son, is not the Father, nor Spirit, determines the meaning of 'like the Father in all things'.

An interesting theological point hangs upon the Son being, paternity apart, like the Father in the Father's being essentially unlike creation. Even in his earliest works, Athanasius will note that, as God, the Logos 'is unlike in nature to us' (*D.I.* 34). An inference is that anything that is like in nature to us is not God, and worship as very God of such, the Arians' creaturely Logos included, is idolatrous.

'PROPER'

This term was hardly used for theological purposes prior to Athanasius' using it. Yet Athanasius saw no need to defend its introduction. The term's use in relation to characteristics and their subjects is educative. Athanasius speaks of invisibility, omnipotence and immutability being 'proper' to God (*D.I.* 32; *Ad Serap.* 2); he writes of not existing before their creation, of being ignorant and mortal as 'proper' to creatures. 'Proper' stresses the natural oneness of a characteristic and its subject. The characteristic does not accrue from without, but is part of the subject's very definition. Supportive analogies are found in lights and fountains: radiance is 'proper' to light and a stream is 'proper' to a fountain, but those things 'proper' to light and fountain respectively are not theirs in a transferred sense; they are correlatives. When then Athanasius uses 'proper' of the Son's and Spirit's relation to the Father, he does so to stress their correlativity with the Father, and their common distinction from creation, to which the divine Creator, although Creator and Sustainer, is essentially 'external', 'foreign' or 'alien' (*C.Ar.* 1.20). Hence, repeatedly, Athanasius notes that the Son is 'not foreign, but proper to the Father's essence' (*C.Ar.* 1.58; 2.82; 3.3; 3.36; *Ad Serap.* 1.25; 4.3) — a comment as important for its denial of the Arian view that the Logos is essentially 'other' than God (*C.Ar.* 1.5) as for its assertion that in being

> different in kind and in essence from things originate [the Offspring of the Father's essence] is proper to the Father's essence and of the same nature with it. (*C.Ar.* 1.58)

Equally Athanasius argues that the Spirit is not 'alien to the Son's nature nor to the Father's Godhead' (*Ad Serap.* 4.3), but 'in essence proper to the Son' (*Ad Serap.* 1.25) and 'proper to the Father's Godhead' (*Ad Serap.* 1.11–12). Moreover, the term 'proper' will ensure that the Logos, who is 'of the same nature' with the Father, and, by extension, the Spirit, is eternally one with the Father. For on account of both the eternal indivisibility of God's essence and the Son's propriety to it, rather than gracious participation in it,

> God is one, and one the faith in the Father and the Son; for although the Logos is God, the Lord our God is one Lord; for the Son is proper to that One and is inseparable. (*C.Ar.* 3.16)

Properly, God is one, eternally indivisible, very Father, very Son and very Spirit.

The term 'proper' serves then to stress that the Son and Spirit are as closely related to the Father as characteristics are to their natural subjects, as radiance to light, and streams to fountains. Yet the Son and Spirit are not therefore but characteristics, however proper, of the Father. The Logos is the Father's Offspring and Image; the Spirit is the Father's Spirit. Indeed, to fail to deny that the Son and Spirit are but the Father's proper characteristics is to deny not only God as very Son and very Spirit but also the very paternity of God. Without a natural Son, God the Father will be but Father in name alone, which he is in regard to all creatures who rightly hold God's teaching, but which, for Athanasius, he is only because he himself is very Father to his only-begotten Son and the Spirit. By the term 'proper' Athanasius seeks to retain both the indivisibility of the one Triad and the eternity of the very Father, very Son and very Spirit.

HOMOOUSIOS[4]

A reading of many Catholic creeds from 325 onwards would suggest that *homoousios* was introduced especially to counter the Arian belief that the Son was not very God. It is surprising then that Athanasius, the great Nicene, employs the term but once in his three central anti-Arian treatises, in *C.Ar.* 1.9. This single reference seems all the more surprising when it is remembered that Athanasius acknowledged that the Nicene fathers 'pronounced the Arian heresy to be the forerunner of anti-Christ and drew up a suitable formula against it' (*De Syn.* 5). Indeed, he unequivocally asserted that

> the precision of this phrase detects [the Arians'] pretence whenever they use the phrase 'from God' and gets rid of all the

subtleties with which they seduce the simple ... this phrase only, as detecting their heresy, do they dread, which the fathers set down as a bulwark against their irreligious notions, one and all. (*De Syn.* 45)

If *homoousios* was so splendid a bulwark against Arian irreligion, one cannot but ask why the champion of Nicaea did not use it more frequently and obviously. The answer seems to lie in a number of factors. The term may have been an anti-Arian bulwark, but only to those who had eyes to see; it is not one which readily commended itself even to mid-fourth-century Catholics; and the particular contexts of the various Athanasian works colour its usage. Throughout his *De Synodis* Athanasius refers to the problems or pretexts which his contemporaries found and which led to their not approving the term's usage. Sirmium II (357) drew attention to Isaiah 53:8, which was taken as proof that 'no one can declare the Son's generation' (*De Syn.* 28), and therefore that terms like *homoousios* should be withdrawn from ecclesiastical usage. Sirmium III (359) favoured saying that 'the Son is like the Father in all things, as also the holy Scriptures say and teach' (*De Syn.* 8). Seleucia (359), Nice (359) and Constantinople (360) each also wished to acknowledge the 'likeness' of the Father and Son 'as the divine Scriptures say and teach' (*De Syn.* 29–30). Ecclesiastical affirmation was to be limited to scriptural vocabulary. Indeed the very fact that Athanasius was eager to explain the Nicene term and to justify its use, despite both Isaiah 53:8 and the term's non-scriptural form, confirms that there was doubt about the term's use even amongst those sympathetic to Athanasius' theology. Confirmation that there was confusion as to the term's meaning is found variously: Athanasius recognizes that not the Nicene term but the perverseness of those 'who misinterpret' it (*De Syn.* 33) is to be excluded; he further notes that the fathers in the Church, through no perverseness, 'have spoken variously concerning the term *homoousios*' (*De Syn.* 46). This confusion is not surprising. The term, which had been used in Origen's writings of material things, was now being used of the Son of the incorporeal Father, to defend the Son's recently affirmed immateriality against the Arian belief in his natural materiality. This term the fathers, who were not trained philosophers, introduced at Nicaea. To be historically accurate, one must remember both that these fathers were quite unfamiliar with the Aristotelian distinction of *ousia* as *either* individual, the primary form of being, *or* generic, and that they only half understood the variety of senses which *all* the terms that they then had available might carry. To suppose that Athanasius' readers then had a choice between clearly defined alternatives of Aristotle is to be quite unhistorical.[5] The readers' confusion was further exacerbated by the inclusion of *hypostasis* in the Nicene creed's anathemata as an alternative to *ousia*, an alternative which Athanasius himself employs when he writes that the Logos is the 'Expression of the Father's *hypostasis* ... the very image of the Father's *ousia*' (*C.Ar.* 1.9). Amongst many different meanings, *hypostasis* could mean either a thing's underlying reality, which it will probably share with other things — such as the common metal which coins share — or the emergent, perceptible reality, mainly seen as individual. Indeed, later Greek theologians could speak of the Father, Son and Spirit as three *hypostaseis*, three distinct individual beings. For them the assertion that there was only one divine *hypostasis* might suggest either that only the Father was divine, as in Arianism, or that the Father, Son and Spirit were of the same divine *hypostasis* in the sense that the Son and Spirit were but modes of the Father, as is surmised by Sabellians, supporters of the view that God is by nature a monad, the Father, Son and Spirit being assigned the status of modes or manifestations of the one divine being. It is not surprising therefore that many of the councils mentioned in the *De Synodis* draw attention to the fact that the term *homoousios* was a source of confusion to the laity.

Politics seems to have added to this confusion. The various Arian parties wished to be recognized as part of the Catholic Church in the post-Constantinian empire. The Eastern emperors wanted peace, even amongst the ecclesiastical parties. The Arians therefore tried to persuade the emperors to exclude from tests of Christian orthodoxy the term *homoousios*, which they particularly disliked, and to settle for scriptural terms, which they knew that they could interpret in an Arian manner, and which, they argued, all Christians should accept. In short, the lowest common denominator should achieve the widest degree of unanimity and peace within Church and State. What these Arians wanted was political acceptance; what Athanasius desired was theological orthodoxy. Local politics also coloured the debate. In Antioch in Syria in the 360s, for example, there were two main anti-Arian groups, the followers of the late hard-line Nicene Eustathius, and those of Melitius. The latter were converts from Arianism who were fearful of a Sabellian deity, a monad revealing himself under the modes of Father, Son and Spirit; they preferred *homoiousios*, 'of like nature', to *homoousios*, seemingly because the former, through its referring to similarity, implied distinct persons while the latter might allow modalism, if *ousia* was interpreted as 'individual'. Given the politics and the variety of meanings of the terms, *homoousios*, *homoiousios* and *hypostasis*, none of which was biblical, many a layman might well have thrown up his hands in despair at the arguments of the various Catholic and Arian parties, and agreed with the declaration of the Arians at Sirmium II that

> the whole faith is summed up and secured in this, that a Trinity should ever be preserved, as we read in the Gospel, 'go ye and baptize ... in the name of the Father and the Son and the Spirit'. (*De Syn.* 28, referring to Matthew 28:19)

Those who knew Athanasius' arguments based upon Matthew 28:19 might have been forgiven for having thought that at last the followers of all the parties could leave aside the many diverse terms and build an ecclesiastical unity upon this precious common ground.

Both Arians and Athanasius believed that there were only two conditions of being, godly and creaturely. For the former the Logos was God's freely willed creature, and for the latter he was essentially God. Athanasius' main concern *vis-à-vis* Arianism, therefore, was not with God's internal relationships but the Father and Son's essential oneness over against creation. It is in the light of this that Athanasius asserted that the Logos is

> very Son of the Father, natural and genuine, proper to his essence, only-begotten, Wisdom, and very and only Logos of God ... not a creature or work, but an Offspring proper to the Father's essence. Wherefore he is very God, existing *homoousios* with the very Father, while other beings, to whom he said, 'I said, ye are gods' (Psalm 82:6), had this grace from the Father only by participation of the Logos through the Spirit. (*C.Ar.* 1.9)

This single reference to *homoousios* maintains that the Father and Son, whatever their relationship one with the other, are united in their both being very God and so their both being 'unlike' creation. They are not creatures; the Son is not 'divine' in the same way as creatures may be. This concern to distinguish both the unbegotten Father and the only-begotten Son from the generated creation is reflected in the distinguishing of 'I am' sayings from instances of 'he became'; in stressing the indivisibility of God; in rightly interpreting texts such as Proverbs 8:22, Luke 2:52 and Mark 13:39; and the like. The precise definition of *homoousios* did not matter, provided it asserted that the Father and Son both were of another essence to creation. Indeed, this point Athanasius explicitly states:

> The Son is the Offspring of the Father's essence ... therefore the Son is different in kind and different in essence from things originate, and ... is proper to the Father's essence and one in nature with it. (*C.Ar.* 1.58)

In this sense *homoousios* served the same purpose as 'form', 'like' and 'proper': each stressed the essential oneness of the Father and Son and the essential otherness of the Father and Son from all creatures, made by the Father through his Logos, the Son.

Athanasius did believe that the Son

> preserves the Father's likeness and unvarying Image, so that he who sees him sees in him the subsistence of which he is the Expression. (*C.Ar.* 2.33)

'Likeness' was a scriptural term, which plainly countered those who believed that the Logos was 'unlike and foreign' (*C.Ar.* 2.43) to the Father's essence, as indeed Seleucia recognized in rejecting those who maintained the Son's unlikeness to the Father (*De Syn.* 29). Yet Athanasius held that *homoousios* was preferable to 'like'. For he knew that there are things which are outwardly 'like' but are 'in some respect or wholly ... other in essence'. Thus

> brass shines like gold, and silver like tin. [But] these are foreign or of another nature, and are separated off from each other in nature and virtue ... Although they are considered 'like', yet they differ in essence. (*De Decret.* 23; cf. *De Syn.* 41)

In short, things that are 'like' need not be of the same nature. Thus, while it is right to counter the belief that the Logos is 'unlike' the Father by asserting that he is 'like' the Father, such an assertion is not wholly sufficient to counter Arianism, not precluding the Son being a creature. Even Athanasius will allow that men and women are 'like' God, insofar as they participate in God.

This point Athanasius drives home when he states that 'like' properly should not be predicated of 'essences' but of 'habits', 'qualities' and 'character'. In the case of essences one should properly speak not of 'likeness' but of 'identity'. Hence, for example, properly one should say that 'in essence man is of one nature and *homoousios*' (*De Syn.* 53). Initially this may seem pedantic. Yet Athanasius is here making serious theological and soteriological points. Maintaining that the Son is 'like' the Father is equivalent to saying that the Son shares the Father's attributes. If the Son 'shares' the Father's attributes, they are not his very own but his by participation. This Athanasius highlights by noting the use of 'like' of creatures to God. By partaking of God they are made like God, ' "like", that is, not in essence but in sonship in which we partake from him' (*De Syn.* 53, referring to 1 John 3:2). Hence, if the Son be the Son by participation and not by nature, 'he is not Truth ... nor Light ... nor in nature God' (*De Syn.* 53), but is 'like' the Truth, 'like' the Light, 'like' God. He resembles the divine Reality but is not that divine Reality. Strictly speaking, if the Son is but 'like' God, he is not God.

This theological point has a soteriological consequence. If the Son is 'like' God by participation, he may, like all others who participate in God, 'undergo a change for the worse and can be separated from those [others] who [yet] participate in the sharing [in God]' (*De Syn.* 53). Not only his very deity but also his filial relationship to the Father, his saving role towards others and his fellowship with redeemed mankind would thereby be put at risk. If what he has is not his own and is barely sufficient for himself, he cannot be in truth ignorant humanity's effective Illumination and corrupt mortality's Saviour (cf. *De Syn.* 51). For Athanasius, then, the Son is not *homoiousios* with us, like us in essence, and like God by participation. He is like God in essence; he is indeed God by nature.

If the Son is 'like' God in essence, we may wonder why Athanasius does not allow *homoiousios*, like in essence, equally with *homoousios*, of the same essence, especially when, at least once, Athanasius virtually equates 'likeness' and *homoousios* when he remarks that inasmuch as the Son has no likeness to things originate and has as his own properties all that belong to the Father, 'it follows that he will be *homoousios* with the Father' (*Ad Serap.* 2.5). Athanasius' arguments concerning the preferability of *homoousios* hinge upon the matter that 'like' properly does not refer to essence, and especially upon the issue that those who employ *homoiousios* and similar phrases are partially mistaken. They are indeed opposed to the Arian doctrine that the Logos is a creature. Yet, while their hearts are in the right place, they 'have taken their proof against [the Arians] from the illustrations of son and father' (*De Syn.* 41). Their mistake is to allow the introduction into the God-head of the 'division' which exists between a human father and his son, and so to render possible the sacrifice of God's simplicity. Not that these anti-Arian users of *homoiousios* intended such. Their intentions are clear.

> They have called the Father the Fount of Wisdom and Life, and the Son the Radiance of the Eternal Light and the Offspring of the Fountain. (*De Syn.* 41)

Yet their use of *homoiousios* does not preclude the loss of divine simplicity. To safeguard this divine simplicity, implied but not stated in their image of Life which cannot be sundered from Fount, and of Radiance which cannot be separated from Light, it is, Athanasius believes, better to employ *homoousios* than *homoiousios*. *Homoousios* is preferable as, at least in this context, it is less liable to error.

Nevertheless, it is true that Athanasius is concerned more with the theological point which lies behind this matter than with ter-minological strictness. In *C.Ar.* 1–3 he frequently refers to the Son being 'like' the Father, albeit this Son is also called the Father's 'proper' Son, a qualification which Athanasius would not use of even the most holy saint. He castigates Arius, Eusebius and others who

> as to the oneness of likeness between the Son and the Father did not confess that the Son is like the Father according to essence, or according to nature, as a son resembles his father. (*De Syn.* 45)

In Antioch anti-Arian Melitians were concerned to defend the Father and Son's essential oneness; but they were also concerned lest that defence should slip into a form of Sabellianism. They therefore preferred *homoiousios* to *homoousios*, as the former maintained the Son's oneness in essence with the Father while also maintaining that the Son was not simply a mode of God but was eternally distinct from his Father. Addressing these Melitians Athanasius requires them not to relinquish *homoiousios*, but only to interpret it in the sense of *homoousios*, so making clear that their desire to distinguish the Father from his Son did not amount to dividing the Father from the Son and to sacrificing God's essential

simplicity. The nature of the debate and the practicalities of ecclesiastical politics seem to account for this 'laxity'. In an ideal world,
however, the Son, 'being by nature and not by participation Son will
properly be called not *homoiousios* but *homoousios*' (*De Syn.* 53).
Indeed, even in this less-than-ideal world, when the hearts of those
addressed are not in the right place and seek to capitalize upon
others' naïve terminology, the Son is to be known as *homoousios*
with the Father. For thus

> the bishops assembled at Nicaea, with a view to the craft of the
> parties ... and as bringing together the sense from Scripture,
> cleared up the point by affirming *homoousios*, that both the
> genuineness of the Son might be known, and to originate things
> might be ascribed nothing in common with him. (*De Syn.* 55)

Even the Nicene statement that the Son is 'of the Father's essence'
Athanasius began to realize was not wholly equal to the demands of
the Arian debate. The Arians themselves understood this phrase as
being synonymous with 'of God'; and in the Pauline remark that
'there is one God, the Father, from whom are all things' (1 Corinthians 8:6), they found support for their belief that the Logos was
'from God' and yet a creature. There was a further problem with 'of
the Father's essence'. Some opposed to the Arian doctrine that the
Logos was a creature took

> their proofs against [the Arians] from the illustrations of son and
> father, with this exception, that God is not as man, nor the
> generation of the Son as the issue of man. (*De Syn.* 41)

A human son is 'from his father's essence'; and insofar as a human
son is connatural with his father, this illustration is apposite to the
divine Son's generation from his Father. Yet these anti-Arians were
liable to being seduced into a different error by the very attractiveness of their defence. For insofar as a human son is separate and
separable from his father, this illustration is not apposite, not
underlining that the divine Son is 'the genuine Son' (*De Syn.* 41).

Athanasius' main concern is to show that the Arian reading is not
admissible. Yet his argument also wishes to stress God's simplicity,
and hence the dangers of reading 'of the Father's essence' in a
pluralist way. Athanasius proceeds on two grounds, one exegetical
and one theological. 1 Corinthians 8:6, referring to 'of the Father',
is, according to Athanasius, a counter to those who consider that

the world was held together by random chance, or by a spontaneous combination of atoms of similar structure, an uncaused combination, or by a cause other than God's Logos. It seeks to certify that God was the world's true maker, at whose good will it was framed. Temporarily Athanasius' argument turns to the theological issue, God's simplicity. He notes that the Arians themselves acknowledged that the 'Son is generated from the Father' (*De Syn.* 34). This, Athanasius maintains, is to acknowledge, with Nicaea, that the Son is 'of the Father's essence'. For, being simple, God's fatherhood and essence are inseparable. God is not first God, who then becomes Father. Athanasius is working with the idea of a person's 'essence' being of the character which it must have and which it can neither become nor cease to be; this essence retains its identity despite changes of condition. In a man's case, 'essence' is 'humanity'; 'paternity' here signifies something about a man's nature, but is not that self-same essence itself. In the case of the eternal and immutable Godhead 'paternity' is of the divine essence itself. This Scripture reveals in witnessing to

> nothing else than the very simple, blessed and incomprehensible essence itself of him who is. For though we are unable to master what he is, yet hearing 'Father' and 'God' and 'Almighty' we understand nothing else to be meant than the very essence of him that is. (*De Syn.* 35)[6]

This the Nicene Fathers also recognized when they remarked that

> the Son is 'from the Father's essence', considering that it is all one to say rightly 'from God' and to say 'from the essence'. (*De Syn.* 35)

God does not become Father; nor does he alter in his fatherhood by creating or redeeming. Whereas there is a contrast in man's case between the significance of the verb 'to be' in 'he is man' and 'he is a father', in God's case there is no such contrast. God is God and ever is Father. To suggest that paternity is not of God's essence is in fact to transpose creaturely categories to the creative, divine essence. Thus, if the Son is 'from the Father' and God is simple, both of which even the Arians note, the Son is 'of the Father's essence', as Nicaea and Athanasius conclude. Only were God creaturely and compound, which he is not, would the title 'Father' not be of his essence but a 'name', an epithet, accidental to God's being. Such an understanding of the Son's generation 'from the Father's essence' stands in marked contrast with all being 'of God', as Paul attests. This all, *which came into being through the Son*, is to the Son as creature to Creator. The creature is other in nature than the Creator, the argument again being that the Creator cannot by definition be one of the *all* which came into being from the Father through the Son; it once was not and was brought into being, and the Creator ever is God, eternally begotten 'of God' (cf. *De Decret.* 19).

Given then that the Son is generated 'of the Father's essence' and that that essence is simple, immutable and indivisible, the Son is naturally one with the Father's essence and is eternally inseparable from the eternal Unbegotten Begetter. Hence Athanasius' hesitancy towards not only the Arians but also those who limit their response to Arianism to asserting that the Son is 'from the Father's essence'. Properly understood, it rightly asserts the Father and Son's oneness. Yet its obtuseness and openness to misinterpretation do not lend it easily to the right asserting of the Father and Son's inseparable, essential oneness. It is such oneness alone which guarantees that the Son is 'the genuine Son' of the Father (*De Syn.* 4) and the Complete Image, whom having seen one has seen the Father (cf. John 14:9). So Athanasius finds himself again preferring the Nicene term *homoousios*.

Homoousios did carry a variety of senses which its fourth-century users only half understood. Yet this need not render us helpless in our present quest to understand Athanasius' use of the term. Athanasius himself recognized that the term was obscure. Yet he would not relinquish the term, but sought to explain it. Writing to those 'who accept everything else that was defended at Nicaea and have doubts only about *homoousios*' (*De Syn.* 41), he remarked that they,

> confessing that the Son is 'from the Father's essence' and not 'from another's subsistence', and that he is not 'a creature' nor work, but his genuine and natural Offspring, and that he is eternally with the Father as his Logos and Wisdom, are not far from accepting even the term *homoousios*. (*De Syn.* 41; cf. *Ad Serap.* 2.5)

The point here, confirmed in *De Decret.* 20, is that *homoousios* seems to distinguish the Logos from creation, of which he is not an essential member, as the Arians maintained, and not to elucidate primarily what the Son's essence is. The controversial term stresses what the Son is not, a fact tallying with the assertion that God is 'very simple ... an incomprehensible essence' (*De Syn*. 35). As Athanasius elaborates in his first letter to the monks, although it is impossible to comprehend what God is, it is yet possible to say what he is not: God is not a man, nor of any originated nature (*Epist*. 52.2). Hence, insofar as the Logos is not a creature, and as there is no other existent than a simple God, if the Logos exists, he is one with that simple, indivisible God. He is not even one of several gods, but is God. God's essence is his [7]

Given then that *homoousios* is introduced partly to stress the essential distinction of the Logos from all creatures, it follows that the term is not to be interpreted in a material sense, 'after the manner of bodies' (*De Syn*. 42). *Homoousios* may not then be understood as allowing any partitions or divisions within the Godhead (*De Decret*. 24). For it belongs only to the nature of creatures to be of parts and to be divisible. For this reason Athanasius excludes certain illustrations of *this* aspect of divine paternity and includes others. Human generation, being 'passible', is not illustrative of divine generation, which is 'impassible and without division' (*De Syn*. 41).[8] Human utterance is admissible. For a person's word is

> not a part of [a person], nor does it proceed from him according to passion ... much less does God's Word, whom the Father has declared to be his own Son. (*De Syn*. 41)[9]

So too are the images of life and fountain and of radiance and light. The Father and Son's indivisibility lies behind Athanasius' statement that 'the sense of "Offspring" and *homoousios* is one ' (*De Syn*. 42). For whoever considers the Son an Offspring — and God being simple, the Offspring from the Father is one and proper to his essence — rightly considers him also to be *homoousios*.

Homoousios further precludes the Son being divine either by participation in God or by moral obedience. According to Athanasius, the Arian Logos was a creature who was made divine by participation in God's graciousness, through his obedience and openness to God; he was divine to the utmost extent that a saintly creature could be divine. Athanasius counters by reflecting that the assertion that the Logos is *homoousios* with the Father stresses that he is not a creature and hence does not become divine, as creatures do, by participating. Rather than not becoming divine as creatures become divine, the Logos is he who deifies those who partake of the Father through him (*De Syn.* 51; cf. *De Decret.* 24). It follows then that

> he, being the deifying and enlivening Power of the Father, in whom all are deified and enlivened, is not alien in essence from the Father, but is *homoousios*. (*De Syn.* 51; cf. *De Decret.* 24)

The arguments twist and turn; in fact, they are circular. Yet, to Athanasius' mind, they are no less true for that. These truths are so interrelated as only to be true if each is true.

Homoousios equally preserves the distinct oneness of the Logos with God. Even those who 'imitate' the Logos are one with God only as a result of agreement; their unity with their Maker is 'possessed only by influence and by participation and through the mind' (*De Syn.* 48). The oneness of the Logos with the Father is inseparable and indivisible, as that of Radiance and Light. Laudable as the oneness of saints and angels with God is, of none of them may the Johannine statements, 'I and the Father are one' and 'he who has seen me has seen the Father' (John 10:30; 14:9), be made. Only of the Logos may such be said, and only if the Son is *homoousios* with the Father. For Athanasius is convinced that

> it does not belong to what is other in essence [to God] to possess such prerogatives [as being God, Almighty, Light, Operative Cause or Creator]. (*De Syn.* 50)

For these properties are properly not external to God's being, but are part of his self-definition, without which God is not God. Certainly a creature may partake by grace of these properties; yet these properties he will then have 'from without'; and so even then he cannot truly and fully express and image God. He may reflect him inasmuch and as fully as any creature can. Yet he reflects God, and is not the one reflected. To that extent he who has seen even the most godly creature has not seen God. To maintain otherwise would be to introduce 'another essence foreign to [God] yet capable of the properties of the First essence' (*De Syn.* 50), to conceive a second God and to challenge God's sovereign oneness. Hence, if the Son is not one with God even as God the Father is, he cannot truly and genuinely reveal the Father. So it is that Athanasius maintains that 'if ... he who has seen the Son has seen the Father, reasonably is [the Son] called by the fathers [of Nicaea] *homoousios*' (*De Syn.* 50; cf. *Ad Serap.* 2.5–6).

In short, *homoousios* seems to be saying that the Son is not a creature, naturally open to division and separable from God, liable to changing allegiances, and 'divine' in his oneness with God by participation through grace, founded and manifest in agreement. Corollaries of the assertion that the Logos is of another essence to creatures are the very oneness of Father, Son and Spirit, the immutability of the Logos as very God, and the security of both God's revelation through the Logos and humanity's deification by participation in the very Son. Interestingly, these are the very ideas that appear in that one reference in *C Ar.* 1.9 to *homoousios*. The Son is

> very Son of the Father, natural and genuine, proper to his essence
> ... not a creature ... he exists *homoousios* with the very Father,
> while other beings had the grace [of being gods] from the Father
> by participation of the Logos through the Spirit.

Athanasius' problems concerning *homoousios* were not yet over. Some suspected that admitting that the Son was *homoousios* with the Father meant admitting three essences, 'one pre-existing essence, and ... [the Father and Son] who are generated from it' (*De Syn.* 51). Further, they feared lest those who originated from the one, pre-existing essence should be reckoned not Father and Son but two brothers. Athanasius' crucial counter is to insist that 'there is no need to seek for three essences, but merely to seek whether "this" is true from "that" ' (*De Syn.* 51). When 'this' is truly from 'that', even when 'this' offspring is the sole offspring, this one offspring

> would not be called alien in essence [to his father] merely
> because there was no other from that [originating] essence than
> he. Though alone, he must be *homoousios* with him who begat
> him. (*De Syn.* 51)

For co-essentiality is a 'property of children with reference to their parents' (*De Syn.* 51). So it is with the only-begotten Son of the Father. Hence Athanasius concluded that 'when the [Nicene] fathers said that God's Son was "from his essence", they have reasonably spoken of him as *homoousios*' (*De Syn.* 51). Nor need the co-essential Father and Son originate either in a pre-existent essence, or even in an infinite regression of essences. For Athanasius equates the essence from which the only Son is generated as the uncaused essence, beyond or above which there is nothing. Others were fearful of using *homoousios* lest it meant implying not one but two Gods, analogous to two co-essential human beings. In a scarcely veiled reference to the Arians' intermediary Logos of a wholly transcendent God, Athanasius replied by rejecting the idea that 'God attached to himself the Son from without as though needing a servant' (*De Syn.* 52). God is 'Father'; and 'if God be "Father", he must be Father of one who is by nature a Son and *homoousios* with him' (*Ad Serap.* 2.6.). Hence the Son calls God 'begetter' and not 'maker' and God calls him whom he begot 'son' and not 'creature'. The Father and Son are not, however, two co-essential Gods, whose oneness is simply 'in likeness of teaching'; it is 'according to essence and truth' (*De Syn.* 52); it is 'as light and its radiance is one' (*De Syn.* 52). No one, Athanasius exclaims, can be so foolish as to suppose that either the sun and its radiance are two lights or are of different essences, or the sun's radiance accrues to the sun from without. Rather, the radiance is 'the sun's simple and pure offspring' (*De Syn.* 52; cf. *De Decret.* 24). While the sun and its radiance are distinct, the sun not being its radiance nor the radiance its source, they are one. As then the radiance is indivisible from its source, the sun, much 'less divisible is the Son's nature from the Father. The Godhead [does not accrue] to the Son ... Wherefore', Athanasius challenges the suspicious, 'should not such a one be called *homoousios*?' (*De Syn.* 52; cf. *De Decret.* 24).

Yet others were wary of *homoousios*, as it was not found in Scripture, and its meaning seemed to be not very obvious. Whether or not a term was found in Scripture, Athanasius maintained, was immaterial, so long as the term's meaning was 'religious' (*De Syn.* 39). Indeed, one may compose a credal statement of only scriptural terms and yet be heretical. The Nicene fathers did not devise novel, private sentiments: 'what they wrote down was no discovery of theirs, but is the same as was taught by the Apostles' (*De Syn.* 5), whose teaching was clear. This they safeguarded by a creed, which rightly included *homoousios*. If the Arians' faith had also confessed

> the Father as truly Father, ... the Son to be genuine Son and by nature ... true Logos and Wisdom of the Father ... [understanding] him to be the proper Offspring of the Father's essence as the Radiance is from Light, then not one of them would have

found fault with the [Nicene] fathers but would have been confident that the Council wrote suitably and that this is the right faith concerning our Lord Jesus Christ. (*De Syn.* 39)

The communion of being of the Father and Son which Athanasius was thus trying to describe was not an abstract conception. It is the basis of Athanasius' theology. Upon it rests the eternal relationship of the divine persons. It undergirds the Father's delighting in the Son with the same joy as that with which the Son rejoices in his Father; their delight in each other is reciprocal and complete; and the Son and the Spirit delight in the Father for none other than the Father's sake. Certainly the Son and Spirit do not delight in the Father in order to lay claims upon him for their 'promotion'; and being *homoousios* they do not respond to claims laid upon them as they might were they God's creatures. Their communion of being and their delight in one another complement each other, showing that God — Father, Son and Spirit — does not exist for the sake of anything other than God. The simplicity of being of the Father, Son and Spirit, a simplicity which does not exclude the eternal giving and receiving of being and love, is the basis for understanding the gracious acts of creation, providence and salvation. Particularly it is the basis for the Son's ability to reveal the Father. This is so in the sense both of the Son's comprehensive knowledge of the Father and of the Son's approachability. Unlike creatures, and especially the Arians' creaturely Logos,[10] which cannot fully see or know the Father who so transcends their sight and knowledge, the Son knows the Father as the Image knows him whom he images, and of whose nature the Son fully is; and unlike a solitary, wholly other God, God's Image is never distant from his creation, and never hesitant in his giving himself, and through him his Father, to needy creatures, that they may live and move and have their being in God.

HYPOSTASIS

By the beginning of the last quarter of the fourth century, philosophically astute Christian theologians like Basil of Caesarea (*c.* 330–379), Gregory of Nazianzus and Gregory of Nyssa tended to argue that there was one divine 'being', or *ousia*, and three *hypostaseis*, individual realities, the Father, Son and Spirit. This thinking arose from their desire to describe the Father, Son and Spirit as a Trinity of being. Some Greeks, however, did accept that

God was 'one *hypostasis*', taking the term in the wider generic sense. This they did, to some extent, through recognizing that three *hypostaseis* might suggest three Gods.

The Nicene fathers lacked philosophical training, and the various senses of the term *hypostasis* then current surface in the anathemata appended to the Council's creed, wherein the Logos' everlasting co-existence with the Father is asserted: for the Son 'is not of another essence or *hypostasis*, but proper to the Father's, as the bishops of the Council said' (*De Decret.* 27; cf. *De Syn.* 41). Initially this seems, whatever the situation, a straightforward rejection of the Arians' understanding *hypostasis* as signifying subsistences which are 'foreign, strange and alien in essence from one another' (*Tome* 5), each of which is 'divided apart by itself' (*Tome* 5). Such thinking lay behind the Arian view that the Son was a creature, 'alien in essence' from God his Creator.

In the later 350s and early 360s matters were anything but straightforward in Antioch in Syria. Although the followers of Melitius and of the late Eustathius had a common enemy in the Arians, they were not in harmonious relations. Ecclesiastical politics apart,[11] the one group portrayed God as being 'three *hypostaseis*', three individual realities: for them the Father, Son and Spirit were *homoiousioi*. The other group described God as 'one *hypostasis*', meaning one essence or *ousia*; for them the Father, Son and Spirit were *homoousioi*. Athanasius' interest was not in terminological strictness but in right theology. He was therefore pleased that those who understood God as being three *hypostaseis* were both anti-Arian and anti-Sabellian. They believed in a holy Trinity 'not in name only but existing and subsisting in truth' (*Tome* 5). The Father, Son and Spirit were recognized to be neither confused nor simply 'names' within the Godhead. Athanasius was further pleased that, while noting the individual realities within the one God, they not only denied 'three Gods or three beginnings' but also acknowledged

> one Godhead and one Beginning, and that the Son is *homoousios* with the Father ... while the Spirit is not a creature nor external, but is proper and inseparable from the essence of the Father and Son. (*Tome* 5)

What Athanasius was so eager to maintain in the *De Synodis* and *De Decretis* is here maintained, through different terminology, to preclude both Arianism and Sabellianism. The other anti-Arian group denied that theirs was a Sabellian God, the Trinity existing 'in name only'. They did assert that God is one *hypostasis* but interpreted *hypostasis* as 'essence'. So God is one,

> on account of both the Son being 'of the essence of the Father' and the identity of nature. For ... there is one Godhead and ... it has one nature, and ... there is [not] one nature of the Father, from which that of the Son and the Spirit are distinct. (*Tome* 6)

In phrases very reminiscent of Nicaea, they countered Arianism.

Athanasius is ready to recognize the orthodoxy of both these groups. What is of importance for him is 'the faith confessed by the fathers at Nicaea ... [rather] than the said phrases' (*Tome* 6). The fact that the forms in which these two groups expressed their common theology were ambiguous Athanasius was prepared to tolerate, partly for pastoral reasons and partly for ecclesiastical reasons. The pastoral issue concerned distinguishing essentials from incidentals in a very fraught situation in Antioch. The ecclesiastical issue concerned the view that

> it is undesirable that a second creed be promulgated lest that drafted at Nicaea should be deemed imperfect and lest a pretext be given to those who were often wishing to draft and define a creed ... [with] no motive save only contentiousness. (*Tome* 5)

The dangers of tinkering with the language, but not the faith, of Nicaea were deemed greater than those of retaining the seeming ambiguity of the Council's formulae.

Notes

1 Cf. Irenaeus' argument that if, besides God, there is a second principle, there must be a dividing third principle, which, since it embraces both God and the second principle, must be greater than the two that it embraces, and so must be God (*Adversus omnes Haereses* 2.1–2); Eusebius, Bishop of Caesarea (*c.* 260–*c.* 340), argues similarly: if there are two principles, there must be a dividing third; and between this dividing third and each of the first two principles there must be a dividing fourth, and so on, *ad infinitum* (*Praeparatio Evangelica* 7.22).

2 Note, for example, Telemachus' appeal jointly to 'Olympian Zeus and Themis' in Homer, *Odyssey* 2.68–69; cf. R. J. Bonner and G. Smith, *The Administration of Justice from Homer to Aristotle*, vol. 1 (Chicago, 1930), esp. pp. 10–11. Plato argues, by implication, against any more

TRINITY, TERMS, TRIBULATIONS AND TRUTHS

ultimate principle beyond the deity: the Godhead, which is good
'always, altogether and in all ways, ... is perfectly sufficient' (*Philebus*
60C). See also J. Moltmann, *The Crucified God: The Cross of Christ as
the Foundation and Criticism of Christian Theology* (ET; London,
1974), pp. 267–8.

3   Cf. *De Syn.* 52: there are not 'two Gods but one God, there being but
one form (*eidos*) of Godhead, as the light is one and the radiance'.

4   Traditionally this term is translated as 'consubstantial'. It is not
translated here as its meaning was initially much debated, as will be
seen in succeeding pages.

5   See G. C. Stead, *Divine Substance* (Oxford, 1979), esp. pp. 131ff.;
242ff.

6   Cf. *De Decret.* 22: in saying 'God' or naming him 'Father', 'we name
nothing as if about him but signify his essence'. In asserting that
paternity is of the divine essence itself, Athanasius is not equating
paternity with the divine essence in such a way as to permit paternity
to belong to the Son *qua* God. His acceptance of the givens of God
being only unbegotten Father, only begotten Son and only Spirit
prevent such. His point is primarily that God does not become but
eternally is Father, even as the Son does not come into being but
eternally is God the Son. For this see P. Widdicombe, *The Fatherhood
of God from Origen to Athanasius* (Oxford, 1994), esp. pp. 159ff.

7   One may know of the Son's generation; for it has been *revealed* that
the Son is only-begotten. One may also thereby know that the Son is
not the Father, nor the Spirit. But what this generation is has not been
revealed. Hence any study of it remains essentially apophatic.

8   Although the philosophical background in Alexandria is complicated
by the usual early Christian dual inheritance of Greek thought, from
Plato as well as from Aristotle, it appears that Athanasius is here
working with Aristotle's belief that the male seed contained the entire
foetus in embryo; this a father 'planted' in the woman's womb, as in an
incubator that the child might grow; cf. Aristotle, *De Generatione
Animalium* 1.729A–730B and Plato, *Timaeus* 91A–D.

9   The illustration of a man's word needs qualification in that a human
word exists only insofar as the speaker utters it. The divine Logos, or
Word, exists even as the divine Father, who utters him, exists, and not
just insofar as the Father utters him. Unlike the human word, the
divine Logos is not wanting in self-existence, but is the living Logos,
the substantive Wisdom of God (*De Syn.* 41).

10 Cf. Arius, *Thalia* 35aff.; it is impossible for [the Son] to explore that
Father who exists by himself ... for clearly it is impossible for what has
a beginning to encompass by thought or apprehension the one who is
unbegun.

11 Cf. A. L. Pettersen, 'Making sense of Athanasius' *Tomus ad
Antiochenos* 7', *Journal of Ecclesiastical History* 41, no. 2 (1990), pp.
183–98.

7

The Triune God

THE FATHER

Fatherhood is central for Athanasius' understanding of God. It orders titles such as 'unoriginate', 'unbegotten', 'Son' and 'Spirit', and makes intelligible their significance for the divine nature. Primarily it describes the relation internal to the divine being; only secondarily does it refer to God as Father of his adopted children. Indeed, it is as eternal Father of the Son, as the very source of all goodness and life, that God is who he is. Fatherhood is that without which God is not; it is a given; God *is* Father, 'ever and now' (*C.Ar.* 1.11). Hence this Fatherhood is not adventitious to this immutable God. He is neither imperfect nor incomplete, the paternity proper to his divine essence being added to him. He does not lack, even in the sense of finding his meaning as 'Father' through another. Divine simplicity precludes such. Otherwise 'does not each supply the deficiency of the other?' (*C.Ar.* 1.26). It is Arians, Athanasius maintains, who allow God's Fatherhood to be contingent and incidental. For them it is brought into being and given meaning by God's creative act. Creation is that which causes God to become and to be *called* Father. Athanasius will not allow God's Fatherhood, in any sense whatsoever, to be dependent upon creation. For it is defined by none and defines all else. So Athanasius stresses God's Fatherhood as that which defines God as the Source and End of creation, and which underwrites men and women's becoming his sons and daughters. Athanasius, it is true, does not use the Platonic description of God as the 'Father of all'. Yet this does not mean that

Athanasius uses 'Father' as a trinitarian and soteriological term which is inapplicable to his relation to 'all things'. For the trinitarian description, with the appreciation of the Father as him who, being very good, envies nothing its existence, lies behind the belief that God is the Creator and Sustainer of all.

So, while it is important to recognize the relation of God the Father to the world, it is also crucial to distinguish the Father's relation to the Son from God's to the world. It is with this understanding that Athanasius approached the question of how to interpret God as 'unbegotten' and 'unoriginate'.

THE FATHER, UNBEGOTTEN AND UNORIGINATE

The terms 'unbegotten' and 'unoriginate' the Arians understood as synonyms; similarly they interpreted their opposites, 'begotten' and 'originate'. For that 'begotten' clearly had an origin. Hence, as Scripture suggests that the Son is the begotten One, they argued that he cannot be unoriginate and therefore must be essentially one with the 'originate', created world. Their argument found support in the thesis that there could not conceivably be two unoriginates. Athanasius, meanwhile, was beginning to appreciate possible distinctions between 'unbegotten' and 'unoriginate' and between 'begotten' and 'originate'. Athanasius too held that there could not conceivably be two unoriginates. He did, however, recognize that 'unoriginate' might be variously interpreted, and depending upon its particular sense might have a different point of reference. When the term signified 'what is not a work but was always' 'the Son, as well as the Father must be called "unoriginate"' (*C.Ar.* 1.31). When, however, it meant 'existing but not generated of anything, nor having a father' 'the unoriginate in this sense is only one, namely the Father' (*C.Ar.* 1.31). Athanasius then rounds on his opponents, pointing out that these two meanings of 'unoriginate' were not synonymous.

> To say that God is in this sense 'unoriginate' [i.e. not generated of any nor having a father] does not show that the Son is a thing 'originate' [i.e. a work which was not always], it being evident ... that the Logos is such as him who begat him. Therefore if God is unoriginate [i.e. what is not a work but was always], his Image is not originate [i.e. a work which was not always], but an Offspring ... For what likeness has the unoriginate [i.e. the increate Creator] to the originate [i.e. creation]? (*C.Ar.* 1.31)[1]

165

Athanasius' thinking may be Platonic in hue, but its inspiration is biblical. Scriptural revelation takes precedence in theological enquiry. He therefore recognized that God the Father is naturally other than creation. He also acknowledged that the Son, being the Father's Offspring, naturally is like his Begetter. Hence Athanasius began to understand the term 'unoriginate', meaning 'that which was always', as referring not to a person or the persons within the Godhead, but to the divine essence, distinguishing the divine, unoriginate essence from the originate, creaturely essence, which once was not but now has come into being, and manifestly has an origin. In short, for Athanasius, the 'unoriginate' is specified not by contrast with the Son but with things which come to be through the Son, the Origin of all things, even with him who, by implication, is other than the all which came to be through him. Thus, in contrast especially with later Arianism, Athanasius understands the Father to be the 'unbegotten', the Son the 'only-begotten', and them both to have a common, unoriginate essence, which always is and has no origin. The strict verbal distinction between 'unoriginate' and 'unbegotten' is not always maintained; the ideas behind such a distinction are.

It follows that, while the Arians think that 'unoriginate' dictated the understanding of 'paternity', Athanasius is convinced that 'paternity' expounds the meaning of 'unoriginate'. A consequence of the Arian thinking is to reinforce the solitary, almost sterile sense of God: God is distanced from the Son, and from all other lesser creatures. A consequence of Athanasius' thought is to undergird the expansive, bounteous perception of God: the eternally unbegotten Father eternally begets the Son; through him, who 'is other than the things originated and alone is the Father's proper Offspring, all things came to be' (*De Decret.* 29).

For the Son is the unoriginate Father's proper Image. The idea of God being 'unoriginate' does not distance the Father from the Son, nor the Godhead from that which is originate. Indeed, in the unbegotten Father is the begotten Son, and in the generative deity is the origin of all creation. As P. J. Widdicombe powerfully argues,[2] the centrality of the ideas of 'Father' and 'Son' in Athanasius' theology concentrates the theologian's mind upon the idea of 'begetting' as entailing relationship. As 'Father' the divine nature is identified as inherently good, radically generative. The eternal relationship of being of the Father and Son is one of mutual giving and receiving and is the eternal source of both creation and salvation. Father and Son are determinative subjects in Athanasius' theology. Without a divine, generative nature, precluded by the Arian denial of the Son's essential oneness with the Father, the existence of creation is problematic. With the assertion of the Son, who is not external to the Father but is his proper, creative agent, creation is secure, not in and through itself, but in and through God's inherent generative fruitfulness. The extraordinarily generous, divine act of bringing all into existence from nothing is conceivable and indeed possible for Athanasius, since the divine being exists first as the dynamic relationship of Father and Son. Hence there is the all-important connection of the Father as the Son's origin, of God as the source of goodness which envies nothing its existence, and of God mercifully wishing even fallen humanity its salvation. God's Fatherhood is the Source of divine and creaturely reality; and only if the Son is the Father's Offspring, rather than however noble a thing originated, which has no essential likeness to God unoriginate, can God's character as Creator, Sustainer and Saviour be maintained.

THE SON

God, for Athanasius, is not viewed as a monolithic and static abstraction, but as consistently dynamic. Divine simplicity there is, and it belongs to God as Father, Son and Spirit. Hence God exists as Light, with its divine Radiance, as Being, with its Expression and Image, and as Father, with the Truth, his Son. This dynamic God, being 'unalterable and perfect and ever what it was, neither [adds] to it what is more, nor [suffers] any loss' (*C.Ar.* 1.18). Hence, Athanasius emphasizes both that the Son is not simply an attribute of the Father and that the Son is not merely *called* Son. For Athanasius God *is* Son, *is* Logos, *is* Wisdom; in relationship to the Father, the Son *is* the Father's eternal and proper Offspring. Just as it belongs to a fountain's nature that it cannot be dry, so it belongs to God, the Fountain of Wisdom and Life, that he cannot ever be without Life and Wisdom, who is the Son (*C.Ar.* 1.19; cf. *Ad Serap.* 2.2). It is impossible then to say that God was ever 'without the Logos' (*C.Ar.* 2.32). This last statement the Arians could also voice, although interpreting it differently. They maintained that God never wanted in Wisdom and Rationality. These however were God's eternal, divine attributes, but not the divine person, the Logos; in accordance with these attributes God created the supreme creature, his Logos. In contrast, Athanasius' God the

Father never was without God the Son, his true Logos, where 'true' does not carry simply the sense of the genuine, authentic Logos, over against a 'veracious' Logos, one who might be supposed to be a Logos, and who indeed, in a sense, but not the ultimate, eternal and essential sense, is a Logos. The 'true' Logos is the non-contingent Logos, who is true and faithful in his own character to his Father. So being very God, he is truly the Father's Son and Logos, who genuinely and fully reveals his Father. He is then not the Logos only in name. He is the Logos in that he 'utters' and makes known the Father; he is the divine Power in that he acts for and as God; he is the Son, in whose Image the Father is always to be seen. Clearly, the Logos then is distinct but not divided from the Father. 'The Logos is in his Begetter; and the Begotten co-exists with the Father' (*C.G.* 47). Given this eternal filial relationship with the Father, where all giving and receiving is reciprocal and complete, and which exists, not selfishly, for its own sake, the Son is not seen as but a cosmological principle connecting a transcendent God with creation; nor is the Son conceived as but God-in-his-immanence. He is a given of the Father–Son relationship, rooted in God's eternal goodness or paternity, that essential part of the definition of the 'God'. The 'Son' is the eternal correlative of the eternal 'Father'.

This generative community is one where knowledge of the Father is through the Son, and of the Son from the Father, and where the Father delights in the Son and the Son similarly rejoices in the Father. They are eternal correlatives, the eternity protecting the divine goodness and power and ensuring it as the matrix for both the secure expression of God's creativity and the secure basis of people being made God's children through deification. Yet Athanasius clearly does not see these two persons as but replicas, one of another. The Father is not the Son nor the Son the Father. For the Son has his 'Cause' in the Father while the Father is 'uncaused'. This is not to say that the Son is subordinate to the Father, as is made very manifest when Athanasius interprets the text 'The Father is greater than I' (John 14:28) as meaning 'greater' not 'in greatness, nor in time, but because of his generation from the Father himself' (*C.Ar.* 1.58). Indeed, continuing this exegesis, Athanasius suggests that comparatives are used only of things of the same nature. Hence, 'in saying "greater" [John] again shows that [the Son] is proper to [the Father's] essence' (*C.Ar.* 1.58). Central to the understanding of the divine community then is the philosophical belief that the Son is 'second' to the Father, in the sense that the Father is the eternally uncaused cause and the Son the eternally caused cause, or, as Athanasius traditionally puts it, the Father is unbegotten and the Son is only-begotten. Clearly, 'in view of the asymmetry and distinctiveness of function, we cannot claim that there is any consistent suggestion of numerical identity in the strict sense'.[3] This asymmetry of the uncaused Father who eternally begets his only Son is a belief not simply stated but also used theologically. Athanasius supports his contention that, since the Logos is not subject to time's limitations, he is ever the Son by reference to the Father's immutability. What the Father is, that he ever continues to be. Hence it follows that

> the Image also continues to be what he is, and will not alter. Now he is the Father's Son; therefore he will not become other than is proper to the Father's essence. (*C.Ar.* 1.22)

As the Father is eternal, is he who is, is almighty and true God, so also is the Son. For 'there are not some things in the Father and others in the Son; those which are in the Father are also in the Son' (*Ad Serap.* 2.2). Even as in the case of the terms 'unbegotten' and 'unoriginate', so here the eternal Fatherhood of God defines the very nature of Sonship.

Corollaries of God's Sonship being neither an epithet nor an attribute surface in Athanasius' understanding of the Son's relationship to the Father and to creation, and of the Son's and creation's relation to the Father. There is both continuity and discontinuity between the Son and people as 'sons' of God. 'By reason of the Logos in us is God called "our Father". For the Spirit of the Logos in us names through us his own Father as "ours" ' (*De Decret.* 31; cf. Galatians 4:6). The Logos' Sonship is essential; ours is graciously given, a distinction marked in a poignant analysis of worship.

> While he is adored, because he is the adorable Father's Son, we [sons of God] adore, confessing him Lord and God, because we are creatures and other than him. (*De Decret.* 11)

This continuity and discontinuity extends beyond the realm of soteriology. For the Son's immutability and inseparability from the Father is crucial to the Son's being the Truth and to creation's continuing existence. 'How can what alters and changes ... be true?' (*C.Ar.* 1.36). If the Son is not unalterably the Son, no contemplative shall be able to see the Father; for how can the unchangeable be clearly seen in the ever changing? If the Son is not perfect and has 'no stay in one and the same condition' (*C.Ar.* 1.46), creation may not be assured of its security and will not attain its perfection. Hence while the Father 'defines' the Son's very nature, the Son's very nature 'defines' creation.

There is, however, a crucial difference between creation and the Son in their respective relation to God. Creation is totally dependent upon God; its non-existence is not to God's diminution. It is not part of his definition. For God is sovereign and free. However 'for the Offspring not to be ever with the Father is a defect in his essence's perfection' (*C.Ar.* 1.29). The Son is part of the definition of God, who is neither alterable nor incomplete nor open to addition.

Accepting that the Logos therefore is neither God's attribute nor constituent nor complement, but is the Father's Son, Athanasius is convinced that the Son is the result neither of the Father's willing his being nor of the Father's being compelled to permit his being, nor of his participation in the Father. This tallies with Athanasius' thinking concerning God's simplicity. Clearly necessity exerted upon God confounds his simplicity. Equally certainly so does free will. For whatever is peculiar or 'proper' to God, which the Logos is, cannot be 'by will'. Otherwise God's simplicity is risked by questions of mutability and of multiplicity. Firstly, if a being is free to will a particular thing, the same being is free not to so will. If it is then believed that the Father, in his good pleasure, wills the Son to be, the Father

> begins to be good and ... his not being good is possible. For to counsel and choose implies an inclination two ways and is incidental to a rational nature. (*C.Ar.* 3.62)

Such a thesis would place God's immutability at stake and render his goodness not essential but incidental. Secondly, while there is correlativity between one who wills and that willed, the relation is not one of being: the former's existence does not necessarily entail the latter's existence. Athanasius even uses the analogy of a man who freely wills to build a house (*C.Ar.* 1.26–27): the house freely willed into existence is external to the maker. Hence, as the correlativity between him who wills and that willed is not a relation of being, and as anything willed is thus external to God, than whom there is none other but creaturely beings, that willed is creaturely.

170

Further, no matter how superb a creature, what is willed, once was not. For 'by will' suggests a 'coming into being' (*C.Ar.* 3.61). It may even suggest that, if the Logos was willed into being, there was a 'time' before the Logos came into being. For ' "by will" is to place times before the Son. For counselling goes before things which once were not, as in the case of all things' (*C.Ar.* 3.61). Yet more may therein be suggested. That willed implies a Logos before the willed Logos. For if the Logos came into being 'by will'

> it follows that the will concerning him consists in some other Logos, through whom he in turn comes to be. For it has been shown that God's will is not in the things which he brings into being, but is in him through whom and in whom all things are brought into being. (*C.Ar.* 3.61)

The suggestion therefore that the Son is 'by the Father's free will' would thus render God compound, divine and creaturely, and multiple.

Nor is the problem removed by thinking in terms of an eternal willing by God. For if willing implies that that willed is essentially other than God and is truly creaturely, eternally willing merely allows that the Son so willed is an eternal creature. The creature's eternity is an idea which Athanasius' belief in creation-from-nothing would find self-contradictory; and, even were that creature ever in harmony with the Father, its essential and numerical difference from the one, true God would still constitute a serious challenge to the integrity of God's simplicity.

Athanasius therefore rejects the assertion that the Logos came into being 'by will'. All things everywhere witness to the 'being of the Logos', while nothing anywhere witnesses to his 'being "by will" or to his being made' (*C.Ar.* 3.60). Scripture, when referring to the Son, employs the description 'he was', with the implication of eternal being, rather than 'he became', and refers to him uniquely 'being in the Father and being the Father's Image' (*C.Ar.* 3.60). Athanasius even extends his argument that if, as the Johannine Prologue records, the Logos is the Framer of *all* things, he cannot himself be one of these *all* things framed by the Father's will, by noting that he must be the Framer even of those 'times' of counselling which precede the framing of *all* things. The Logos therefore must be everlasting, co-existing as the Father's Will; he is 'external to the things which have come to be by will, but rather is himself the Father's living Counsel, by which all things have come to be' (*C.Ar.*

3.64). The Logos *is* the Father's Will, and is not the consequence of the Father's will.

Athanasius then resists the suggestion that if the Father does not beget the Son 'by will' he does so 'unwillingly' or 'by necessity' (*C.Ar.* 3.66). He neither decided to be what he is, nor was he constrained from without to be good. For necessity is an improper and unseemly category for God, that which is necessitated being not 'at the Father's pleasure'. He did not begin to be good but rather is naturally so in accordance with his will and pleasure. In short, what God is is his delight and pleasure. His being and his act are one. This natural goodness, which is naturally envious of no one's full existence, is akin to the Father's natural paternity. God did not decide to be the Son's Father but is so, naturally and in accordance with his will and good pleasure.

> As [the Father] is of his own subsistence, so also is the Son, being proper to [the Father's essence], and is not without [the Father's] pleasure. Hence permit the Son to be the object of the Father's pleasure and love. (*C.Ar.* 3.66).

The Father thus truly and naturally delights in the Son whom he has begotten by nature; or, as John writes, 'the Father loves the Son' (John 3:35).

Athanasius seeks to understand 'will' and 'good pleasure' in accordance with the subject of this willing and good pleasure, one whose being and act are one. This is Athanasius' normal exegetical custom of reading texts in accordance with the revealed truths of their subject.[4] Athanasius begins by remarking that,

> it is one thing to say, through will [the Logos] came to be, and another, that the Father has love and good pleasure towards the Son, who is his own by nature. (*C.Ar.* 3.66)

The former permits that once the Son was not and that the Father could have chosen not to have willed the Son's coming into being. The latter proposes that the Father is always good by nature and so is always generative by nature. The naturally good Father never envies his natural Son's existence, naturally begets his Son and delights in his only-Begotten. An image of this oneness of being and act, of nature and good pleasure Athanasius finds in light and ray.

There is no will preceding radiance in the light; it is its natural

172

offspring, at the pleasure of the light which begat it, but not by will and consideration, but in nature and truth; so also in the instance of the Father and Son one might rightly say that the Father has love and good pleasure towards the Son and the Son has love and good pleasure towards the Father. (*C.Ar.* 3.66)

Thus Athanasius concludes that to say that the Son exists as a consequence of will is folly, the Son being the Father's Will. Consequently, the Father's Son, or Will, is not 'by necessity' and the Son is the Father's Good Pleasure. As P. J. Widdicombe notes,

> As naturally generative, 'what [the Father] does in producing the Son is the enactment of what he is; and as his acts are not temporal and episodic, he always and necessarily "does" what he is — by the necessity of his own being, not by any intrusive compulsion' ... the generation of the Son is both free and natural.[5]

The relation of the Father and Son is then not by participation nor modes. In a very early work Athanasius gives a summary of the apostles' teaching:

> being the good Offspring of a good Father and being true Son, he is the Father's Power, his Wisdom and Logos; not so by participation, nor do these properties accrue to him from outside in the way of those who participate in him and are given wisdom by him, having their power and reason in him. But he is absolute Wisdom, very Logos, himself the Father's own Power, absolute Truth, absolute Justice, absolute Virtue, and indeed Stamp, Effulgence and Image. (*C.G.* 46)

Even at this early stage Athanasius is leaving aside both Origen's belief that the Logos is a 'second god' to the very God (*Contra Celsum* 3.41; 5.39) and the second-century philosopher Numenius' thinking that the First God is 'absolute God' and the second god is 'good' (*Fragment* 25). Athanasius is siding with the Nicene thinking that the Logos is 'true God from true God', essentially one with the Father and distinct from all creatures which depend upon the Logos for life and reason. He is what he is, and is that not 'by participation'. This thinking, although conveyed, because of the debate's context, without a strict terminological exactness, Athanasius still maintains in his later anti-Arian debates. 'Participate' and its cognates both Athanasius and the Arians agree may describe the relation of *any* creature with God, wherein in grace it becomes divine.

> If, as [the Arians say], the Son is from nothing and was not before his generation, he, of course, as well as others, must be called Son and God and Wisdom only by participation. For thus all other creatures consist and by sanctification are glorified. (*C.Ar.* 1.15)

Where Athanasius differs from the Arians is in denying that the Son is a creature, and divine only by grace through participation.

> The Son himself participates of no one; but that of the Father of which there is participation is the Son. For in participating in the Son we are said to partake of God. (*C.Ar.* 1.16; 1.28)

The idea that the Son *is* God and does not become God dominates the argument. The Son is God; and those who participate in the Son 'are said to participate in God', a real but not essential participation.

Athanasius' strongly voiced beliefs are not however such as limit his use of vocabulary. He fully engages the Arians in debate. They 'have to tell us of what [the Logos] is partaker' (*C.Ar.* 1.15). Using the Arian controversialists' term 'partake' Athanasius continues: the Logos cannot 'partake' of the Spirit, as do all other creatures. For the Spirit, as John's Gospel suggests, takes from the Son and not the Son from the Spirit. If, Athanasius continues, the Son does not partake of the Spirit, he must 'partake' of the Father. For he is the only other of whom he may 'partake'. Athanasius then offers two possible explanations of this participation. If the Logos 'participates' in some external attribute of the Father, the Logos will not partake of the Father but of that external to the Father. He will be 'second' not to the Father but to that external attribute; he will be called Son not of the Father but of that external attribute. This explanation is rendered vain by the Father's calling the Logos his 'beloved Son' (Matthew 3:17) and the Son's saying that God is his Father. Hence, Athanasius deduces, there is no other possible explanation but that 'it follows that that of which there is participation [by the Logos] is not external, but of the Father's essence' (*C.Ar.* 1.15). For the sake of winning the argument Athanasius tolerates terminology which properly should be excluded. The theology, and not a strict, narrow use of particular terms, dictates the form of the argument.

Thus the distinction between the Son and God's adopted children is maintained. For the Son shares in the divine nature and properties, paternity excepted, exactly as the Father does. Humanity's sonship, meanwhile, is not part of the definition of who and what we are, but is a quality which we graciously receive. Further, the truth and security of revelation is ensured. If the Son is both to be the Father's Image, a term which Arius avoids in his credal statements, and to reveal the Father as he truly is, the Son must be God in exactly the same way as the Father is. To be the Son but nominally or notionally will not suffice. Nor will Origen's sense of the Son having a continuity of being with the 'higher' being, the Father, and thus being the Father's Image. For Athanasius, if the Son is truly to 'image' the Father, he must share fully in the divine nature and properties, paternity aside. Equally, unless the Son 'participates', not in something external to the Father, but in the Father's being, he shall not be able to grant creation, which is wholly other than God, that gracious, saving participation. Salvation is not, to Athanasius' mind, possible through an hierarchical chain, from the Father through an intermediate Son to creatures. For an intermediary separates as much as he unites creatures with the Father. A particular ecclesiology is also retained. The paradigm of church unity is that of the Father and Son. The Son, through his Spirit indwelling us, wills us to call his proper Father 'our Father'.

Because of Athanasius' strong belief in the persons of Father, Son and Spirit not being accidents or metaphorical descriptions, in the Son and Spirit's possessing the Father's properties in not merely a transferred sense but as theirs essentially, and in the Father being the divine uncaused Cause, he rejects certain theological beliefs. A tritheism in which the Father, Son and Spirit are seen as co-ordinates belonging to one genus is precluded by the identity of God as Father, the source of the Son and Spirit, as witnesses his attempt to unite the anti-Arian parties in Antioch in the early 360s; also evident from these events in Antioch is Athanasius' taking a strictly anti-modalist stance. Rather, he emphatically believed in the eternity and immutability of the persons. The Father is, and is not only called, Father. This he ever is. The Son is the eternally and only-begotten Son; and the Spirit is ever Spirit, proceeding eternally of the Father and given through the Son. The eternal interrelationship of the Father, Son and Spirit stresses their eternal distinction as much as their eternal unity.

Not surprisingly Athanasius will have no truck with the supposition that if the Father and Son are co-eternal, they are not Father and Son but two co-eternal brothers. Athanasius begins his argument by noting that while the Son may be described as being 'with' the Father, such is properly interpreted by reference to the description of the Son being 'eternally begotten of the Father' (*C.Ar.* 1.14). The Begetter is not the Begotten.

> The Father is the Son's Origin, even his Begetter. Thus the Father is the Father and is not born the son of another; and the Son is the Son and not a brother. (*C.Ar.* 1.14)

Indeed, just as titles such as 'unoriginate' and 'maker' and 'framer' imply what is 'originate' and 'made', so that of 'Father' implies not a 'brother' but 'the Son' (*C.Ar.* 1.33). The Arians' 'third man' argument that, if the Father and Son are consubstantial (*De Synod.* 51; cf. *C.Ar.* 1.14), there must be a third being from which these two are both begotten as consubstantial brothers Athanasius rejects. As is obvious from the case of human beings, what is generated is consubstantial with what has generated it, and the generator is not the brother of that generated. How much more is that the case in the unbegotten Father's begetting the only Son.[6] It is also evident that a co-essential relationship does not necessarily mean that the participants in that relationship must necessarily share *all* the same properties; the begetter and the begotten are co-essential and yet still father and child. Besides recalling what is evident from human co-essentiality, it is to be remembered that tradition speaks of the 'Father' and 'Son', so preserving the individual and distinct identities. Implicit in their titles is their relation, one to the other. The 'Father' signifies God as the uncaused Cause of all, anterior to which there is nothing; it certainly does not suggest a regression to a common cause, as in the Arians' 'third man' argument. The 'Son' is Son in view of his generation by the Father: the Son is so, *because* he is the Son of the Father, the Source of all. God, Father, Son and Spirit, being eternal, has no predecessor; and their relations are the incontrovertible 'givens' of God's self-disclosure.[7]

In *Contra Arianos* 1 Athanasius confronts the suggestion that if the Son is the Father's Image, like him in all things, he must be like the Father even in what characterizes the Father as Father, namely the act of begetting. If this is so, then the Son will become a father, 'begetting' the Spirit. In *Ad Serap.* 1 Athanasius continues to face this issue, only there it surfaces in the suggestion either that the Spirit is the Son's brother, both the Son and Spirit being begotten of the Father, or that the Spirit is the Father's grandson. These suggestions Athanasius quickly dismisses.

> Just as we cannot ascribe a father to the Father, so we cannot ascribe a brother to the Son. Other than the Father ... there is no God. There is no other Son than the Son. For he is only-begotten. Hence the Father, being one and only, is the Father of a Son who is one and only; and in the Godhead alone the terms 'Father' and 'Son' keep to their meaning and are ever thus. (*Ad Serap.* 1.16)

Central to Athanasius' thinking are three themes: God is simple; God is he who defines all else, and all else does not define God; and God's self-revelation through Scripture is not to be challenged. In *Ad Serap.* 4.4 Athanasius notes that 'the things above the creation [have] an eternal stability'. The notions then of the Son becoming the Father of the Spirit or the Father being both the 'Father' and becoming a 'Grandfather' are inconceivable. What is true of God is true eternally, immutably and perfectly. God's Fatherhood, his Sonship, his Spirit are not adventitious to him. Unlike a man, who may be 'called' a son or a father, God the Father 'is called and is Father'; the Son 'is called and is Son'.

> In the Godhead alone the Father is and was and always is, because he is Father in the strict sense, and only Father. The Son is Son in the strict sense, and only Son ... and the Spirit is always Spirit. (*Ad Serap.* 4.6)

The characterizing of God's very nature as Father, Son and Spirit is then used without sacrificing the divine properties of eternity and immutability. Indeed, fatherhood and sonship are fully, properly and eternally realized in God and contingently in God's creation, in humanity, God being Father and Son 'in the strict sense' while 'with men the names "father" and "son" are not kept to their strict meanings' (*Ad Serap.* 1.16; 4.6). A man may rightly be called 'father', while at the same time being another's 'son'; and each man, when begotten, receives a part of his father that he may himself become the father of another, men being divisible, 'parts of one another' (*Ad Serap.* 1.16; 4.6). These truths may not, however, be transferred to the immutable, indivisible Creator, who is without parts. A good theology then does not argue in an unqualified way from human to divine generation, but acknowledges that creaturely reality reflects, but only darkly, divine reality, its causal exemplar. If however these arguments cut no ice, Athanasius assumes scriptural witness will.

> The faith of the Catholic Church ... the Lord grounded and rooted ... in the Triad, when he said to his disciples, Go ye and make disciples ... baptizing them in the name of the Father and the Son and the Spirit. (*Ad Serap.* 3.6, quoting Matthew 28:19)

In the light of this dominical statement, it is pure folly to envisage a brother to the Son, or to believe the Father to be a Grandfather.

> The Spirit is not given the name of 'son' in the Scriptures lest he be taken for a brother, nor 'son of the Son', lest the Father be a Grandfather. The Son is called Son of the Father and the Spirit of the Father is called Spirit of the Son. Thus the Godhead of the Holy Triad and faith therein is one. (*Ad Serap.* 1.16; 4.3)

In *Ad Serap.* 4 Athanasius' patience is wearing thin. Only a madman, who 'is searching the unsearchable' (*Ad Serap.* 4.4), will ask why the Son is so named and the Spirit so called and why they are not given the same name; only an impious fool will dare to rename what God has named or to reorder what God has ranked together in the Matthean declaration of the baptismal faith. Such people reveal their impertinence in giving more weight to their own ideas, born of analogies of human generation, than to divine unveilings through the Son incarnate.

While therefore Athanasius is concerned to stress the eternal distinction of the only Father from the only Son from the only Spirit, he is yet concerned to assert God's oneness and the three persons' unity. Eternal distinction within the Godhead there is; even occasional division there is not. For 'God is not composed of parts, but being impassible and simple, is impassibly and indivisibly the Father of the Son' (*C.Ar.* 1.28).

IMAGES OF DIVINE ONENESS

The relation of the Father and Son is one of a generous being, which exists eternally in relationships. The Father's and Son's and Spirit's existences necessarily entail each other, each existing simultaneously and eternally with the others. For both polemical and theological reasons Athanasius is willing critically to consider images of this oneness. These include human generation, a light's radiance and the human word.

Athanasius forbids the transference of creaturely categories to the divine, when it results in denying what is natural and proper to the Father.[8] Rather than divine paternity and generation being read anthropomorphically, human paternity and generation are to be understood from the divine standpoint. Yet, because human paternity and generation can be so understood, they may help to elaborate upon truths concerning God, which are confirmed elsewhere. The title 'son', for example, in the nature of things suggests 'what is naturally begotten from anyone and does not accrue to him from without' (*De Decret.* 10). The begotten is properly related to the nature of the begetter. Hence, even as a human son is of one nature with his father, so the only-begotten Son is not naturally other than his Father. Extending this argument against the Arian thesis that the Logos is the Son of the essentially divine Father and yet is a creature, Athanasius contrasts the relation of a father and son with a maker and an artefact.

> A man by counsel builds a house, but by nature begets a son; and what is being built began to come into being at will and is external to the maker; but the son is a proper offspring of the father's essence and is not external to him. (*C.Ar.* 3.61)

As is suggested even by human paternity and sonship, if the Logos is the true Son of the divine Father, he cannot be a creature; and if he is a creature, he cannot be the true Son. Such thinking lies behind such statements as

> The Son is the Offspring of the Father's essence ... therefore the Son is different in kind and different in essence from things originate, and ... is proper to the Father's essence and one in nature with it. (*C.Ar.* 1.58)

In short, the rule of faith is the framework within which human generation may or may not be used as an analogy of God as Father and Son.

Light's radiance is another image which Athanasius employs. When, in *Ad Serap.* 4.6, Athanasius emphasizes that God is not composed of parts but is indivisible, and hence the Son is not a part of another, the result of begetting by division, Athanasius makes a significant shift in *exempla*. Rather than continuing to speak of

Father and Son, he speaks of light and radiance. With its implied, constant oneness, this corrects an abuse of the analogy of human generation. Even as none can ever rightly imagine that the 'radiance' of the 'light' ever was not, so the right-minded may never suppose

> that the Son was not always, or that the Son was not before his generation. For who is capable of separating the radiance from the sun or to conceive of the fountain as ever void of life? (*De Decret.* 12)

This image is the more pointed for the rejection of the suggestion that the Logos is related to God

> as fire kindled from the sun's heat ... For this is an external work and a creature of its author ... but the Logos is related to God as radiance, thereby signifying both his being 'from the essence', proper and indivisible, and his oneness with the Father. (*De Decret.* 22)[9]

Not only is this image used to stress God's indivisible co-eternity, but also the Father and Son's asymmetrical distinction. So Athanasius can write

> what the light enlightens, that the radiance irradiates; and what the radiance irradiates from the light is its enlightenment. So also when the Son is beheld, so is the Father; for he is the Father's Radiance, and thus the Father and the Son are one. (*C.Ar.* 3.13)

This asymmetrical distinction is all the more emphasized in Athanasius' denying that he teaches many gods or three origins or Fathers (*C.Ar.* 3.15). His choosing the analogy of the sun and its radiance, and not three suns, is not accidental.

In as early a work as *Contra Gentes* Athanasius notes that, while the Logos may proceed from the Father, that Logos is not like 'the word of humankind, which is composed of syllables and expressed in the air' (*C.G.* 40). Later, Athanasius expands upon this. God's Word is unlike a person's.

> For many and various are men's words which pass away day by day; because those that come before others continue not, but

vanish. This happens because their authors are men and have seasons which pass away and ideas which are successive; and what strikes them first and second, that they utter, so that they have many words and yet after them all nothing at all remains. For the speaker ceases and his word forthwith is spent. (*C.Ar.* 2.36)

The divine Word neither once did not exist nor now exists from nothing, nor reverts to nothingness; it is of God, yet 'not before nor after, as human words are in sequence, but existing the same always' (*C.Ar.* 2.36). Being God's eternal utterance, the Logos is not composite but simple; and it is not dissoluble, but is stable and effective, not solely in signifying the speaker's intention but also in creatively calling into being things naturally dissoluble. Yet God's Word is not so dissimilar to the human as not to be illustrated by the human word. A human word uttered implies no diminution of the human mind. For 'the word which men utter is neither an affection of them nor a part of their mind' (*C.Ar.* 1.28). The human word is 'begotten' of the human speaker, 'without partition or passion' (*De Decret.* 11). How much less then does the immaterial and indivisible Father's utterance of his divine Logos imply passions, parts, affections and diminution. So, just as a human word 'is proper to us and is from us and not a work external to us, so also God's Word is proper to him and from him and is not a work' (*C.Ar.* 2.36).

Athanasius will however go beyond such images of the Godhead. God's oneness surfaces in the persons' being implied the one in the other, and in their having one common action. Since God is indivisible and one in himself, the distinct persons of the one Godhead are implied in their distinct relations one to another.

> When mention is made of the Father, there is included also his Logos and the Spirit, who is in the Son: if the Son is named, the Father is in the Son and the Spirit is not outside the Logos. For there is from the Father one grace which is fulfilled through the Son in the Spirit; and there is one divine nature and one God 'who is over all and through all and in all'. (*Ad Serap.* 1.14, quoting Ephesians 4:6)

So, even when, for example, the apostle Paul charges Timothy before 'God and Jesus Christ' (1 Timothy 5:21), the Spirit, Athanasius maintains, is not excluded from the one Godhead and included amongst creaturely angels. The Spirit, the 'Spirit of Sonship', 'of Wisdom and Truth', 'of Power and Glory' is implicit in the reference to Christ, the incarnate Logos, who is the Father's Wisdom, Truth, Power and Glory. Equally, since the Father, Son and Spirit are one indivisible Godhead, they have one divine action, in which the distinctions are yet preserved. Hence Athanasius can write both that 'when we partake of the Spirit, we have the Son; and when we have the Son, we have the Spirit' (*Ad Serap.* 4.4), and that what we graciously have, we receive from the Father through his Son in the Spirit. Indeed, this oneness of action and this particularly qualified distinction within the Godhead is stressed in *C.Ar.* 3.11.

> One and the same grace is from the Father in the Son, as the light of the sun and of the radiance is one, and as the sun's illumination is effected through the radiance.

What is significant about this example is its underlining the particularity of the divine oneness. Athanasius is not envisaging divine unity as lying in a generic divine nature, of which there are three individual examples collaborating exactly in a given task, as in that human unity where three people sharing one common nature comply and work together. Athanasius' sense of divine oneness stems from the one source and end, the Father. All that the Son and Spirit are and do, they are and do from the Father, the Father himself acting only through the Logos, the Father's only and proper Offspring, and in the Spirit, the Father's only 'Spirit of Sonship'. Hence the Father graciously gives through his Son in his Spirit; and humanity in the Spirit beholds the Father through his Image, the Son. 'Proof' that this oneness of activity cannot be understood in multiple terms Athanasius finds in 1 Thessalonians 3:11, 'Now God himself, even our Father and the Lord Jesus Christ, may he direct our ways unto you'.[10] Paul, Athanasius maintains, here guards the Father and Son's oneness.

> For [Paul] has not said, may *they* direct, as if a double grace were given from two sources, this and that, but, may *he* direct, to shew that the Father gives it through the Son. (*C.Ar.* 3.11)

No division, no separation, only distinction is permissible in this oneness. Indeed, given the Father and only Logos are one God, indivisible, inseparable, immutable and not open to variation, 'it is madness even to place will and consideration between them' (*C.Ar.*

3.66). Citing again the analogy of radiance and light, Athanasius notes,

> in the case of the radiance and the light, one might say that there is no will preceding radiance in the light, but it is its natural Offspring. (*C.Ar.* 3.66)

Even so the Son is not united to the Father by sharing a common will. Rather than sharing the Father's Counsel and Will, the Son is the Father's 'living Counsel and Offspring in truth and nature, as the radiance from the light' (*C.Ar.* 3.57).

Here are two very different models of unity. The Logos is God; by nature he is the Father's Will and Counsel; theirs is one good pleasure, from the Father through the Son in the Spirit, extended to the whole creation. In contrast, creaturely beings, whether celestial or terrestrial, may be 'one' with the Father in that 'neither in judging nor in doctrine are they discordant, but in all things are obedient to their Maker' (*C.Ar.* 3.10) and may rightly be called the 'sons' of God. They may even be titled 'gods' (*C.Ar.* 3.19). Yet their sonship, divinity and shared judgements are not natural to them. Even the most sublime creature's unity with God stands in marked contrast with the Son's with the Father. 'He is the Truth ... but we by imitation become virtuous and sons' (*C.Ar.* 3.19). Once again, Athanasius' principle is that the paradigm for understanding divine unity is not to be saints' union with God, highly to be praised though it is. For 'in truth, neither are we Logos and Wisdom nor is he creature or work' (*C.Ar.* 3.18).

THE SPIRIT

Athanasius, though stressing the divine oneness, will yet strongly defend the belief that the Father is not the Son, who is not the Spirit. His understanding of divine unity precludes division, but not distinction. Hence he will note

> lest a man, perceiving that the Son has all that the Father has, from the exact likeness and identity, should wander into the religion of Sabellius, considering the [Son] to be the Father, therefore hath he said, 'was given me' [cf. John 3:35] ... only to show that he is not the Father, but the Father's Logos and the eternal Son who, because of his likeness to the Father, has

eternally what he has from him, and because he is the Son, has from the Father what he has eternally. (*C.Ar.* 3.36)

That there is a giver and a recipient precludes any absence of distinction within the one Godhead. The Father receives of none, but is the unquenchable and ever generous Source and Giver. The Son is the eternal recipient, receiving all that he has from the Father. The Spirit, meanwhile, though having the same oneness with the Son, as the Son has with the Father (*Ad Serap.* 1.2; 3.1), does not have a relationship with the Father identical with the Son's. The relation of the Son to the Father may be analogous to that of a stream to a fountain and of radiance to light (*Ad Serap.* 1.19). The relation of the Spirit to the Father is not, however, but a replication of the Son's relationship. The Spirit originates in the Father; for the Father is the sole uncaused Cause. Yet the Spirit is not a second Son, a brother of the Son. Hence Athanasius extends the above analogy of the Son's relation to the Father to illustrate the Spirit's relation to the same Father. Where the light is, there is radiance; and where the radiance is, there is its 'activity and lambent grace' (*Ad Serap.* 1.30). Indeed, illustrations from Scripture tumble over one another to illustrate the distinction of the Spirit within the Godhead. The Father is light, the Son radiance and Christians are enlightened by the Spirit (cf. John 1:9); the Father is fountain, the Son stream and Christians are made to drink of the Spirit (1 Corinthians 10:4); the Father is very Father, the Son very Son and Christians are adopted and made God's children in the Spirit (John 1:12); the Father is only wise, the Son Wisdom and Christians are made wise in receiving the Spirit of Wisdom; the Father is Father, the Son Life and Christians are quickened by the Spirit. These all tally with the assertion that God's work 'is derived from the Father, through the Son and in the Spirit' (*Ad Serap.* 1.20) and find confirmation in the beliefs that the Son does the works of the Father and so witnesses to him who sent him, and that the Spirit does the deeds of the Son who gave him, so effecting that those in whom he works cry 'Jesus is Lord' (*Ad Serap.* 1.32). Interestingly, however, Athanasius does not use the term 'procession' and its cognates in a strict sense. Athanasius, though using these terms of the Spirit in both his essential life and his ministry and not at all of the Son, does not contrast 'procession' with 'being begotten', useful as such would have been to distinguish the Father's Spirit from the Father's Son. Indeed, the emphasis seems to be upon the Spirit's relationship with the Son rather than with the Father. Thus the

Spirit is 'said to proceed from the Father because it is from the Logos who is confessed to be from the Father' (*Ad Serap.* 1.20). This connecting the Spirit with the Son surfaces when Athanasius argues that the Spirit is not external to the Logos, but is

> in the Logos and through him ... in God [the Father]. So the spiritual gifts are given in the Triad ... For the Father himself through the Son in the Spirit works and gives all things. (*Ad Serap.* 3.5)

Mirroring this is people's 'coming' to God. 'Inasmuch as we partake of the Spirit we have the grace of the Logos and in the Logos the love of God' (*Ad Serap.* 3.6).

This absence of a stress upon the distinction of the Spirit and Son is explained by the context of the works concerned. Athanasius' argument here is not against Sabellianism,[11] but for the Spirit's essential divinity. The argument runs along particular lines: as, the Son having a proper relationship with the divine Father, the Son must be co-essential with the Father, so, the Spirit having a proper relationship with the divine Son, the Spirit must be co-essential with him. The shape of the argument for the Spirit's divinity required stressing the oneness of the Spirit and Son and not their distinction. Yet distinction is not excluded: the Spirit is given from the Father through the Son.

Athanasius' arguments that the Spirit is not 'alien to the Son's nature nor to the Father's Godhead' (*Ad Serap.* 4.3) are in form not unlike those employed to establish the Son's divinity. They centre upon God's oneness, upon tradition and upon the divine works. The Triad is one; it is indivisible and self-consistent, not admitting within itself anything that is creaturely and essentially foreign to it. Hence, if the Spirit is the Son's Image, and the Son is not a creature but of God, the Spirit is very God. For 'as the Image, so also must be he whose image it is' (*Ad Serap.* 1.24). Indeed, if the Spirit is a creature and is believed to be either the Son's Image or one of the Triad, divine self-consistency is sacrificed. It is sacrificed in retaining either self-consistency but not divinity or a divinity but without self-consistency. For if the Spirit is a creature and yet is the Son's Image, who is the Father's Image, then the Father is a creature. If however the Spirit is both a creature and one of the Triad, God's self-consistency or eternal immutability is put at stake. For a creature once was not and then is brought into being. If then a creaturely Spirit is one of the Triad, God must be understood as a

Dyad which expands into a Triad, when that creaturely Spirit, which once was not, is brought into being. Yet it is great impiety, Athanasius thinks, to maintain

> that the Triad owes its existence to alteration and progress, even that it was a Dyad and waited for the birth of a creature which should be ranked with the Father and Son and with them become the Triad. (*Ad. Serap.* 3.7)

Tradition, Athanasius asserts, confirms this. Referring to Matthew 28:19, he understands tradition to maintain that the Spirit proceeds from the Father and belongs to the Son (*Ad Serap.* 1.2); tradition rightly works with the knowledge that

> it is absurd to name together things which are by nature unlike. For what community or what likeness is there between creatures and the Creator? (*Ad Serap.* 1.9)

Hence through this oneness of the Spirit with the Father and Son, tradition places the Spirit with the eternal Godhead and not with creatures. So tradition observes that it is 'not lawful ... to divide [the Spirit] from the Logos and to reduce the Triad to imperfection' (*Ad Serap.* 1.21).

It is no surprise then that Athanasius will argue that if the Father, through the Son, in the Spirit creates *all* things, the Spirit cannot be one of the all things created (*Ad Serap.* 3.4–5). If by the Spirit the Logos seals and anoints in baptism and instructs *all* things, the Spirit is not one of these all. Rather he is he in whom all partake, and so 'are made "partakers in the divine nature", and thus all creation partakes of the Logos in the Spirit' (*Ad Serap.* 1.23, referring to 2 Peter 1:4). In contrast with creatures, who are sanctified, renewed and quickened by partaking in the Spirit, the Spirit sanctifies and is not sanctified. 'Our spirit is renewed; but the Spirit is [God's] Spirit, whereby ours is renewed' (*Ad Serap.* 1.9). The importance of divinity to renewal is stressed over and over again. A creature, even the highest angel, 'is outside God's essence and came into being from that which is not' (*Ad Serap.* 1.26). If then any people were joined to him by participation, they all 'should be strangers to the divine nature in as much as [they] did not partake therein' (*Ad Serap.* 1.24). In short, if the Spirit makes people participants in God's nature, 'it is not to be doubted that his nature is of God' (*Ad Serap.* 1.24). The same conclusion is reached in a kindred but new argument in *Ad Serap.* 1. The Spirit is the yardstick against which moral declension is measured; and he is the guarantee of a creature's moral progress in the saintly life. This he could not be if he were a creature. For creatures, being outside God's essence and having come into being from nothing, are capable of both moral progress and declension, insofar as they partake in and fall away from God. The Spirit's being the guarantor of moral security lies in his being proper to the simple God; he is simple, ever the same, partaking of nothing and no one. There being nothing and no one of which he may partake, he is incapable of that progress or declension which comes of partaking or not partaking in God. Rather, he always gives himself that all may partake of him and may walk in the Spirit. Even as we have noted in regard to the Fall, the Spirit is one with God in being both the Judge and the Renewer, constantly being the Spirit of Wisdom, Light and Life, by turning from whom people bring judgement upon themselves and by partaking of whom they open themselves to the gift of God himself, the life in the Spirit.

It seems therefore that the Spirit's divinity is a necessary inference from that of the Son, and that every argument for the Spirit being a creature is an argument for the Son also being a creature.

The faith then upon which Athanasius believed that the Church was founded was faith in one God, even three distinct persons. The Spirit was even as the Father and Son in not being just a divine attribute or epithet. He was not external either in an essential sense or in that of being the 'spirit', the 'influence' or 'immanent presence' of the Logos, an accident or attribute of the Son. This was the

> tradition, teaching and faith of the Catholic Church, from the beginning, which the Lord gave, the Apostles preached and the Fathers kept. (*Ad Serap.* 1.28)

Athanasius will therefore claim that 'he who should fall away from [this faith] would not be a Christian and should no longer be so called' (*Ad Serap.* 1.28). What is important to remember here is that Athanasius' concern is not just right beliefs. His concern includes right beliefs, but also right relationships. In his debates with the Arians, who denied the Son's essential divinity, and with the Tropici, who maintained that the Spirit was a creature brought into existence from nothing, what is at stake is not just a theological theory but people's salvation. Remarking that the Arian baptism is into not the Father and Son, but the Creator and creature, into Maker and made, Athanasius suggests that the sacrament's virtue is 'hazarded'; it is 'without guarantee'. For baptism's efficacy depends upon the very divinity which the Arians deny the Son. For 'if the Son were a creature, man had remained as before, not being joined to God' (*C. Ar.* 2.69; cf. 1.34; *De Syn.* 36). The Tropici's baptism is likewise undermined in that, having a Spirit who is but a creature, there is want of someone to unite the baptized to God. For 'who will unite you to God if you have not the Spirit of God, but the Spirit which belongs to creation?' (*Ad Serap.* 1.29). The fundamental issue is that only very God can unite a creature to God. For a Christian to be a Christian, each must be baptized into that one God, Father, Son and Spirit.

Athanasius expands upon his arguments with the beliefs of the Tropici and upon their fatal consequences for salvation. Athanasius has marshalled his argument that if God is one and if the Spirit is a creature, the Father and Son are also creatures. Baptism into this Father, Son and Spirit is then not into life in God but into another creature's life. Even baptism into a Godhead with which is ranked the Spirit as a created angel is not satisfactory, as 'by reason of variegation it is without guarantee' (*Ad Serap.* 1.29). For where there is plurality, Athanasius maintains, there is the possibility of division and inconsistency. Hence, even if baptism into such a Godhead were tolerated, its security could not be maintained. Properly conceived, God is one, an 'indivisible and consistent Triad' (*Ad Serap.* 1.30) and so his 'holiness must be one and his eternity one and his nature immutable' (*Ad Serap.* 1.30). Therein lies the baptismal life's security. The possibility of the saving God altering is removed and his salvation is made ever the same. Neither choice nor a mutable nature affects the Sanctifier.

Athanasius, however, will not tolerate baptism into a Godhead with which is ranked the Spirit as a created angel. This he will not tolerate not only because its efficacy could not be guaranteed, but also because baptism is not, for it cannot be, initiation into part of God. For God is one, indivisible and without parts. Hence,

> he who takes anything away from the Triad and is baptized in the name of the Father alone, or in the name of the Son alone, or in the name of the Father and Son without the Spirit, receives nothing but remains wanting and imperfect, both himself and he who is supposed to initiate him. For the rite of initiation is in the Triad. So, he who divides the Son from the Father, or who

reduces the Spirit to the level of the creatures, has neither the Son nor the Father, but is without God. (*Ad Serap.* 1.30)

So dividing the indivisible Triad by conceiving a creaturely Spirit with increate Father and Son, the Tropici divide the baptized from life (*Ad Serap.* 1.32). In short, there is one faith in one Godhead, indivisible, wholly God. There is then one baptism, given in the name of very God, Father, Son and Spirit. Nor could it be otherwise. For God, being indivisible and consistent, cannot have the Spirit separated from it and cannot have a creaturely Spirit included in it. Put another way, God minus the Spirit does not equal the Father and Son; God minus the Spirit equals nothing. Hence the denial of either the Son or the Spirit being very God results in those baptized into either the Arian or Tropici's God remaining necessarily 'without God'. The only salvation and sanctification comes, Athanasius insists, of recognizing a consistent Godhead, which is indivisible. For a creaturely Spirit cannot renew; and a 'mixed' God is not God at all. The gifts of God are given by the Spirit from the Father through the Son. They are not given 'differently and separately by each person but ... given in the Triad, ... all are from the one God' (*Ad Serap.* 1.31). So the baptized

can have no communion in the gift except in the Spirit. For it is when we partake of him that we have the love of the Father and the grace of the Son and the communion of the Spirit himself. (*Ad Serap.* 1.30)

The simplicity of God is then, for Athanasius, the basis of his understanding of God and the security of our holy salvation. Thus the simplicity of God is not abstraction; and the communion of the Father, Son and Spirit is no collection of individuals. That there is one God, Father, Son and Spirit, is no mere academic matter, but that which permits and enables a person's living a godly life. Athanasius has been seen as an individual *contra mundum*, over against the world. It is because of his strong connection between theology and a godly life that he stands *contra mundum*. Otherwise he would think that he was indeed being *contra mundum*, agreeing with the world in its error, but with the awful result of not showing the world its folly and that folly's fatal consequence. Allowing the world to fall, to remain in ignorance not only about God but also of God, and spiritually to die, would be truly to be *contra mundum*.

189

Notes

1 The confusion lies partly in the similarity of spelling in the words concerned. There is *agenētos*, unoriginate, not having an origin, and *agennetos*, unbegotten; and there is *genētos*, originate, having an origin, and *gennetos*, begotten.

2 P. J. Widdicombe, *The Fatherhood of God from Origen to Athanasius* (Oxford, 1994), pp. 159ff.

3 G. C. Stead, *Divine Substance* (Oxford, 1977), p. 266.

4 Cf. *The Fatherhood of God*, pp. 155ff.; 212ff.

5 Ibid., p. 186, quoting R. D. Williams, *Arius: Heresy and Tradition* (London, 1987), p. 229.

6 Cf. Aristotle, *Metaphysics* Z.7.1032a, 23–24; Porphyry, *Sententiae ad Intelligibilia ducentes* 13.

7 This anticipates the later ideas that the divine persons, Father, Son and Spirit, are constituted as such by relation. Cf. Aquinas and K. Rahner.

8 Cf. Origen, *De Principiis* 1.2.4 and Athanasius, *De Decretis* 10–12 for the differences between human and divine generation: the former is in time; offspring are 'portions' of their fathers, whose bodies are not simple, but 'in a state of flux and composed of parts; and men lose their substance in begetting' (*De Decret.* 11); implicit are 'parts and divisions'; it is marked by affections, passions and even diminution. The latter is eternal, impassible and indivisible: the Father is Father of the Son 'without partition or passion. For there is neither effluence of the Immaterial nor influx from without, as amongst men' (*De Decret.* 11); it is without addition or subtraction.

9 Cf. Arius, *Letter to Bishop Alexander of Alexandria* (Epiphanius, *Panarion* 69.7) where Arius repeats Hieracas' view that the Son was from the Father as a light from light.

10 Athanasius highlights the singular verb 'direct'. The RSV translation fails to distinguish between the singular and plural and so is not used here.

11 The use of *homoousios* of the Father and Son can be interpreted in terms of Sabellianism, as can John 3:35.

Conclusion

In order to safeguard a strongly monotheistic sense of God, who is unique, beyond human comprehension, wholly free and supremely sovereign, Arianism employed a very particular sense of transcendence and simplicity. This proved, however, to be limiting rather than liberating. For while it asserted that God was transcendent in being other than creation, it maintained that this God was 'constrained'. In being simply one, God was not essentially Father, nor obviously of a generous, communal nature. In being other than the universe, in the sense of being outside the universe, God was limited by it and excluded from it. God no longer was seen as infinite, not limited by anything. Athanasius resisted precluding God being Father and Son, as the Arians did, on a preconceived notion of divine oneness. He would not forbid God creating and sustaining and becoming incarnate on the basis of a very strict sense of transcendent simplicity. He acknowledged that God, being infinite, cannot be fully comprehended, but can be known. In contrast with the Arians' limiting God to concepts, through their 'protecting' divine simplicity, Athanasius recognized both that, being infinite, God can and does reveal *himself* in the human sphere and that people are brought to know God and not to knowledge of conceptions of deity. Equally, whereas the Arians' preconceptions of a simple transcendence lay very heavy constraints upon divine freedom, Athanasius' sense of an infinite God, who is not curtailed by the universe in either being excluded from or limited to it, is the very basis of divine, sovereign freedom.

Unlike Arius, for whom God was neither naturally nor necessarily Father, Athanasius held that 'Father' and 'Son' are not attributes, not just names with which to address God, but are part of the definition of who and what God is. Indeed, they are of primary importance in God's definition. In relation to these all other definitions are considered. Thus, for example, while it is proper to speak of God as Creator, Saviour and Sanctifier, it is also appropriate to recognize that this is to speak of God's acts and of his relationship with creatures. They are not arbitrary ascriptions but terms of Scripture, which, to be interpreted aright, are to be understood in terms of the *being* of the God who acts and who initiates the processes of creation, salvation and sanctification. For Athanasius the divine *will* to create, save and sanctify is not to be considered apart from the divine being. Our experience of being created and sustained, of being saved and sanctified begins and ends in a relationship with the One who *is* Father, *is* Son and *is* Spirit. For being Father, Son and Spirit, God is the ground and source of the divine properties of creating, saving and sanctifying and of their expression. God's eternal purposes arise from and are given effect by the eternal nature of God as Father, Son and Spirit.

For Athanasius the eternal Fatherhood of God identified the immutable being of God as the relationship of mutual generosity, of Father, Son and Spirit. This divine being was further conceived as existing in its own right. So illimitable, dependent upon nothing, and eternally generous, the sovereign God existed for the sake of all others. Being perfect and self-existent, God did not need creation; and being unbounded, generous goodness, Father, Son and Spirit did not envy anything a full, wholesome existence, but delighted in bringing all into being, sustaining, redeeming and sanctifying all. Since God *is* Father, Son and Spirit, very goodness, the wholly illimitable source of all goodness, creation *comes to be* and to be other than, but reflective of, its Maker.

This sense of one, eternal, inherently good, generative and generous God lies behind not only God's bringing things into being but also his self-manifestation, his salvation of man and the nature of the Christian life. For Arianism, the work of Christ was not the very work of very God. Their God was not directly involved in the world and was known only indirectly, through a creaturely intermediary. Against this, Athanasius held that, since the Son was very God, the revelation of the Son was truly the revelation of God. In the Incarnation, through the Spirit, people are brought into the very presence of God; they are granted to participate in the Son's eternal knowledge of his Father. So brought to know God as Father, all might stand before God, not in terror, but in confidence, although not self-confidence but trust in the good Father. For, graciously, through divine generosity, each was brought from being a creature and servant of the Creator and Lord to being also a child of the heavenly Father. Indeed, God's goodness lies behind not only God's self-disclosure for people's benefit, but also the manner of God's self-disclosure, the oblique, challenging but not dazzling and so confusing, self-revelation. The same goodness also lies behind the manner of people's deification. This is not a quasi-physical sharing in the divine nature but a participation in the divine life by enjoying, insofar as a creature may, the divine *relation* of the Son to the Father. Unless the relationship of the Father and Son is eternally true of God, the Source and the End of people's salvation falls. Otherwise, there is neither the infinite goodness which wishes all people's salvation nor the relationship into which they may in salvation be brought. That is why, when writing against Arianism, Athanasius' main concern is to secure the Son's natural divinity as the basis of salvation, a divinity seen in relation to the divine Fatherhood. Salvation, as Athanasius argues, is possible only if the Son is divine, or, more accurately, is very Son. Without the relationship of Son to Father, people's deification cannot be realized and secured.

Athanasius' description of God as Father is crucial to understanding the Christian life. The priority of the description of God as Father makes sense of the idea of God both as unoriginate first principle, the uncaused Cause, and as directly involved in the processes of this world. The relation of God as first principle to humanity, of the Father in his simple perfection to mutable creature, demands discipline. This discipline is grounded in the truth that God is to be loved above all the good gifts that he gives, loved for himself as the source and goal of creaturely existence. The relation of God as the uncaused Cause to his creation equally demands a person's not being ruled by this world's pressures but by obedience to the transforming One who is both within and beyond space and time. The Christian life, which arises and is sustained by the divine goodness, is lived in imitation of this enlivening goodness through the Spirit's presence. For to receive the Spirit of the Logos is simultaneously to receive the Father and to be drawn into participation in the eternal, divine tranquillity, wherein one is enabled to face creation's chaos and to establish the divine order in place of human disorder. In short, the Trinity allows people to live

193

a trinitarian life, which is good, generous, creative and fulfilling. The 'Father', 'Son' and 'Spirit' allow and undergird the faithfulness and constancy of God towards his whole creation. For it is improper that what the Father, Son and Spirit bring into being should slip from that happy existence. Hence, in and through godly goodness, he sustains and saves it, a goodness whose constancy is absolute and not compromised a whit by sin and consequent mortal corruption. For this goodness is an expression of the eternal, immutable divine Being. The Christian life, then, is a person's living this life of divine constancy, a Christian's faithfulness and goodness similarly being neither weakened nor withheld on account of the sins of others. As God's faithfulness to them is unvarying, ever willing their well-being, so their faithfulness to their neighbour is to be constant, ever wishing their neighbour's well-being, in and through the one God, Father, Son and Spirit.

What is particularly significant here is that God's immutability does not lead to his being viewed as uncaring and non-responsive, but as immutably caring. Indeed, were God not ever good, the Father not ever the Son's Father, creation, revelation and salvation would be endangered, if not rendered void.[1]

When we reflect upon Athanasius' thinking concerning creation, we must note that he has a strong sense that creation includes both the material and the spiritual, and that both are from nothing. By acknowledging that both matter and spirit are creatures, Athanasius eliminates any antithesis between them. The spiritual is not to be pursued at the expense of the material. Loving God and loving one's neighbour are but two sides of the one coin. Nor do works like *The Life of Antony* undermine this. Certainly the monk flees the city and abides in his cell. This, however, is not tantamount to flight from the material to the spiritual. The flight is not a 'washing one's hands' of the State or the Church, but a critique of it. Witness Antony's supporting the Nicene rather than the Arian churchmen in Alexandria and his exposing the vacuity of the Greek philosophers.[2] Further, by fleeing to his cell, the monk seeks to live and to learn to live with his own inner darkness, and especially with his bodily temptations and sexual fantasies. Within the city, boredom, unsatisfied desires and unhealthy ambition may be overlooked through the individual's being busy with new tasks and novel ideas, and at the cost of sealing off from God's transforming grace these areas which are in fact but the marks of deep-seated human problems. Being busy may enable one to forget the problem but it will not cure it. In the monastic cell, along with the wholly 'unspiritual' routine of limited, trivial tasks, the daily tedium and the continuing solitude, there is no diversion and every opportunity of confronting human nature. The monastic cell is no flight from the material to the spiritual, but a move to a particular, disciplined life where illusions are exposed and every aspect of humanity is brought into God's healing light.

The distinction of both matter and spirit from their common Creator precludes any form of anthropomorphism. For Athanasius, God certainly is not physical. Equally, however, he is not a purely spiritual being, like other spiritual beings but somehow infinitely superior. God is not just an individual's greatest spiritual concern, but is his sole concern; he is that in terms of which all other spiritual concerns are to be understood and appreciated. God is not pictured, like the old Greek gods, as human in character, but as immortal and invisible. For he is not a purely mental being who, however sophisticated and sublime, thinks and decides and feels and acts as human beings. Rather he alone is God, alone the Creator of all things, material and spiritual. Such thinking lies behind Athanasius' argument that the Logos is very God since, being the creator of *all* things, he cannot be one of these *all*. This also tallies with the terms 'Father', 'Son' and 'Spirit' not being used univocally by Athanasius of God. For Athanasius, human fatherhood, the sonship of adoption by God, and the human spirit reflect God. Such language has its primary meaning in reference to God and, because of that reference, is applicable to human creatures made in the divine likeness, and confirms the essential distinction of the Creator from all creatures, celestial and terrestrial, spiritual and material.

Athanasius' sense of our knowing God through his self-revelation is not unusual. He stresses that we know God, and not simply that God exists. Where Athanasius is perhaps unusual, at least from a twentieth-century perspective, is in his sense that knowledge of God is a religious and not an academic matter. People share in the Son's eternal knowledge of the Father as they live the godly life of the redeemed community. For knowledge of the Father is granted to those who believe in the Son; and those who do not believe in the Son neither hear nor have seen the Father. Only he who has truly seen the Christ as the Son of God or heard the divine Word active throughout the world knows the Father. The revelation of God is thus not immediately accessible and assessable. People cannot, as it were, sit in judgement upon it and then decide whether or not to believe. A person must first believe in the Logos, through whom one enters into the knowledge of the Father. Athanasius is working with two groups of ideas. Firstly, his trinitarianism is strongly relational: our deification is our sharing in the Son's relation to his Father, and our knowing God is our participating in the Son's knowing his Father. Knowing God is entering a relationship with God. Hence, one cannot know God apart from commitment. Secondly, the truth of God in Christ is self-authenticating in the Christian's experience.

God allows himself to be known by the believer. Significantly, however, he allows himself to be known only indirectly. He is never known face to face, but always as hidden in what is not God. Believers do not begin from innate ideas of God. Even when they know God in and through their own human soul, they do not begin from an intuitive sense of the Absolute. Rather, Christians are drawn into that knowledge; each is wooed to a transformed life, in which the inexhaustible God who draws is gradually discovered in the life which becomes ever more godlike. As their life more truly reflects their Maker, and as their life more fully imitates Christ's, each discovers more and more of the God who is present and active in all but, being infinite, is not exhausted by any. Hence it is that Athanasius has so little time for what he sees as the private opinions of heretics and so much time for those who submit their minds to the Truth incarnate in Christ. Hence also it is that he thinks both that good behaviour reflects good theology, and that bad behaviour reflects bad theology. It is customary to connect the good works and the holy countenance of the monk Antony with his orthodoxy. It should be customary to recognize a similar connection between the 'uncaring' attitudes of the Arians and their theology. Clearly there is a polemical dimension in passages such as that in which the Arians are criticized for their absence of pity for and sympathy with the poor.[3] Probably there is also a theological dimension: by a person's works the onlooker shall know an individual for what he is. As though echoing John's Christ in his statement 'even though you do not believe me, believe the works, that you may know and understand that the Father is in me and I am in the Father',[4] Athanasius' point in *Hist. Ar.* 62 and like passages seems to be 'even if you do not believe my word of criticism of Arian theology, note their works, that you may know that the one true Father is not in them nor they in him'. The issue here is not hypocrisy, not failing to practise what one preaches, but misguided sincerity. Sincere works witness to particular values or 'gods'; and so a theology may rightly be tested by its works and found to be true or otherwise. This is not an anti-Pauline stance, a version of 'salvation by works' rather than 'by faith alone'. It is a recognition of the proper inseparability of beliefs and actions, which indeed allows Athanasius, when writing of the final judgement, to side with Paul in noting that 'we must all stand before the tribunal of Christ, that each may receive according to what he has done in the body, whether good or evil'.[5]

Athanasius' treatment of humanity has been open to negative comment.[6] There is no stressing the psychological force of fear and the like; there is the awkward juxtaposition in Jesus' life of divine and human activities. Yet, when viewed in context, Athanasius' treatment is substantial. The Arians believed that God could release people from sin simply by *fiat*. For them it was therefore unimportant, as regards salvation, whether or not the Son was a creature; and it was of no consequence that their God could not be and was not directly involved in the work of salvation. For Athanasius salvation by *fiat* was no real salvation. By *fiat* grace did not become internal to and securely joined with needy humanity. If the divine Logos did not associate himself inextricably with a human body which was ignorant, fearful and mortal, and so become one with the contingent worldly order, these areas of human life and death would have remained untouched and untransformed by God. That Athanasius is so concerned about God's capacity to involve himself in the contingent world through the Incarnation, a concern all the more pronounced given the Arians' absence of such concern, suggests that at least in early-fourth-century Alexandrian terms Athanasius took humanity and human history seriously.

Within this context of taking humanity seriously is the noteworthy point that while human actions are important, they are not all-important. Being human is more than being active, activity being, as it were, symptoms of being human. If we look at Athanasius' portrayal of Christ we find a person who is wholly open to God. He is generally portrayed as receiving grace rather than as doing good, although good he does. When we look at humanity's salvation, we find that God is not prepared to treat people's problems symptomatically, by simply forgiving sins. God rather deals with the *root* of the problem, humanity not being strong enough, even in the comparative safety of Eden, to abide ever with God; God is not content to deal just with the Fall, the consequence of people's folly and weakness. God is concerned with their *sins*, but especially with the people whose sins they are. Hence salvation is not a return to a prelapsarian state, but to a higher, more secure

197

state, wherein in Christ people are securely deified. When, moreover, we look at Athanasius' sense of human maturation in God, we find the same emphasis. Especially in the *Festal Letters* there is a stress upon human activity. Yet even there human maturation before God, though found in and through trials and tribulations, and through good thoughts, ideas and acts, is not dependent upon them. It is by coming to terms with the individual's own being, allowing a person's own most secret darkness to be expelled by the divine grace, that each is transfigured and transformed. What is at stake here is a view of humanity appreciated in God's not applying his saving love symptomatically, meeting a person's needs rather like the missionary visiting a primitive tribe with a box of medicines. Herein the whole person, and not just that person's acts, is transformed. Herein fallen humanity is seen as that which lacks the enlivening, generous, good God, of which human ignorance of the divine, mortality and corruption are real symptoms, but only symptoms; such can be wholly healed not by a simple *fiat* but by God's presence, which makes up for that lack. The symptoms of this divine presence, given us at infinite cost, are forgiveness, knowledge of God, enhancement of life, resurrection and incorruption.

Athanasius, it must always be remembered, was a fourth-century theologian. His theology employs fourth- and not twentieth-century ideas. Hence for the twentieth-century reader he poses questions rather than supplying answers. He suggests priorities. He invites us to ask again, for example, whether Christ's being a window into God, though true, is the whole truth. He asks us how important God's *becoming* man, rather than his coming upon a person, is for humanity's secure salvation. He suggests further reflection upon the issue of whether an immutable God need be uncaring. And he questions whether we can afford to be without a truly trinitarian God, one God, Father, Son and Spirit, whose natural and eternal goodness is the basis and guarantee of creation, redemption and sanctification.

Notes

1   Athanasius' high evaluation of divine immutability is not widely shared by twentieth-century theologians, despite his anticipating many of their later objections. For the contemporary debate see R. P. C. Hanson, 'The grace and the wrath of God' in *The Attractiveness of God: Essays in Christian Doctrine* (London, 1973); J. Moltmann, *The Crucified God: The Cross of Christ as the Foundation and Criticism of Christian Theology* (ET; London, 1974); D. G. Attfield, 'Can God be

crucified? A discussion of J. Moltmann', *Scottish Journal of Theology* 30 (1977), pp. 47–57; R. M. Edwards, 'The pagan dogma of the absolute unchangeableness of God', *Religious Studies* 14 (1978), pp. 305–13; W. McWilliams, 'Divine suffering in contemporary theology', *Scottish Journal of Theology* 33 (1980), pp. 35–53; K. Surin, 'The impassibility of God and the problem of evil', *Scottish Journal of Theology* 35 (1982), pp. 97–115; R. Bauckham, 'Only the suffering God can help', *Themelios* 9 (1984), pp. 6ff.; P. S. Fiddes, *The Creative Suffering of God* (Oxford, 1988); D. A. Pailin, *God and the Processes of Reality* (London, 1989).

2   *Vita Ant.* 68–71; 72–80.

3   *Hist. Ar.* 62.

4   John 10:38.

5   *D.I.* 56, quoting 2 Corinthians 5:10.

6   E.g. M. R. Richard, 'S. Athanase et la psychologie du Christ selon les Ariens', *Mélanges de Science Religieuse* 4 (1947), pp. 5–54; J. N. D. Kelly, *Early Christian Doctrines* (4th edn; London, 1968), pp. 284–9; H. E. W. Turner, *Jesus the Christ* (Oxford, 1976), pp. 34–6.

Index